# NARRATIVE

Paul Cobley

Routledge
Taylor & Francis Group

LONDON AND NEW YORK

First published 2001
by Routledge
2 Park Square, Milton Park, Oxon, OX14 4RN.

Simultaneously published in the USA and Canada
by Routledge
270 Madison Ave, New York, NY 10016

Reprinted 2003, 2004, 2005, 2006 (twice), 2008 (twice)

Transferred to Digital Printing 2009

*Routledge is an imprint of the Taylor & Francis Group,
an informa business*

© 2001 Paul Cobley

Typeset in Garamond by Taylor & Francis Books Ltd
Printed and bound in Great Britain by
TJI Digital, Padstow, Cornwall

*British Library Cataloguing-in-Publication Data*
A catalogue record for this book is available from the British Library

*Library of Congress Cataloging in Publication Data*
Cobley, Paul, 1963-
    Narrative / Paul Cobley,
    Includes bibliographical references and index.
    1. Narration (Rhetoric) 2. Fiction–History and criticism. I. Title
    PN3383.N35 C63   2001
    700~.423–dc217   2001                                        019652

ISBN10: 0–415–21262–6 (hbk)
ISBN10: 0–415–21263–4 (pbk)

ISBN13: 978–0–415–21262–5 (hbk)
ISBN13: 978–0–415–21263–2 (pbk)

*To*
*Auntie Rene*
*1915–1992*

# NARRATIVE

Human beings have constantly told stories, presented events and placed the world into narrative form. This activity suggests a very basic way of looking at the world, yet, this book argues, even the most seemingly simple of stories is embedded in a complex network of relations. Paul Cobley traces these relations, considering the ways in which humans have employed narrative over the centuries to 're-present' time, space and identity.

The guidebook to narrative covers a range of narrative forms and their historical development from early oral and literate forms through to cyberspace, encompassing Hellenic and Hebraic foundations, the rise of the novel, realist representations, narratives of imperialism, modernism, cinema, postmodernism and new technologies.

Written in a clear, engaging style and featuring an extensive glossary of terms, this is the essential introduction to the history and theory of narrative.

**Paul Cobley** is Reader in Communications at London Guildhall University. He is the author of *The American Thriller* and *Introducing Semiotics* (with Litza Jansz), and editor of *The Communication Theory Reader, The Routledge Companion to Semiotics and Linguistics* and (with Adam Briggs) *The Media: An Introduction* 2nd edn.

# THE NEW CRITICAL IDIOM

SERIES EDITOR: JOHN DRAKAKIS, UNIVERSITY OF STIRLING

*The New Critical Idiom* is an invaluable series of introductory guides to today's critical terminology. Each book:

* provides a handy, explanatory guide to the use (and abuse) of the term
* offers an original and distinctive overview by a leading literary and cultural critic
* relates the term to the larger field of cultural representation

With a strong emphasis on clarity, lively debate and the widest possible breadth of examples, *The New Critical Idiom* is an indispensable approach to key topics in literary studies.

Also available in this series:

# CONTENTS

# SERIES EDITOR'S PREFACE

*The New Critical Idiom* is a series of introductory books which seeks to extend the lexicon of literary terms, in order to address the radical changes which have taken place in the study of literature during the last decades of the twentieth century. The aim is to provide clear, well-illustrated accounts of the full range of terminology currently in use, and to evolve histories of its changing usage.

The current state of the discipline of literary studies is one where there is considerable debate concerning basic questions of terminology. This involves, among other things, the boundaries which distinguish the literary from the non-literary; the position of literature within the larger sphere of culture; the relationship between literatures of different cultures; and questions concerning the relation of literary to other cultural forms within the context of interdisciplinary studies.

It is clear that the field of literary criticism and theory is a dynamic and heterogeneous one. The present need is for individual volumes on terms which combine clarity of exposition with an adventurousness of perspective and a breadth of application. Each volume will contain as part of its apparatus some indication of the direction in which the definition of particular terms is likely to move, as well as expanding the disciplinary boundaries within which some of these terms have been traditionally contained. This will involve some re-situation of terms within the larger field of cultural representation, and will introduce examples from the area of film and the modern media in addition to examples from a variety of literary texts.

# ACKNOWLEDGEMENTS

This volume would not have happened without the vision of John Drakakis. Not only has he presided over an excellent series to which I'm honoured to contribute, he has given immeasurable help with this book. I have learned an immense amount from him. Where the cover notes of early Queen albums were able triumphantly to proclaim 'no synthesizers!', I hope I am able to reward him with 'no parentheses!'. (Well, only a few.)

Approaching the thorny issue of the origins of narrative was always going to be difficult, but it was made that much easier by the suggestions of my level-headed interlocutor on the subject, Myrdene Anderson. Although he may not know it, Federico Bonfanti gave me some valuable help; as did Kalevi Kull during a breakfast interrogation in Finland. I've benefited from discussions with Marcel Danesi and Christina Ljungberg. Also, my attempts to understand the consequences of heteroglossia and Bakhtin's work in general have been enhanced by Susan Petrilli and Augusto Ponzio, both through discussion with them and through their crucial writings. My many hundreds of first-year students of the last eight years or so have been a fruitful source of ideas whenever I have even entertained the notion that there might not be anything new to say about the theory of narrative.

My colleagues at Routledge, Liz Thompson and Talia Rodgers, have been extremely patient while this book was being brought to completion. However, it is unfair simply to characterize them by their patience: they are also hard-working, committed and they share John Drakakis' vision. If I have been the cause of anxiety to any of the above, it should be said that I would have been worse were it not for the love of Alison and Gemma.

# 1

## IN THE BEGINNING: THE END

In a fit of bombast all too typical of contemporary features journalism, Bryan Appleyard of the *Sunday Times* asserts that

> We tell stories to ourselves; of our journey from birth to death, friends, families, who we are and who we want to be. Or public stories about history and politics, about our country, our race or our religion. At each moment of our lives these stories place us in space and time. They console us, making our lives meaningful by placing us in something bigger than ourselves. Maybe the story is just that we are in love, that we have to feed the cat or educate the children. Or maybe it is about a lifelong struggle for salvation or liberation. Either way – however large or small the story – the human impulse is to make sense of each moment by referring it to a larger narrative. We need to live in a world not of our own making.
>
> (*Sunday Times Magazine* 7 February 1999: 39)

Omnipotent, pretentious, unsubstantiated and obvious: all these things are true of Appleyard's opening paragraph. Facing the millennium, and seeking to account for the previous thousand years of human endeavour, he obviously wishes to utter something grandiose, exaggerated even. Yet, for all our recognition of this, there also appears to be an unavoidable kernel of truth in what he says. Human beings, especially after the development of the verbal faculty, have constantly told stories, presented events and squeezed aspects of the world into narrative form.

Wherever there are humans there appear to be stories. It is true that people tell stories about life history (Gee 1991) and about their psyches (Schafer 1983; Spence 1987); people read stories when they consume various media, including the one in which Appleyard operates (Kunelius 1994); different media, such as musical notation, might embody stories (McClary 1998); and, even when thinking about the world in an 'objective' fashion, scientifically or ethically, the tendency to 'storify' remains (Harré 1990; Levine 1997). Yet, as soon as we start to look more closely at this phenomenon, it is evident that the apparently natural impulse of storytelling and storylistening (or reading) is far from simple. Pronouncing that certain events in the world of human experience 'make a good story' invariably carries with it the contention that those events can be reduced to a few crude principles, that stories are very 'basic' ways of thinking about the world.

This book is dedicated to the opposite premise: that even the most 'simple' of stories is embedded in a network of relations that are sometimes astounding in their complexity. This is not to say that those relations are beyond the ken of all but the most technically orientated academic minds. The opposite, once more, is the case. The most familiar, most primitive, most ancient and seemingly most straightforward of stories reveal depths that we might hitherto have failed to anticipate. That we do not anticipate them is usually because we do not attend to the network of relations in which a story resides; but this is definitely not to say that we do not partake of these depths and the potential pleasure they yield.

So far we have referred to stories, but, strictly speaking, the chief object of our focus in this network is 'narrative', a communicative

relation which is often conflated with straightforward understandings of what a story is. We will see that narrative is a particular form of
representation implementing signs; and in the rest of this chapter we
will consider how it is necessarily bound up with sequence, space and
time. Chapter 2 reflects on early narratives and confronts some of the
thorny issues involved in the search to discover them, while Chapters
3 and 4 focus on arguably the most pre-eminent narrative form, the
novel. Chapter 5 continues to focus on print fiction but discusses different forms of consciousness arising from inter-cultural
exchanges, technology and the advent of 'modernism'. Then, in
Chapter 6, another embodiment of narrative, the cinema, is discussed
in relation to 'modernism'. Chapter 7 considers the phenomenon
called 'postmodernism' and how it has impinged on the manifestations of narrative. Finally, Chapter 8 surveys recent developments
in narrative technologies, considers 'openness' and 'closure' and
suggests one direction for the future study of the narrative sign.

Throughout, we will be interested in narrative as part of the
general process of *representation* which takes place in human discourse. Hall (1997) suggests that there are three general
approaches to the question of the work done by representation.
The 'reflective' approach sees meaning as residing in the person
or thing in the real world; a representation such as narrative
'reflects' that meaning. The 'intentional' approach sees meaning
in the control exercised by the producer of a representational
form such as narrative; *s/he* uses representation to make the world
'mean'. The 'constructionist' approach sees meaning neither in
the control of the producer nor the thing being represented;
instead, it identifies the thoroughly social nature of the *construction* of meaning, the fact that representational systems, rather
than their users and objects, allow meaning to occur. The following chapters will be mostly concerned with the 'constructionist'
perspective on narrative as representation but will also consider
some arguments regarding 'reflection' and 'intention'. They will
also more specifically discuss some of the possible reasons for

changes in the components of narrative representation; among these is a concept so frequently synonymous with narrative that it must be defined now: 'story'.

## STORY, PLOT AND NARRATIVE

To be sure, story and narrative are closely related; but even the most preliminary of investigations reveals that there are three fundamental items which, while they sometimes blend in a most pleasing way, are really separate. These are 'story', 'plot' and 'narrative'. Rather than relying on technical descriptions of each, let us turn to a reasonably familiar kind of contemporary illustration. In 1999, a four-part series, *Oliver Twist*, was broadcast on the commercial television channel ITV in Britain. As is well known in the literate world, *The Adventures of Oliver Twist* is an early novel of Charles Dickens, originally published in 1838. The *story* concerns a young orphan boy, Oliver, brought up in a workhouse, thrust out into the evil world and then preyed upon by Fagin, a small-time racketeer whose principal source of income is garnered from the petty criminal activities of a group of street urchins over whom he presides. The story of the character Oliver Twist, his adventures, what happens to him and the events connected with these, is therefore central to the novel.

The *plot* of *Oliver Twist*, the circumstances which involve Oliver in a specific series of events, is not quite the same as the story. The reason that Oliver is victimized by Fagin and his associates has to do with Oliver's parenthood. He is the illegitimate product of a union between Edwin Leeford and Agnes Fleming, both of whom are dead as Oliver takes his first breath in the world. Leeford, incarcerated in an unhappy marriage when he met Agnes, already had a son, Edward, by his wife. This shadowy young man, under the alias of 'Monks', later haunts Oliver and, in turn, is haunted by the orphan's very existence, a fact which could prevent him getting his hands on the considerable Leeford inheritance. 'Monks' is determined to gain what he considers to be his birthright. He is, therefore, the main catalyst of the plot and, concomitantly, the events of the story.

In Dickens' novel, the full account of the events which bring Oliver Twist into the world and the web of circumstances in which he is enmeshed is not actually given until near the end. Although the events precipitating Oliver's genesis will, ineluctably, precede in a temporal sequence the events of his life, the *narrative* chooses not to disclose them. In short, the *narrative* of Oliver's story and the plot which drives it only reveal the relevant wider circumstances surrounding them in Chapter XLIX, 'Monks and Mr. Brownlow at last meet. Their conversation and the intelligence that interrupts it' and in Chapter LI, 'Affording an explanation of more mysteries than one, and comprehending a proposal of marriage with no word of settlement or pin-money'. Even with such an account, it can be seen that the narrative separates the revelations of these chapters with a chapter devoted to the narration of Sikes' demise.

The 1999 television version, dramatized by Alan Bleasdale, has a different narrative. The first episode of the four-part series consists of a detailed narration of the love affair between Oliver's parents, Edwin and Agnes. This narrative not only moves the facts of their story to the beginning, unlike Dickens' novel which leaves them at the end, but it also depicts the affair 'first-hand', with the characters speaking their own dialogue and acting out the events, rather than having them retold by 'Monks' and Leeford's friend, Brownlow. The narrative of the TV version also has additions: the *murder* of Leeford and the continued existence through subsequent episodes of Leeford's wife.

We glean from this example a sense of how narrative is different from 'story' and 'plot'. Put very simply, 'story' consists of all the events which are to be depicted. 'Plot' is the chain of causation which dictates that these events are somehow linked and that they are therefore to be depicted in relation to each other.

'Narrative' is the showing or the telling of these events and the mode selected for that to take place. As we saw above, the Dickens novel about Oliver has a narrative with certain key events narrated towards the end; the TV version has a narrative with those events appearing at the beginning. The novel's narrative tends to 'tell' what those events were through a scene involving the verbal testimonies of Monks, Brownlow and others. One could argue, though, that this is a 'showing' because the narrative selects for depiction this particular scene with these particular characters. The TV version 'shows' what happened between Oliver's father and mother; it presents them in a depiction at 'first hand'. At the same time, though, one could argue that this is a 'telling' because only certain scenes in the love affair and the genesis of Oliver are offered; the narrative 'chooses' to present some events and not others.

This example shows how narrative maintains the fragile distinction between 'showing' and 'telling', an issue to which we will return on more than one occasion in what follows. Yet we must also note that the act of selecting what is depicted here is also crucial in the process of narrative, and provides a demonstration of a general fact about representation: that representation allows some things to be depicted and not others. In order to prefigure some of the arguments about this, consider the following example. The film *Pleasantville* (1998) features the story of a contemporary American brother and sister in their teens. Near the beginning of the movie they find themselves inserted into the world of a late-1950s television sitcom, a world that is self-contained, black and white, squeaky-clean and ideologically unquestioning. Having reconciled themselves to their fate, they play the roles of son and daughter to their fictional parents, and the roles of friends to their fellow pupils at school. But this is not without its problems: in one humorous moment early in the film, the sister decides to go to the Ladies' Room while she is in a diner, only to find, once she is beyond the door, that there are no facilities there for answering the call of nature. The incident wryly tells us what we all know: that, on television, people never (or very rarely) empty their bowels. More accurately, in the terms of the present discussion, we could say that narrative *selects* some events and omits others.

These comments should offer a few preliminary insights about narrative as it might be distinguished from the terms with which it is often juxtaposed and often confused, 'story' and 'plot'. Yet it remains to ask what is fundamental to narrative and what some of its chief components might be. In light of the above comments about selection and the (re)arrangement of events, it should be clear that the concept of sequence is crucial.

## SEQUENCE

At the lowest level of simplification, narrative is a sequence that is narrated. As an example, we might consider any documentary series on television. Since the success of 'Life on Earth' in 1980, BBC 1 in Britain has made sure that the autumn schedules will be graced with a major 'life' documentary such as 'The Living Planet', 'The Life of Birds' or 'Walking with Dinosaurs'. Customarily we will assume that these consist of a series of pictures which we watch on the screen and which are *narrated* by a voice-over commentator. Quite often, in wildlife documentaries, the latter is a popularly recognized authority such as Sir David Attenborough. Thus, the narrative seems to come from the authoritative voice-over. But one might ask whether the actual pictures on screen and the way that they are organized into a sequence also constitute a narrative. This 'showing', in addition to the voice-over 'telling', might equally possess a narrative orientation.

By asking this question it is not necessarily implied that verbal and visual narratives are the same. The Russian semiotician, Jurij Lotman (1977), usefully illustrates that the verbal arts such as literature are characterized by sequences whose individual elements are themselves discrete units of meaning (words or phrases). The iconic or pictorial arts, on the other hand, realize their meaning through their existence as an isolated *whole*, while music does it not through individual elements *or* through isolation but through its very sequence; film, television and video, in yet another way, combine these characteristics. So, with the simplest of definitions which aims to cover all media, serious questions begin to arise.

It is probably the fact that we rarely acknowledge such questions that makes us take narrative for granted; or even believe that it is natural and just happens for our instant gratification. Organized stories, once more, *seem* to be intrinsic to the fabric of everyday existence (cf. Forster 1962). On the other hand, as soon as we begin to think a little bit more deeply about the issue, we might easily reach the conclusion that the whole storytelling impulse is illusory: catching the bus, going out with friends, performing mundane tasks at work, watching football – none of these come to fruition as stories unless we choose to impose some kind of narrative form on them.

The contradictory coupling of these insights leads to the most fundamental observation that can be made of narrative: that it consists of signs. A sequence of any kind might exist in the world, but if that sequence is to consist of meaningful relations it requires human input; it needs to be understood as being made up of signs. A cat, for example, may jump onto a wall and, in so doing, nudge a terracotta pot which falls onto the concrete on the other side, spilling its load of compost and shattering into the bargain. This sequence of actions exists, but until I become aware of the breakage by being told or by actually witnessing the desolate fragments of the pot, I am unable to interpret it as a sign of the cat's clumsy wall-scaling activities.

What is apparent, then, is that as soon as we advance on the task of seeing relations between things, we are operating in the domain of signs. Moreover, these are thoroughly human signs. Undoubtedly, signs between and within animals, and signs between plants make up the bulk of communication on this planet; but while it is possible that a second cat might pass by the broken vessel and catch the sign of another cat's scent, we have no way of knowing whether it could make the interpretation that we do on the basis of the breakage alone. Human signs, or what humans interpret as signs, therefore stand in for something else in the world. Put another way, they *re*-present it (Hall 1997).

This dynamic, which is so obvious that we tend to forget it, has been depicted most economically by the literary theorist Wolfgang Iser. Referring to the way in which representation works, he has stated succinctly, "no rendering can *be* that which it renders" (Iser 1989: 251). Put another way, as it is here by the historian David Carr, "real events do not have the character of those we find in stories, and if we treat them as if they did have such a character, we are not being true to them" (1991: 160). In the second quote we can see that there is much at stake in recognizing the transformations which take place in *re*-presentation. Yet, not only is the 'real' world different from the world as it is represented, as even 'reflective' and 'intentional' approaches would acknowledge, but representational systems such as narrative *work* to facilitate the recognition of such phenomena as sequence and causality. They facilitate the meaningful relations which will transpire with human input.

The general work of representation as we have described it can also be carried out by non-narrative forms such as statuary, still photography and even music. Therefore we are compelled to ask what is specific to narrative representation. At their simplest, all narratives are the movement from a beginning point to a finishing point. Narrative is just a sequence which starts and moves inexorably to its end. To understand this is to understand the most important principle behind narrative. Of course, any straightforward movement from start to finish runs the risk of being tedious; yet, as most of us are aware right from our first experiences of fairy tales as infants, narrative has the potential to be thoroughly captivating. Furthermore, even tedious narratives cannot consist of an untrammelled journey from A to B; it is impossible, just as it is impossible to imagine an object that has only one dimension. The most crude and flimsy narratives must have something between their beginnings and ends.

The best way to indicate what makes up the body of narrative, or what comes between the beginning and end, is through the use of examples. We will start with one from probably the most famous contemporary writer of popular narratives, Stephen King (b. 1947). In his 1992 novel *Gerald's Game* Gerald and Jessie are a middle-aged married couple who own a country cabin where they go for weekends away from it all. Whilst there they have fallen into the habit of playing sado-masochistic games which invariably involve Jessie being tied up or handcuffed to the bed as a prelude to sexual intercourse. On the occasion narrated in the novel, however, Jessie has become sweaty and irritated, and demands that Gerald remove the handcuffs. Advancing naked to the bed, Gerald thinks she is just playing along in the game and makes no effort to release his wife. This only makes Jessie more angry and when Gerald is within striking distance she lashes out, kicking him in the groin.

Unfortunately, as a result of the kick, Gerald has a heart attack and dies on the spot, leaving Jessie chained to the bed with no clothes on and a dead husband on the floor. It is just after this point in the novel that the following sequence is narrated, in which a stray dog enters the cabin:

> The stray began to advance slowly into the room, legs stiff with caution, tail drooping, eyes wide and black, lips peeled back to reveal a full complement of teeth. About such concepts as absurdity it knew nothing.
>
> The former Prince [!], with whom the eight-year old Catherine Sutlin had once romped joyfully (at least until she'd gotten a Cabbage Patch doll named Marnie for her birthday and tem-

porarily lost some of her interest), was part lab and part collie ... a mixed breed, but a long way from being a mongrel. When Sutlin had turned it out on Bay Lane at the end of August, it had weighed eighty pounds and its coat had been glossy and sleek with health, a not unattractive mixture of brown and black (with a distinctive white collie bib on the chest and undersnout). It now weighed a bare forty pounds, and a hand passed down its side would have felt every straining rib, not to mention the rapid, feverish beat of its heart. Its coat was dull and bedraggled and full of burdocks. A half-healed pink scar, souvenir of a panicky scramble under a barbed wire fence, zigzagged down one haunch, and a few porcupine quills stuck out of its muzzle like crooked whiskers. It had found the porker lying dead under a log about ten days ago, but had given up on it after the first noseful of quills. It had been hungry but not yet desperate.

Now it was both. Its last meal had been a few maggoty scraps nosed out of a discarded garbage bag in a ditch standing beside Route 117, and that had been two days ago. The dog which had quickly learned to bring Catherine Sutlin a red rubber ball when she rolled it across the living-room floor or into the hall was now quite literally starving on its feet.

Yes, but here – right here, on the floor, *within sight!* – were pounds and pounds of fresh meat, and fat, and bones filled with sweet marrow. It was like a gift from the God of Strays.

The onetime darling of Catherine Sutlin continued to advance on the corpse of Gerald Burlingame.

(King 1992: 77)

What is obvious about this undoubtedly gruesome scenario is that it does not have to be presented in this precise way. A minimal way to narrate the scene would be to write 'A dog came in and started to eat the dead body.' Slightly more satisfying might be 'A *starving* dog tentatively entered the room and, seeing that it was safe, approached the corpse, its appetite whetted.' The addition of the word 'starving' introduces a little bit of motivation.

The much longer digression in the passage above, however, offers a great deal of detail of the dog's recent past, all of which is germane and much of which it is quite diverting to hear about, including the fact that the dog, like a famous contemporary 'artist', was formerly called Prince. Perhaps more important than the mere information, though, is the fact that the readers of the novel, when supplied with the necessary details, will most likely be able to make up their own minds about what might happen in this room with this starved animal and this pile of meat on the floor. Despite this, a fine balance is imperative: King himself admits that he has "been accused over and over again of having diarrhea [sic] of the word processor" (King 1991: ix). These are matters of selection, once more, but there is a further matter of importance.

The progress of fictional narrative must, necessarily, be impeded; and this is the key point. Narrative must entail some kind of delay or even diversions, detours and digressions. Moreover, these can yield a certain amount of pleasure for the reader. Crucially, however, such delays or digressions are not foolproof mechanisms which guarantee enjoyment; instead, the space between beginning and end in narrative is where the reader will be involved in doing work. Immediately, then, in this simple definition, two further facts arise about narrative which demand some investigation. These are that a narrative might be said to possess 'space' in the movement from beginning to end, and that narratives enact in this movement a relation to 'time'.

## SPACE

The whole notion of narrative progression or a movement from 'A' to 'B' implies that there is such a thing as 'narrative space'. A narrative must advance to its end whilst simultaneously delaying it, and in lingering, as it were, a narrative occupies a 'space'. This dynamic has been most cogently expressed by the French critic and cultural theorist, Roland Barthes: in *S/Z* (1974) he analyses a Balzac short story, 'Sarrasine', by elaborating five codes through whose matrix the text passes. There is a code of action, the 'proairetic', which is concerned with the linear relation of narrative events; a code of character traits, the 'semic'; and a code of binary oppositions, invoking a specific meaning according to some latent and opposed, but nevertheless present, meaning, the 'symbolic'. All of these codes are germane to the study of narrative and assist Barthes in making a robust analysis of the Balzac story. But the fifth of these codes, the 'hermeneutic', is of particular interest to the present discussion as it has a dual function in relation to the establishment of narrative 'space': to push the narrative forward towards disclosure and simultaneously to retard the narrative's progress by way of 'equivocation', 'snares' and 'false replies'.

Peter Brooks (1982) suggests that the individual retardations on the way to a narrative's end which Barthes has recognized in his discussion of 'Sarrasine' and identified by way of the 'hermeneutic' code, can also be understood as *detours*. *Detours* are woven so imperceptibly into narratives that they may not be instantly apparent as pure delays but rather as snatches of dialogue or sequential description. In the popular genre of narrative known as the thriller, for example, *detours* are components of the process that creates the phenomenon known as suspense. Will the hero uncover the extent of the conspiracy? Will s/he survive this threatening situation? Will s/he triumph over the villain? These are fundamental questions about the *dis*pleasure that is created by stoppages, by the problems in story events and by the yield of pleasure in their resolution. Clearly, then, *detours* are a crucial site of potential enjoyment in a narrative.

Yet, this is not always an easy point to understand; consider the following statement by the American hard-boiled writer, Mickey Spillane:

> A fiction story is like a joke. The reason you listen to a joke is to get to the punchline. Pacing a story is like sex: you start off with the teasing, then work up to the rough stuff and then all of a sudden you get the real boom-da-boom-da-boom-da-BANG, the big explosion, then you're finished. The closer to the last word you can get the climax, the better. Nobody reads a book to get to the middle, you read a book to get to the end and you hope the end is good enough to justify all the time you have spent reading it.
>
> (Miller 1989: 36)

On the one hand, Spillane wishes to contradict those points about the necessity and potential pleasure in *detours* which we have made so far; but, on the other hand, by means of the analogy with sexual intercourse, he unwittingly makes our point for us by stressing the necessity of a build-up in any narrative. An alternative reading of the quote might suggest that Spillane has a pretty instrumental understanding of the act of sex.

There is more to delay, as well, than simply pulling back from the climax. Brooks notes that the movement towards disclosure in narrative, its linear dynamic, is equivalent to the poetic effect of metonymy, the sequential linking of items according to their common association in part or whole; for example, a shot of the Houses of Parliament and Big Ben in a film stands for 'London', or the phrase 'the Pentagon' may be used to refer to the US military establishment rather than simply its headquarters. Here, one thing calls upon another by linear association, thus linking narrative progression to sequence. In addition, though, Brooks states that narrative has a metaphorical aspect where something different is offered in place of the expected item. Love, for example, might be presented as a red rose. So, on the one hand, the movement towards conclusion is effected by a *re*-presentation which is culturally coded in a relatively general way and, on the other, by a trope which is more specifically culturally coded.

It is worth noting that, in pursuing this argument, Brooks utilizes two concepts distinguished by the Formalists, a group of literary theorists operating in Russia directly after the First World War. For them, *fabula* refers to the chronological sequence of events which make up the raw materials of a story; *sjuzet* is the way the story is organized. It is important to acknowledge here that these influential terms are usually translated as 'story' and 'discourse' respectively, conflating 'plot' and 'narrative' in the process (see Chatman 1978), although they are sometimes translated into 'story' and 'plot' (Shklovsky 1965; Hawthorn 1997). Either way, they fall into the difficulties we noted above. However, *fabula* and *sjuzet* have been crucial terms in the analysis of narrative, especially for Brooks. The reason that the concept of *fabula* is helpful is because it designates the prior events that are to be narrated; at the same time, however, such events are always *organized* in a way that presents itself as 'the same' as those events but, of course, is quite 'different'. That is, it is always *re*organized to highlight some events and downplay others, an activity designated by the term *sjuzet*. In purporting to relate a sequence of prior events, Brooks argues, narrative is therefore a transformation: like metaphor, narrative is "the same-but-different", and the level of unfamiliarity entailed by this formula also results in a temporary halt to the movement towards disclosure.

Some of the representation in a narrative, then, is based on principles which are fairly familiar and expected: metonymy, sequence; other aspects forge new associations: metaphor. Although this version of representation based on a dual formulation of *fabula* and *sjuzet* fails to tally with our identification of the separable entities 'story', 'plot' and 'narrative', it is instructive when considered in relation to our earlier observations about narrative as an ensemble of signs. The examples we used suggested that signs have reference to something real in the world which might actually be available for scrutiny; signs then act to *re*-present, in different ways, that to which they refer. Equally, though, signs refer to things that are not easily available (for example, Utopia, Sherlock Holmes, the USS Enterprise) and, even so, they still *re*-present that to which they refer. This is the case with *fabula* and *sjuzet*. According to Brooks' argument there is a rationale for the *fabula/sjuzet* combination which lies in narrative's completion; but rather than Spillane's desultory vision of an impatient sexual journey to the climax, Brooks sees the *anticipated* "structuring force of the ending" in the movement through narrative space (1982: 283). A corollary of this is that the *detours*, all those delaying factors on the way to the ending of a narrative, are 'bound' to an end point. 'Binding' is the process by which a *detour* is created and a 'binding effect', therefore, is something that also produces all those retardations of the narrative's progress to denouement that Barthes discussed under the terms of the 'hermeneutic code': 'snares', 'equivocations', 'false replies'. What we might add to this is that story events will be caught up in this complex and often be bound 'in space' by a plot; but we must also say that the specific ways in which that binding will be related are due to narrative.

## TIME

While the movement of narrative implies 'space', it must always also involve 'time'. Moving a football from one end of a field to another, moving the pieces of a broken terracotta pot from the ground to a dustbin, and moving through a narrative, are all activities which must take place within a particular time-frame. Yet the vicissitudes of time are notoriously difficult to understand, especially in light of the fact that all humans tend to apprehend time through its discrete measurements: days, weeks, years, as well as the way it is imposed on us – by the regularity of work schedules, railway timetables, licensing hours, and so forth. One of the most influential discussions of the nature of time, both in contemporary philosophy and in literary theory, is that of the French thinker, Paul Ricoeur, especially his three-volume work *Time and Narrative* (1984–6). For Ricoeur, time is not just a part of the narrative apparatus; in fact, he understands time and narrative as being on intimate terms precisely because narrative *is* the human relation to time.

This obviously requires some elucidation, so let us consider that there are two types of temporality: 'objective' time and 'subjective' time. 'Objective' time co-exists with the universe, it is embodied in the movements of the heavenly bodies, it always has been and there is nothing that we can do about it. For most people, this is a difficult concept to grasp, although it is integral to modern physics (see Hawking 1988, Davies 1996 and Gribbin 1999 for introductions). 'Subjective' time is temporal passage as it is experienced by humans going about their lives. The obvious problem that arises, then, is that 'objective' time cannot be measured or even conceptualized unless it is done so by a 'subjective' human; similarly, 'subjective' time cannot exist without some reference to the possibility of 'objective' time. The two are linked for humans in an inescapable relation, and it is at this point that narrative comes in.

Commenting on Ricoeur, Stevens (1995) offers, as an example of narrative's mediating role between the two forms of time, the human invention of the calendar. The calendar corresponds to the movements of the heavens but it is also a linear narrative sequence: Tuesday, Wednesday, Thursday; March, April, May; 1886, 1887, 1888. It provides a good starting point for thinking through Ricoeur's reasoning although, as the rest of the present book will make clear, from the very beginning strict linear sequence such as that espoused by the calendar has repeatedly been subverted in narrative.

Ricoeur's perspective on time and narrative is also a 'hermeneutic' one. That is to say it is one which is based on understanding the imperatives involved in the interpretation of phenomena. In respect of time, Freeman says

> We seek to revisit the morning before we arrived at work, or the previous day or month or year; we land back in the present, now informed by the visits just made; we concentrate on what's next, both in the immediate and distant future ... in coming to terms with the past, I can only do so from the present, through the act of interpretation.
>
> (Freeman 1998: 41)

For Ricoeur, this kind of understanding is crucial, especially in the interrogation of the relation of time and narrative.

The two philosophers who are probably most important to Ricoeur's analysis in his three-volume work are Martin Heidegger (1889–1976) and St Augustine (354–430), and a passage from the *Confessions* of the latter opens up the interpretative nature of the issue quite nicely, by introducing the idea of the 'three-fold present':

> Suppose I am going to recite a psalm that I know. Before I begin my faculty of expectation is engaged by the whole of it. But once I have begun, as much of the psalm as I have removed from the province of expectation and relegated to the past now engages my memory, and the scope of the action which I am performing is divided between the two faculties of memory and expectation, the one looking back to the part which I have already recited, the other looking forward to the part which I have still to recite. But my faculty of attention is present all the while, and through it passes what was the future in the process of becoming the past. As the process continues, the province of memory is extended in proportion as that of expectation is reduced, until the whole of my expectation is absorbed. This happens when I have finished my recitation and it has all passed into the province of memory.
>
> (St Augustine cited in Ricoeur 1984–6: 20)

It must be remembered that Augustine, a fifth-century Christian, wishes to say something about eternity in these meditations as well as the origin of the universe. But it is notable that he chooses to use a *text* to conjure up the interpretative triad of 'expectation – memory – attention'.

Ricoeur insists that the kind of temporality encountered in narrative has more to do with the interpretative mode prefigured in Augustine's comments than it has to do with the common-place version of time as a series of instants arranged along a line. Like Brooks, he stresses the importance of the end point of a nar-rative, arguing that the understanding of successive actions, thoughts and feelings in a narrative is dictated by anticipation of the conclusion, and also, that reaching the conclusion enables a backward glance at the actions that led up to it (Ricoeur 1981: 170). Narrative is therefore not just a matter of paying attention to individual incidents on the time-line; it is most importantly about 'expectation' and 'memory': reading the end in the begin-ning and reading the beginning in the end.

It follows from this recognition, then, that the cornerstone of narrative structure is the plot, or what Ricoeur, borrowing from Aristotle and, presumably, to avoid plot/*sjuzet*/discourse difficul-ties, calls 'muthos' or 'emplotment'. Emplotment is the intelligi-ble whole which governs the succession of events in a story and thus "places us at the crossing point of temporality and narrative" (Ricoeur 1981: 167). Moreover, this is so for both fictional narra-tive and historical narrative, according to Ricoeur, and for three basic reasons. First, humans' knowledge of the world is largely framed by narrative. Despite what we said above about the non-story nature of catching the bus, going out with friends, perform-ing mundane tasks at work and watching football, Ricoeur is keen to point out that "we are not born into a world of children … as unspeaking children, we come in to a world already full of our predecessors' narratives" (1981: 181–2), that "The largest part of our information about events in the world is, in fact, owing to knowledge though hearsay" (1985: 156) and that "action is already symbolically mediated; literature, in the largest sense of the word, including history as well as fiction, tends to reinforce a process of symbolization already at work" (1991: 182). Second, history is as shot through with emplotment as fiction, based as it is on a conception of time as 'expectation – attention – memory' rather than simple linear sequence. Third, historical narrative, like fictional narrative, strongly seems to invite these 'narrative-time' conceptions of readers in which movement through the narrative is guided by anticipation, focus and retrospection.

This last point is worth expanding a little in relation to what we have said about both space *and* time in narrative. Ricoeur, Barthes and Brooks begin their analyses in ways which suggest that they are discovering some objective facts about narrative as an empirical entity. All of them, however, give way to an understanding of their task as an exegesis of the status and functions of narratives in interactions which involve readers. With this in mind, Ricoeur's project in particular deserves a brief additional comment. Throughout *Time and Narrative*, Ricoeur delineates the position he is against: the 'semiotics' of narrative. He outlines the way that various narrative theorists, such as Propp, Greimas and Lévi-Strauss, as well as some later 'narratologists', all act to 'dechronologize' narrative and reduce it to a series of dominating 'paradigmatic' functions, leaving sequence to the mercy of the common-sense linear interpretation of time. Lying behind this, I believe, is a critique of the *text-centredness* of such approaches (as opposed to understandings of narrative which are aware of the reader's roles in meaning-making).

In terms of the present book, Ricoeur's designation of the 'dechronologizing' tendency is rather unfortunate. Although 'semiotics' has been the term given to the study of the sign since at least 1969 (see Sebeok 2001), embracing the tradition stemming from the 'semeiotic' of Charles Sanders Peirce and the 'semiology' of Ferdinand de Saussure, the narratological work under criticism from Ricoeur is, with the exception of the Russian folklorist, Propp, actually constituted by the latter, Saussurean, phalanx. Alternatively, the theory of the sign which underpins the earlier comments in this chapter and which will be implicit in the chapters that follow is Peircean. The signs which we will see as making up narratives are signs which have objects (in the world or not), signs which change and become other signs when the circumstances are congenial, and, above all, signs for an interpreting agent. In the case of narrative, this interpreter must be a human.

## PHYLOGENY AND ONTOGENY

The fact that narrative consists of human signs leads to probably the most common questions about narrative: how, why and where did it come from? There are two broad ways of answering the question of where narrative comes from. The first would be to consider the psychology of telling stories: why is it that humans have such a strong propensity to think events in a narrative form as opposed to some other kind of organization? Is it a deep-rooted psychological impulse, or is it cultural habit? Implicit in these questions is the conviction that events do not always take place in the shape of a tidy narrative and that tentative answers or speculations in this area might contribute to lively and ongoing debate. It is a bit of a disappointment, then, to find that the most promising opening comments on the issue in a range of books on narrative tend to gloss over the psychological roots in order to move straight on to the historical progress of narrative (see, for example, Scholes and Kellogg 1966: 3–16; Bettelheim 1976: 3–6; Ong 1982: 5–12; Rimmon-Kenan 1983: 1–5; Brooks 1984: 3–7; Chatman 1990: 6–11; Berger 1997: 1–7; cf. Bell 1990).

The other way that the question is answered is by focusing on the evolution of narrative forms against the background of the evolution of peoples. Needless to say, such work will either be anthropological or heavily influenced by anthropology. It will involve referring to the first known narratives which contain elements that are recognizable as the less-evolved features of modern narratives in an attempt to track historically the development of narrative (and different narratives) from its beginnings to the present.

The first approach, looking for the origins of narrative in psychological or biological constituents of humans, provides an ontogenetic perspective on narrative. The second, relying on evidence of developments from the diversity of humans' cultural heritage, is known as a phylogenetic approach. Occasionally, ontogeny and phylogeny can be seen to overlap; on other occasions, ontogenetic and phylogenetic understandings of human phenomena have been seen as thoroughly reciprocal, such that ontogeny 'recapitulates' phylogeny (see Gould 1977).

Brian Sutton-Smith (1997) takes an ontogenetic perspective on the origins of narrative. Specifically, he focuses on children's play activities. For him, stories are not themselves play, but many of the themes that appear in the narratives told by pre-school-age children are originally to be found in their play: being chased, fighting, and crashing cars (160). More complex narrative formations develop from this. By age seven, for example, he finds that children begin to create central, hero, characters in their stories (164), mirroring the trajectory of games with a winner. More sophisticated narratives such as nonsense, parody and satire stories also develop out of play situations. Indeed, there is strong evidence to suggest that such stories are allied to a propensity to similar play with the building bricks of language in general (see Crystal 1998). Yet Sutton-Smith does not remain fixed to an ontogenetic view: writing of comic and trickster tales, he adds a phylogenetic supplement by suggesting that "it is possible to suppose that these early childhood stories are very basic, perhaps universal, narratives of the human mind" (1997: 163).

Another ontogenetic argument, that of Anderson, is interesting for us partly because it will be replayed in a different guise in

Chapter 2, but also because it is offered by an anthropologist. She points out that

> the communication systems of other creatures permit no negation, no constructive fantasy, no manipulations of other times and places. Other animals cannot 're-call' a pheromone indicating 'fear' and replace it with another saying 'not-fear' or 'hungry'. ... Humans, thanks to language, find it easy to lie and deny, to transport both sender and receiver to other actual and imagined situations, and to construct elaborate shared narratives and simultaneously modify and contradict these stories.
>
> (Anderson 1998: 31)

For Anderson, the capacity for a specific kind of communication among humans not only 'permits' narratives but practically makes them obligatory in the organization of human experience.

Probably the most phylogenetic argument about the origins of narrative, although ontogenetic in some of its implications, is that of Julian Jaynes (1990). Writing on the origins of human consciousness, he argues that it arose from a period when the human brain ceased to be 'bicameral' and became more focused on one or the other of its hemispheres and the mental functions associated with them. In a long, but engaging, dissertation on this topic he comments on the phenomenon of 'narratization', which he sees as intimate and coeval with what we know as human consciousness. Put briefly, his contention is that humans develop a sense of 'self', an 'analog I', which acts in the world; they then see the actions of this 'I' as part of a narrative: "The thief narratizes his act as due to poverty, the poet his as due to beauty, and the scientist his as due to truth, purpose and cause inextricably woven into the spatialization of behavior in consciousness" (Jaynes 1990: 64). But he also suggests that 'bicameral'-minded humans did not have complex introspective thoughts; instead, they heard voices in their heads, the 'gods' of the ancient myths and epics. Around 3000 BCE this began to change with the building of cities in Mesopotamia, the development of writing, and the impulse to narratization which arose from a meditation on, and the desire to record, past events. Although outlandish and sometimes speculative, we will see in the next chapter that this argument is not without its persuasive aspects.

Jaynes' observations on the human impulse to produce a 'meaningful' existence based on a narratization of the past, as well as the maintenance of a sense of self, are echoed in the findings of the Chicago psychologist, Mihaly Csikszentmihalyi (1992, 1994, 1996; Beattie and Csikszentmihalyi 1981). In a range of psychological experiments with human subjects in different situations, Csikszentmihalyi developed the concept of 'flow' based on his discoveries. He found that various humans harboured the capacity to sense an immense satisfaction, commitment, rejuvenation and even joy in certain occupations and pastimes, a capacity that enhanced their lives and their 'selves'. Yet, specifically, he found that this capacity of 'flow', allied with the development of coherent life themes, was frequently spurred by an early engagement with narrative as a tool for making meaning of the world. By contrast, "individuals who never focus on any goal, or accept one unquestioningly from the society around them, tend not to remember their parents having read or told stories to them as children" (Csikszentmihalyi 1992: 236). Narrative in this instance is pre-eminently a matter of human interaction in meaning, rather than simply a process involving 'objective', sequential signs.

This 'humanness' of the origins of narrative can be thought of in two broad ways which invoke phylogeny and ontogeny. In a famous study of myth, Joseph Campbell (1975) considers the figure of the hero in the stories ancient and modern which are told across the globe. His contention is a phylogenetic one: that the human species shares a common story with broadly similar protagonists and events which respond to the riddle of life in the same way. However, Campbell's argument has a strong ontogenetic component, too; as might be expected from a perspective so heavily influenced by (Freudian and Jungian) psychoanalysis, there is an attempt to root the principles of world myths in the putatively common experience of the infant:

> Apparently, the most permanent of the dispositions of the human psyche are those that derive from the fact that, of all animals, we remain the longest at the mother's breast. Human beings are born too soon; they are unfinished, unready as yet to meet the world. Consequently, their whole defence from a universe of dangers is the mother, under whose protection the intra-uterine period is prolonged.
>
> (Campbell 1975: 15)

This prolonged scenario gives rise to the "tragi-comic triangle of the nursery" (15): mother–infant–father. Essentially, the effects of the currents in this fundamental relationship are re-played, according to Campbell, in all myths.

Campbell's argument is not that dissimilar from the 'semiotic' or, more helpfully, 'structural' analyses of narrative that Ricoeur has criticized. Different cultures and different time periods may give rise to seemingly diverse narrative organizations; so, too, might they produce widely differing protagonists and situations. But, Campbell suggests, depth analysis reveals that these seemingly different myths are all the same because they derive from or 'reflect' identical primal relationships among humans. In outline, this is the same kind of reasoning which underpins the analyses of 'structural' theorists such as the anthropologist Lévi-Strauss and the folklorist Propp. It is a universalizing tendency, reducing a complex phenomenon to a limited set of universal principles; also, it may be said to be 'functionalist' in that it elides the possible conflicts within the complexity of the phenomenon in favour of a focus on the root, unifying features.

An opposing perspective on narrative is offered by sociolinguistics and social semiotics. This position is particularly well known in the sphere of literacy study and is notable for the way in which it takes account of localized, but profound, conflicts created by the context of communication. For example, a recent study of children's spelling by Gunther Kress focused on the mistakes made by youngsters at a North London primary school; as Kress shows, there exists considerable competition between the ways in which the children feel inclined to spell certain words and the ways in which they 'should' spell them as prescribed by teachers and the English language. But, at the same time, there is also great creativity in the children's spelling, especially the way in which it so accurately mirrors pronunciations of words in the all-pervasive local milieux outside the school (Kress 1999a, 1999b). In respect of narrative, the anthropologist and sociolinguist Dell Hymes makes an identical point. Analysing certain Native American myths and narratives, especially those told to children, he discerns a very complex patterning which, when placed in printed prose, is based on lines and verses. The effect of this patterning, however, is so subtle as to be inaudible to all but the most trained ear; further, the Native American languages do not provide a means of actually listing, categorizing and talking about these subtle narrative patterning devices. But this fact has not stopped the people steadfastly using them in the highly influential stories which they pass on to children. Why?

Hymes believes that the non-Native American fails to apprehend the localized creativity of the Native American narrative patterning. The conflict, in American schools, for example, between dominant narrative patterns and Native American patterns arises, perhaps, from the latter's basis in a culturally specific understanding of children's capacity for communication; Hymes writes,

Among the Chinookans and some other peoples, children,

when they first gave voice, were believed not to be babbling but to be speaking a special language they shared with spirits. There were shamans appointed who were believed to have the power to interpret this language. The concern was that if the children didn't like it here, they might go back to where they were before. The keeping of children was of tremendous importance. There was tremendous value placed on the individual child, and so, in a sense, children were being wooed into adult life.

(Hymes 1996: 136–7)

For Hymes, this attitude to children differs from modern society, which, through its dominance and its own array of narrative patterning paraphernalia, "does debase local tradition and creativity but does not succeed in eradicating it" (140). More striking than this socio-semiotic tenet, though, is the possibility countenanced by Hymes that "the richness of syntax that linguistics finds in every normal child may be accompanied by a richness of narrative organization" (139).

The psychologist, Jerome Bruner, is one of those who, like Hymes, is keen to confront the idea that there may be an 'innate' human propensity towards narrative. While acknowledging that narrative has been built up through time and through tradition, he asks, "Is it unreasonable to suppose that there is some human 'readiness' for narrative that is responsible for elaborating and conserving such a tradition in the first place?" (Bruner 1990: 45). The notion that there is a 'readiness' in children to adopt syntax or grammatical forms has, since the work of the American linguist, Noam Chomsky, been well established (see Pinker 1994; Salkie 2001). But what Bruner suggests is that there "is a 'push' to construct narrative that determines the order of priority in which grammatical forms are mastered by the young child" (1990: 77). This 'push' consists of, and depends on (a) a means for emphasizing human agency or action; (b) a sequence of some sort;

(c) a sense of what is canonical, that is traditional or permitted in human interaction as well as what is non-canonical; and (d) a narrator's perspective. These features of narrative represent the bottom line for Bruner, and we will see in the chapters that follow how frequently they recur.

The following chapters, then, take a broad look at the history of narrative: how it has been seen to develop and how it has been thought to be used. Yet this is not just necessary to demonstrate how narrative embodies the four features of Bruner's 'push'; instead, it should also show that narrative, especially to its users, is much more than these root features. For, as Bruner adds, "the culture soon equips us with new powers of narration through its tool kit and through the traditions of telling and interpreting in which we soon come to participate" (1990: 80). In addition, as we will discover, there are a number of methodological problems in the enterprise of constructing an overview of narrative forms, some of which are very serious. But, as we will also see, accounts of the trajectory of narrative development are indispensable to the construction of any future, anticipated, hoped-for, 'definitive' account of narrative as a whole.

# 2

---

# EARLY NARRATIVE

The study of narrative, as opposed to the 'pure' study of, say, the novel or film, obviously has a wide compass. Where analysis focuses upon one particular narrative genre it may be forced to neglect commonalities of process across different kinds of text in favour of investigating the specificities of enunciation in the genre in question. The advantage of general narrative analysis is that it identifies mechanisms which may be integral to linguistically or visually based genres without becoming embroiled in parochial questions to do with the 'effectiveness' of given modes, or the relative 'value' of different genres. This also allows narrative analysis to track the development of a specified process as well as its embodiment in a range of generic and technological forms.

Yet narrative analysis is not without its problems, one of the chief ones arising from the fact that narrative is used not only to record fictional events but also to record events that actually happened. At first glance, this fact might seem to pose no difficulty: discerning the difference between non-fictional and fictional narratives often appears to be an easy matter. Narrative accounts of contemporary events in discourses such as news are relatively simple to identify in the present as 'factual' in opposition to, say, the 'fictional' events to be found in drama. In its print and broadcast versions, news has developed a repertoire of devices, ranging from a specific syntax to the authoritativeness of its presentation, which have enabled a quick recognition of it as a discourse distinct from fiction (see Hartley 1982; McNair 1996). Furthermore, in the present it is sometimes possible to verify that events depicted in non-fiction actually happened or occurred in a particular way.

Narrative accounts of events produced in the distant past, however, are another matter. The events that they recount are so remote that there will be difficulties in establishing whether the events depicted actually took place or whether they are embellished, embroidered or plain fiction.

Clearly, this creates a difficulty for the practice of history which seeks to untangle that which is true from that which is demonstrably untrue. But it also has consequences for investigation of the early variants of the kind of narrative with which we are concerned in this book: fiction. The temptation to consider 'narrative' and 'fiction' as synonymous is countered both by the recognition of the role of narrative in historical discourse and the consideration of the possible purposes for the implementation of narrative form by early cultures. Let us briefly expand on these two points.

## NARRATIVE AND HISTORY

Fundamentally, history can be conceived both as an "extra-textual real" and as a set of signs which make up a discourse (Bennett 1990: 53). That is to say, history as extra-textual real entails actual events that *really* happened irrespective of what has been recorded about them; in addition, though, there is also a practice of *writing* history which relies not on objective knowable truth but on a *representation* of "what can be derived from the historical record or archive" (Bennett 1990: 49). That the historical record is itself a discursive entity made up of signs means that it offers a *re*-presented, thoroughly selective account of what actually happened.

The work of Hayden White (1973, 1987) has become synonymous with such questions, and the crux of the matter for him is fictionality. Although devices of narrativity such as plot, story, sequence and space are commonly thought to be appropriate to accounts which are *not* true, historians have deliberately inculcated narrativity into their practice to demonstrate processes and causality in real, true happenings. In the cases of both fiction and historical non-fiction there is always a re-presentation of some prior events, a *fabula* as the Russian Formalists describe it in relation to fictional narrative. Consequently, argues White,

> all written discourse is cognitive in its aims and mimetic in its means. And this is true even of the most ludic and seemingly expressivist discourse, of poetry no less than of prose, and even of those forms of poetry which seem to illuminate only 'writing itself'. In this respect, history is no less a form of fiction than the novel is a form of historical representation.
>
> (White 1987: 122)

For White, then, fictional and factual representation both partake of the same rhetorical devices or tropes. It therefore follows that the devices of narrativity play a large part in facilitating human apprehension of the world.

White is hence led to ask whether events in the world always appear to us as mere sequence, one thing after another, or as narratives with beginnings, middles and ends (White 1981: 23). For him, the narrative impulse, both in fictional and historical accounts, might encapsulate a deeper human desire for a 'moral' representation, a sequence with an outcome. Yet even if this is mere speculation, it provides a clue to the purposes for which narrative became so important to early cultures.

## ORALITY, LITERACY AND NARRATIVE

In referring to the mimetic qualities of narrative, above, it is not insignificant that White stresses the role of *written* discourse in recording history. As opposed to the archaeological record, the historical record predominantly exists in linguistic form and, within this form, written records far outweigh oral records. The obvious reason for this latter point is the superior ability of writing to survive in its physical manifestation and to be passed on from epoch to epoch, either as *non-narrative* artefacts such as account books, bureaucratic registers of such events as births, marriages and deaths, and annals, or as *narrative* artefacts such as contemporary histories, biographies, non-fictional accounts of current events and even avowedly semi-fictional accounts such as myths or ballads.

The ability of written discourse to be stored, intact and safe in its original form to be scrutinized again and again, bestows an advantage that oral discourse cannot enjoy. Oral discourse relies on the faithfulness and memory of its transmitters and receivers, neither of which can be perfect as means of recording events. The imperfections of human memory and faithfulness palpably undermine any attempt by oral discourse to render the totality of events without resort to a high degree of compression and omission.

At first sight this seems to suggest that oral discourse is automatically inferior, or even to grant immediate prestige to the written sign. However, it should not be forgotten that written discourse is equally doomed to compression, to present some events and not others, to render in a record only that which is appropriate to that particular written form, while omitting or playing down those things which do not offer themselves quite so readily for representation. Indeed, the superiority of written discourse in history has not always been readily accepted. Ong argues (1982: 96–101) that oral culture was so strong at various stages in the past that the now commonly assumed authority of the written word continued to remain in question during its early stages of adoption as a means of recording events (cf. Lord 2000: 124).

The reason for this brief excursion into some differences between orality and literacy, and the reason why orality might have been felt at certain times to over-ride the qualities of permanency of written records, is to do with the *purposes* of narrative form. For cultures which did not possess writing and wished to preserve their history, customs and rules for conducting lives, narrative was found to embody precious memory-aiding properties. "Although it is found in all cultures", writes Ong, "narrative is in certain ways more functional in primary oral cultures than in others" (1982: 141). Cultures with writing might be able to record and generate abstract or scientific categories, but oral cultures cannot. They therefore rely more heavily on "stories of human action to store, organize and communicate what they know" (1982: 141). Where writing can bond thought by its physicality, in stone, on paper and so forth, in orality it is narrative, with its structure and processes, which serves to bond thought and make it more permanent

## UNIVERSALITY AND NARRATIVE

These arguments must bear quite heavily on any investigation into early narrative. Where Ong suggests that part of the answer to the question of the origins of narrative lies in necessity, and White speculates that it might reside in human desire for morality, the question has also been addressed in another way within the structural study of the narrative embodiment known as myth. In the work of Claude Lévi-Strauss especially, the internal organization of myths offers some answers to questions about the linguistic origins of narratives in specific societies.

Rather than treating every myth as an individual story, Lévi-Strauss advocates a strategy which involves looking further than the surface of a myth to identify homologies of structure among seemingly different narratives. As an approach, this is not entirely novel: other 'structuralists' such as Claude Bremond and A. J. Greimas, as well as 'proto-structuralists' such as Vladimir Propp and archetypal critics such as Northrop Frye adopt broadly similar procedures in their interrogation of narratives (however, see Coupe 1997: 172–5 on the latter). What is notable about Lévi-Strauss' work, though, is that he purports to identify universal mental principles, based upon the oppositions to be found in language, whose manifestation is the narrative structure of myth.

Taking as his model the analysis of language as a set of oppositions between its smallest possible elements, *phonemes*, Lévi-Strauss' proceeds to do the same for myth. His celebrated dissection of the Oedipus story will serve as a brief example of his method. He identifies various key events, actions or relationships as a myth's fundamental elements, or 'mythemes'; these are then rearranged to demonstrate their identical functions in the narrative. Lévi-Strauss' own analogy illustrates the process well: he suggests that a sequence of numbers appearing in the following way

1, 2, 4, 7, 8, 2, 3, 4, 6, 8, 1, 4, 5, 7, 8, 1, 2, 5, 7, 3, 4, 5, 6, 8

can be rearranged in order to make explicit the repetition of themes among them; thus

| 1 | 2 |   | 4 |   |   | 7 | 8 |
|---|---|---|---|---|---|---|---|
|   | 2 | 3 | 4 |   | 6 |   | 8 |
| 1 |   |   | 4 | 5 |   | 7 | 8 |
| 1 | 2 |   |   | 5 |   | 7 |   |
|   |   | 3 | 4 | 5 | 6 |   | 8 |

(Lévi-Strauss 1977: 213)

Following this procedure for the Oedipus story, it is possible to see that mythemes such as 'The Spartoi kill one another',

'Oedipus kills his father, Laius' and 'Eteocles kills his brother, Polynices' all go together. They are all elements to do with murder in this particular structure. The narrative, when isolated from our surface involvement with its sequence, reveals just a small number of such repetitive relations which reveal the purpose of the story.

Ultimately, such regularity leads Lévi-Strauss to arrive at a mathematical formula for explaining myth (1977: 228; see also Marcus 1997). However, more importantly, he concludes that the quality of thought that produced ancient myths is identical to that which generates modern science:

> What makes a steel ax superior to a stone ax is not that the first one is better made than the second. They are equally well made, but steel is quite different from stone. In the same way we may be able to show that the same logical processes operate in myth as in science, and that man has always been thinking equally well; the improvement lies, not in an alleged progress of man's mind, but in the discovery of new areas to which it might apply its unchanged and unchanging powers.
>
> (Lévi-Strauss 1977: 230)

What is evident here is a view of the impulse to narrative organization as fundamental to humans, a reflection of the minute processes, pairings, oppositions and similarities, that make a language possible. For Lévi-Strauss this entails that there is a degree of continuity across all the narratives that have been produced through history, and that it is a continuity so strong that it even renders redundant the historical circumstances of the production of each myth. Myth, in this formulation, is like a grammar which generates new sentences, or a vessel into which new contents might be poured; the sentences or the contents themselves are not nearly as important as the grammar or vessel which gives them shape.

There are advantages and disadvantages to this approach with regard to early fictional narratives. One of the advantages seems to be the abolition of the problem of the historical record. The most commonly known feature of myths is that some relation might exist between the events and characters depicted in them and events and characters that existed in real life (Goody and Watt 1968: 34, 44–5). This is also the case for modern examples such as so-called 'urban myths', elements of which may be true. If, in Lévi-Strauss' hands, "each myth turns out to be the code of all myths, the metalanguage that informs and constrains all tellings of tales" (Coupe 1997: 149), then the difficulty of distinguishing between truth and fiction arising from the flexibility of *oral* narrative being rendered in less flexible *writing* later in the ancient historical record (Goody and Watt 1968: 45) is no longer a problem. Fiction and history will reveal a 'deeper', common linguistic truth when subjected to analysis. For historians, especially, this is a somewhat dubious advantage.

There are, however, some clear disadvantages to Lévi-Strauss' approach to narrative and these have been expressed in criticisms that are now well-known. If a narrative is to be rearranged according to an identification of its key constituent parts, or if a myth is to be broken down into 'mythemes', then a question arises over how the validity of one narrative event rather than another can be guaranteed. As Coupe says of Lévi-Strauss' work, "the mythemes appear as if from nowhere in his own 'arrangement'" (Coupe 1997: 146). An extension of this problem can be seen in Lévi-Strauss' verdict on the Oedipus myth as a whole: that its narrative organization reveals a universal human concern about origins, consisting in this case of mythemes about human provenance on the earth in contest with mythemes about the role of blood relations in procreation, resolved by the outcome of the myth's narrative. Ong (1982: 164–5), Havelock (1986: 26) and others have criticized Lévi-Strauss for reducing the narrative organization of myth to basic, largely binary, principles and ignoring the specific uses of such organization within the orality of cultures. For them, narrative cannot be broken down into simple binary oppositions: the exigencies of memory and performance in oral cultures meant that narrative had to be both more flexible and more varied than Lévi-Strauss' account would allow.

These points about memory and performance can be taken much further, however. If one were searching for the origins of narrative in human culture by sifting through all extant early narratives, it might seem that Lévi-Strauss's approach would be useful in the identification of recurrent themes. In the great libraries formed in Sumeria by 2700 BCE a tablet was found bearing the Sumerian prototype of the epic of *Gilgamesh*; among the papyri placed in jars in Egyptian libraries was the oldest version of the Sinbad story; also there was the narrative of Sinuhe, a prototype of the character of Odysseus who appears in Greek epics such as those by Homer, who flees from Egypt and wanders from country to country of the Near East, suffering homesickness until he makes his way through many hardships back to his native land (Durant 1935: 131–2, 175). All of these findings seem to suggest that narrative has some basic features, including characters and situations, which might tempt one to identify universalizing tendencies in the narrative process. What such a view would fail to apprehend is the many different uses, for different peoples, at different times, that the world's narratives have had.

## NARRATIVE AND IDENTITY

The key 'use' of narrative concerns identity. It is fairly well known in the modern world that social circumstances, and the existence of the self within them, are to a large extent socially constructed by texts and the narratives they frequently contain (Shotter and Gergen 1989). Yet it seems that narrative has played an important role in identity-formation for a long time. Commentators on oral culture, as we have seen, repeatedly found that oral narrative served a mnemonic purpose. Yet narrative structures, with their repetitions and stock devices which enabled early oral cultures to remember key points about their present and their history, also facilitated something else. Memory embodied in narrative made a significant contribution to the formation and maintenance of the self-image of peoples, especially when writing may not have been available physically to store records of past events and details of a people's most cherished ideals. Narrative is therefore also bound with the notion of large-scale identities such as nation.

To be sure, a sustainable notion of nation requires a historic territory or homeland for a people, a common public culture, common legal rights and duties for all members, and a common economy; but, as Smith argues, it also requires common myths and historical memories (1991: 14). The main vehicle for these latter is frequently narrative, although there are others such as monuments and statues. As narrative is closely associated with human action rather than abstract principles, it is particularly suited to the memorializing of that staple of peoples' self-determination, national or folk heroes (cf. Lord 2000: 7).

Indeed, it is not just heroic figures in epics whose national status is facilitated by narrative; one of the most cited theorists of nationalism suggests that narrative also helps to bind individuals in a nation by offering the concept of a 'meanwhile'. Benedict Anderson argues that the narrative structure whereby characters' lives might be narrated such that some of them are intimately known to each other, and others are not, is analogous to the 'imagined community' of a nation. In modernity, all of the characters inhabit the same landscape, even to the extent that, unknowingly, characters might pass each other in the street (Anderson 1991: 24–33; cf. Bhabha 1990a: 308–10).

Thus, in contrast to Lévi-Strauss' position, narrative does not reveal universality; rather it has been instrumental in the promotion of difference, helping to preserve some memories and not others, and helping to bind some people into a given community and not others. In fact, narrative has sometimes assisted in upholding an absolutist conception of cultural difference, especially in its contribution to the concept of tradition. In Europe since the Renaissance rediscovery of Greek civilization, for example, the narratives of Ancient Greece have been incorporated into a 'Western tradition' which has frequently been held to be the 'first' and the 'best'. However, assertions of the purity of such a tradition have been so fragile that they have had to be protected by intellectual fortifications in order to prevent infiltration.

Through works such as Martin Bernal's *Black Athena* (1987) it is now well known that European historians, in the nineteenth century especially, systematically 'edited out' the non-white elements of the Western past. The emphasis on Ancient Greece as the cradle of Western culture enabled European historians to expunge the Egyptian, Semitic and African roots of the West's history; what remained as a result of this process could be put to contemporary use. "The Greek classics" according to Edward Said, "served the Italian, French and English humanists without the troublesome interposition of actual Greeks. Texts by dead people were read, appreciated, and appropriated by people who imagined an ideal commonwealth" (1994: 235). The 'narrative' of Europe, incorporating *some* traditions, myths and memories, therefore had a specific goal.

In challenging the notion of narrative as revealing universal features of humankind, then, we must be careful not to consider narrative as simply and unproblematically the preserve of one nation. The issue to be addressed is not how narrative might be used to promote absolute distinctions between peoples but how it might represent 'cultural difference' and 'hybridity'. As Said explains, "Far from being unitary or monolithic or autonomous things cultures actually assume more 'foreign' elements, alterities, differences, than they can consciously exclude" (1994: 15). Concurrently, for Bhabha, cultures cannot be self-contained and hermetically sealed from one another, nor can they be united by universalist claims. "No culture is full unto itself" he argues,

> no culture is plainly plenitudinous, not only because there are other cultures which contradict its authority, but also because its own symbol-forming activity, its own interpellation in the process of representation, language, signification and meaning-making always underscores the claim to an originary, holistic, organic identity.
>
> (Bhabha 1990b: 210)

Narrative, of course, is central to the process of representation Bhabha mentions.

There can be little doubt, then, that the 'editing out' of some narratives from a tradition has been an enterprise fraught with contradiction and bad faith. The tasks of identifying the 'great works' and locating the ultimate ancestor of narrative have run the risk of reductionism and ethnocentrism. Yet the chief problem has been the failure to recognize hybridity, that unavoidable mingling of cultures which are presumed to be separate. Where narrative is concerned, this is a matter of recognizing its role in the *construction* of concepts such as 'nation' while not neglecting its experienced effects. When the latter is ignored in favour of a seemingly democratic view of narrative as universal to all peoples, power is still being exercised. Snead argues that Europeans' assessment of African narratives in universalizing terms, by reference to such phrases as 'human nature', for example, is an act of confinement, domination and, ultimately, imperialism. Equally, though, he recognizes a universalizing tendency in European approaches to *European* narratives. He notes that Homer, Dante, Rabelais, Cervantes, Shakespeare and Goethe are often seen as "consummate geniuses" or "founding fathers" because their narratives embody "universal truths" (1990: 233). If these authors stand for a European cultural ideal, the ideal is undermined by the fact that "the actual texts they have written seem radically *mixed*, even syncretistic" (Snead 1990: 233). The narratives are "not so much *universal* as *hybrid*, unifying previously scattered or dispersed dialects, colloquialisms, and oral traditions" (234).

The European tradition of narrative, which includes the novel, film and other narratives discussed in this book, has frequently been assumed to be culturally distinct. It has been assumed to be central to the 'culture' of Europe. In 1869, the English social theorist, Matthew Arnold, famously promoted culture as a palliative for "the ravages of a modern, aggressive, mercantile and brutalizing existence" (Said 1994: xiii). Arnold's formulation of 'culture' rests upon the pursuit of perfection in thought and art, and, for him, the pinnacle of such perfection is to be reached through the fusion of existing elements of the 'Hellenic' and 'Hebraic' foundations of the Western spirit (Arnold 1980: 469–573).

A later humanist scholar, Erich Auerbach, who was to become one of the most influential theorists of the Western narrative tradition, partly endorsed Arnold's perspective. For Auerbach, the results of Western narrative technique were largely to be found in the Homeric narratives of Greece and in the Hebraic tradition of the Old Testament (1968). Even assuming that there is an intermixing of these foundations in the Western tradition, there remains in this view an appeal to limited points of origin. In light of the question of the differences between orality and literacy and the cultural difference which gives rise to hybridity, these foundations should now be considered.

## HELLENIC AND HEBRAIC FOUNDATIONS

The Greek epic poet, Homer, is frequently discussed as the originator of European narrative, specifically in his two long narrative poems *The Illiad* and *The Odyssey* (for example, Havelock 1986: 19). The classical scholar, Jasper Griffin, suggests some of the reasons for this when he says of the latter work that it is "the ultimate ancestor of the novel in Europe" (1980: 46). In the last two hundred years the novel form has had a formidable influence within the field of narrative in the West. Among many theorists there has been a broadly held view that the many complexities of the novel form, its devices and recurrent characteristics, have had a profound impact on the way that literate humans seek to represent the world (see, especially, Bakhtin 1981). Academics have therefore charted the fortunes of the novel through an examination of 'romances', epic poems and, more recently, the 'ancient novel' (Doody 1998).

Yet, at first glance, Homer's narratives seem to be very far removed from those that are consumed in the early twenty-first century post-novel landscape of cinema, television and DVD. Homer was thought to be operating in a remote period in human history, 700–800 BCE, and both *The Iliad* and *The Odyssey* deal in one way or another with the events of the Trojan wars of 1184–83 BCE. As such, the poems therefore exemplify the problems of truth in fictional and non-fictional narratives that we have noted. One might ask: to what extent are Homer's narratives historical, as opposed to fictional, in their bearing?

An initial answer to the question might concern the figure of Homer the poet. Nobody knows who Homer was, whether a man or a woman. It is possible that Homer was two people, or even more (Finley 1979: 31, 34). Nobody knows, either, if Homer was the name of a person: it is thought by some that it was the name of a particular genre or tradition of poem (Sherratt 1992) and by others that Homer was a "poet singer among poet singers" (Lord 2000: 150). Tempting though it may be to imagine a stable vision of Homer as an ageing bearded man, as he is depicted in many classical statues, or as an authoritative voice, it is an untenable idea (Havelock 1986: 14). In addition, *The Iliad* and *The Odyssey* certainly appeared *prior* to the 'invention' of writing. Yet both have had their most sustained existences as written texts: for example, in the present, translations of both works in book form can easily be obtained from mainstream booksellers.

One of the outstanding aspects of the poems, preserved in some verse translations into English (for example, Lattimore's translation of *The Odyssey*, 1967) is the way that recurrent rhythms are used. Children in particular are frequently taken with such rhythms, especially when the epic is read to them; but any reader will recognize the way that key phrases crop up time and time again. In *The Odyssey*, rather than simply referring to the celestial protector of Odysseus by her name, she is always called "the goddess gray-eyed Athene"; much of the action takes place on water which is always referred to as the "wine-dark sea"; frequently, the hero of the narrative is not just a plain soldier but "resourceful Odysseus"; also, characters do not try to pass on messages quickly, rather they rely on "winged words".

Two related conclusions arise from this information. First, the recurrence of the phrases is a reminder that this story is being *narrated* by someone. From the outset, in fact, the reader has been encouraged to presuppose a narrator, a fundamental feature of narrative, as we noted in Chapter 1; consider the opening lines:

Tell me, Muse, of the man of many ways, who was driven
far journeys after he had sacked Troy's sacred citadel.
(Lattimore 1967: I. 1–2)

In spite of such an explicit opening to the narrative, it is often easy to 'forget' the role of the narrator, especially if s/he is not part of the unfolding tale. The recurrent rhythms are a reminder that it is this same narrator that is telling the story.

Second, these recurrent rhythms are indicative of the oral origins of Homer's poems. A collector of oral poetry, Milman Parry, carried out extensive studies in the former Yugoslavia in 1932, and found that an indigenous tradition of oral composition existed. By using recurrent rhythms, set motifs and formulas, Slavic poets were able to generate, remember and recount epic poems of comparable length to *The Iliad* and *The Odyssey* (Lewis 1960: 20; Scholes and Kellogg 1966: 20–2; Finley 1979: 29–31; Ong 1982: 17–30; Havelock 1986: 12, 51; Lord 2000; but see also Hainsworth 1992). The complexity of the rhythm and syntax of these oral poems could be considerable (for an analysis, see Lord 2000, especially 144–6); but, in general, the rhythm was essential for effective memorization of the events to be depicted by the poet or singer (Havelock 1986: 29). In short, epic poetry such as Homer's is an act of "reminder and recall" (Havelock 1963: 91); but it is not just recall of fictional story events. As Havelock explains, "Acting as a kind of versified encyclopedia, Homer recorded and preserved the means of maintaining cultural continuity by putting on record the social mores of the culture" (1986: 29). Clearly, this indicates once more the difficulties of separating fact and fiction in the historical record. In light of these arguments, let us consider the second of Homer's epics in a little more depth.

*The Odyssey* is the story of the difficult return home of Odysseus, a hero of the Trojan war. Because of all the obstacles which he encounters, *detours* in the narrative, the journey takes about ten years. The journey is his 'Odyssey', an attempt to get to the final destination. Back at his home island of Ithaca, Odysseus' wife, Penelope, has tried to remain faithful to her soldier husband but is being preyed upon by a number of suitors who not only wish to have Odysseus' death confirmed so that they can propose marriage to her, but have also moved into the family home while they are waiting. Meanwhile, Telemachos, the son of Odysseus, has grown up and set out on a search for his father.

Since its metamorphosis into a written text *The Odyssey* has been divided up into twenty four 'books' as follows:

| Books I–IV | Telemachos' searches |
| Books V–VIII | Odysseus' attempt to return home |
| Books IX–XII | Odysseus' wanderings after the Trojan war (recounted by himself) |
| Book XIII (first half) | Odysseus' homecoming |
| Books XIII (second half) – XXIV | Odysseus on Ithaca |

The mere fact of division is, in itself, significant. As Hymes observed of the subtle patterning of Native American narratives, division and spacing often serve important functions for the readers and tellers of stories (see Chapter 1). More directly, as Lodge (1992: 163–8) notes, the division into chapters gives the reader a chance to 'take breath', and it allows for scene or time shifts.

Far from being a primitive narrative marked by simplicity of both story and formal organization, *The Odyssey* is a very complex epic which contains many of the key technical features of modern narrative, albeit in different ways from modern narratives. Yet, many of those technical features which now suffuse all manner of narratives in different technologies were originally necessary because Homer's poems were *oral* epics. Lord and Havelock are both scholars who have traced the changes that arise in the movement from oral textuality to written textuality or, as the latter puts it, the events in which 'the muse learns to write'. For Lord, one key difference between oral and written narratives is the extent to which the former relies on "formulaic expressions" (2000: 130). For Havelock, another issue is the social imperatives inherent in oral narratives; "in primary orality", he writes, functional content is cast in verbal forms designed to assist the memory by conferring pleasure: social and aesthetic purposes form a partnership. Once social responsibility starts to be transferred to a literate class, the balance is altered in favour of the aesthetic.

(Havelock 1986: 45–6)

For both scholars, the key features of the Homeric poems might have persisted into contemporary narratives; however, the *purpose* of these features has receded as the oral tradition has "moved further and further into the background" (Lord 2000: 138) with the growth of written narrative.

*The Odyssey* therefore contains elements which will be familiar as aesthetic features to modern readers, thus rendering the ancient narrative less remote. We have already stressed the importance of human action in oral narrative; yet it is also worth mentioning that *The Odyssey* is filled with recognizable characters, as would be the case in a contemporary fictional narrative. It is true that the characters in *The Odyssey* do, to an extent, embody limited characteristics and are not the subject of much development. Nevertheless, it would be wrong to consider them as mere ciphers: they cry, mourn, yearn and are joyful in ways which might be interesting to modern readers.

Other features which might have a specific yield of pleasure for readers today include the use of flashbacks (see, especially, Books IX–XII), a device which is usually associated with modernism and the development of cinematic narrative (see Chapter 6). There are also substantial narrations within the main narration (see especially Books IX–XII), which, potentially, cause tension between different 'voices' in the narrative, a phenomenon which is to be discerned in the history of the novel and, in a more problematic way, in postmodern narratives (see Chapters 3, 4 and 7). The direct representation of the speech of characters which appears in the Homeric narratives was to become absolutely crucial to later epics, romances and novels (see Chapter 3). And the multiple storylines and proliferation of characters in *The Odyssey*, which seemed to reach a pinnacle in nineteenth-century realism, were to be surpassed in the serial narratives of twentieth-century television and twenty-first century computers (see Chapters 7 and 8). Despite these continuities, though, it must be remembered that the purposes of what are now considered common narrative features would have been much different for preliterate cultures and would have been embodied in a particular 'style' of narration.

In one of the most famous essays on the beginnings of Western literature, Erich Auerbach (1968) has identified a specific style in *The Odyssey* which provides one of the foundations of the Western tradition of narrative. He singles out an episode in Book XIX in which Odysseus has gained entrance to his home on Ithaca disguised as an old vagabond. Eurycleia, the maid of the house and Odysseus' old nurse, is instructed by Penelope to wash the stranger's feet; as Eurycleia proceeds to do so she recognizes a scar on the man's leg. It is identical to a scar sustained by young Odysseus during a wild boar hunt and she suddenly realizes who the newcomer is. Auerbach focuses on this sequence because the long digression on the origins of the scar, which takes place between the narration of Eurycleia's recognition of Odysseus and the resolution of the question 'will she give the game away?', demonstrates something significant about Homeric narrative.

Where Lord suggests that the recognition of Odysseus is postponed because it is part of a recurring oral pattern of delay (2000: 170–4), Auerbach argues that the long sequence in which the details of the acquisition of the scar are narrated is offered in the service of full 'externalization'. That is to say, the Homeric narratives are characterized by a desire to get everything out into the open, to narrate everything that can possibly bear on a scene, and to leave nothing in the dark. In Homer,

nothing must remain hidden and unexpressed. With the

> utmost fullness, with an orderliness which even passion does not disturb, Homer's personages vent their inmost hearts in speech; what they do not say to others, they speak in their own minds so that the reader is informed of it.
>
> (Auerbach 1968: 6)

The story of the scar is not presented, either, as a memory in the 'background'; instead, the story is offered as objective fact in the process of putting all details into the present and uniformly informing the 'foreground'.

For Auerbach, Homer's style is fixed on the present moment of both characters and places. Characters may be complex, but they have no histories, development or hidden depth: "Odysseus on his return is exactly as he was when he left Ithaca two decades earlier" (1968: 17). The Homeric style is devoted to concealing nothing, to offering no secret meaning; as Auerbach suggests, Homer's narratives can be *analysed* but they are not really susceptible to *interpretation*. In a sense, they are very much imbued with 'realism' or an apparent faithfulness to the surface manifestations of reality, a fact which is not compromised, but instead assisted, by the narratives' legendary nature. Legend, in Auerbach's estimation, deals with events in a straightforward way, isolates them from the distractions of historical context, and presents characters who act from few and simple motives (1968: 19).

The other foundation of Western narrative style that Auerbach identifies, and which throws the Homeric narratives into relief, lies in the books of the Bible, especially the Old Testament. These latter, Auerbach argues, are an altogether different proposition in that their narration is characterized by a noticeable 'background' quality. Full details of events are not given in the Old Testament narratives. Taking the narrative of Abraham and Isaac, Auerbach shows that the commitment to the externalization found in the Homeric narratives is here absent. God speaks to Abraham but neither of the participants is located in a particular space. God commands Abraham to make a journey with his son in order to make a sacrifice but

> In this atmosphere it is unthinkable that an implement, a land-scape through which the travellers passed, the serving-men, or the ass, should be described, that their origin or descent or material or appearances or usefulness should be set forth in praise.
>
> (Auerbach 1968: 9)

Abraham simply receives the command and makes the journey; there is no embellishment; instead, as Auerbach adds, "Everything remains unexpressed" (1968: 11).

The consequence of so much remaining unexpressed in the biblical narratives is that the reader is invited to make interpretations of the baldly narrated events. The Homeric narratives, on the other hand, offer ample information to dissuade the reader/listener from interpretation. Similarly, Auerbach stresses that the characters in biblical narratives are distinct from their Homeric counterparts. The former have *histories*: Abraham, for example, "remembers, is constantly conscious of, what God has promised him and what God has already accomplished for him – his soul is torn between desperate rebellion and hopeful expectation; his silent obedience is multilayered, has background" (Auerbach 1968: 12). When one considers Jacob, for example, the character in *Genesis* who, as a young man, has swindled a blessing out of his sight-impaired father and, as an old man, has to suffer the sorrow of the report of his own son's death under attack from a wild animal, it is clear that much psychological development is to be interpreted as having taken place between these two events.

The 'multilayeredness' of character in the Bible is not present in the Homeric narratives which, instead, focus more on *events*. As Auerbach argues, Homer's style may attempt to provide as much detail as possible, but the narration of the Abraham story is actually more orientated to a "historically true reality" (1968: 15).

The narrator of the Abraham story is religiously devoted in his depiction to a particular vision of God's will; and this results in a presentation of psychological development, as characters suffer twists of fortune brought on by history and their pursuit of a religious vision. God has not only created these individuals "but he continues to work on them, bends them and kneads them, and, without destroying them in essence, produces from them forms which their youth gave no grounds for anticipating" (18).

One other area of fundamental narrative depiction mentioned by Auerbach concerns the focus on the 'everyday' and the 'sublime' (cf. Lewis 1960: 27) or, to put the matter another way, the elevated and the commonplace. Odysseus' story contains events which embrace sex, food and washing as well as outlandish creatures like the Cyclops, the Sirens and Kalypso. The Bible is not dissimilar in that it constantly depicts God in dialogue with humans on earth. Yet, the concentration on domestic routine as an idyllic, unproblematic realm of everyday existence in the Homeric narratives provides an important contrast with the Bible. Furthermore, the mingling of the sublime and the everyday in Homer takes place "far more exclusively and unmistakably among the members of a ruling class" (Auerbach 1968: 22). The Bible, in contrast, presents a different picture of everyday life through an uncensored depiction of jealousies, rivalries and strife in the domestic existence of common people. Moreover, these conflicts in the domestic sphere, which, unlike the Homeric narratives, where they would be resolved by battle, smoulder precisely *because of* God's permeation of everyday life. God's omnipresence is able to create, for example, a great deal of enmity over who is to receive a blessing within a family.

Above all, though, what the Bible can be said to bequeath succeeding narrative traditions is an originally Hebraic 'explanatory' mode of narrative. Like all the major sacred narratives, the Bible has been framed as a text which needs to be *interpreted*. It is implicit in Auerbach's discussion of biblical style that this kind

of narrative invites the reader's meditation on the relative significance and even moral value of depicted events. Moreover, as
Prickett (1996: 55ff.) maintains, the Bible continually reflects
that part of a Jewish mentality in which humans are constantly in
dialogue with God, seeking explanations and answers. "It is
therefore hardly surprising", he adds "if, in our biblically based
culture, the inherent expectations of a book include not merely
narrative but *revelation*: a sense that some hidden mystery is to be
unfolded and explained" (1996: 6).

## HYBRIDITY AND THE WESTERN TRADITION

The revelatory aspect was not the only important feature of biblical narrative for the development of Western narrative; the Bible
was also associated with the technology of literacy. It is well
known that modes of human communication were profoundly
transformed by the advent of printing and it is perhaps no coincidence that the first printed book was the Gutenberg Bible of
1452–6 (McLuhan 1962; Eisenstein 1979; Havelock 1986: 49;
Lacy 1996: 21–45). Moreover, although Havelock suggests that
oral narratives can be found embedded in the Old Testament, "a
text otherwise devoted to revising them, epitomizing them, and
incorporating them in a theological framework" (1986: 47), it is
clear that much of the Bible *originated* in written form. Homer's
narratives, on the other hand, metamorphosed into written form
sometime in the seventh century BCE; Lord even argues that the
idea for recording the poems came from the Near East, where
other epics and some of the Old Testament books had already
appeared in writing (2000: 156).

   In addition to Auerbach's analysis, these arguments may shed
some light on why Homer and the Bible have so frequently been
cited as the foundations of the Western tradition of narrative. The
Bible's status as a sacred book has made it, to all intents and purposes, unassailable (see Prickett 1996). Its concrete existence as a

written book which can be checked and consulted for the purposes of knowledge make it very different from the early oral versions of *The Iliad* and *The Odyssey*. This is the context in which
the *interpretation* that the Bible's narrative style facilitates will
actually take place. Any reading of the Bible will be preceded by
the context of its status as the written cornerstone of Christianity.

The situation is somewhat different for the Homeric narratives. There is now little doubt that Homer was not by any means
the earliest epic poet (see Lord 2000: 158). But the Homeric narratives have become representative because of the way that they
look back to the early oral cultures and the way that their appearance in writing has enabled them to 'look forward'. Havelock
writes of Homer's epics,

> Regardless of the date of their original composition ... they
> were the first compositions to achieve alphabetisation, an
> event or process which can be placed approximately between
> 700 and 650 BC. This appears to have ensured their canonisa-
> tion, and certainly has given them an effective monopoly as
> presenting the preliterate condition.
>
> (Havelock 1963: 115)

Further, this movement into writing brought the Homeric narratives into closer relationship with the diametrically opposed style
of the Bible.

The written version of Homer ensured that the oral basis of
the narratives would remain less apparent and even recede into
the background, as Lord and Havelock argue. The dominance of
the *aesthetic*, as opposed to the *social* purpose of the narratives,
despite the differences in narrative style from the Bible, would
invite interpretation or the search for 'universal truths' in their
texts. It is for this reason that Lord echoes Snead in asserting that

> From ancient times until the present we have been misled
> about the true nature of Homer's art and greatness. And the

reason has been that we have tried to read him in our own
terms, which we have labelled 'universal terms of art'.

(Lord 2000: 147–8)

Yet there is another issue to do with hybridity that must be
mentioned in relation to these foundations of Western narrative.
The Greek culture that produced the Homeric narratives was not
'purely' Hellenic, as Matthew Arnold and others would have it. As
Havelock argues, it was heavily influenced by Mycenaean culture,
which itself bore strong affinities with the Near Eastern cultures:
Sumerian, Assyrian, Hittite and Palestinian (1963: 116). As such,
the Homeric narratives are not the product of one culture, either
'literate' or 'Hellenic'.

## A VOYAGE TO THE SELF

Given the hybrid nature of the Homeric narratives it might seem
difficult to understand why they have been so important to establishing a specifically 'Western' tradition. Undoubtedly, Homer's
narratives could be framed and re-contextualized by accounts
which attempted to expunge 'alien', non-European elements or
by the eschewing of commentaries on their multiple origins.
However, this might take place in respect of any surviving oral
narratives. The question remains that there might be something
integral to the Homeric narratives which has proved indispensable to the forging of a Western tradition.

In Chapter 1 we encountered Julian Jaynes' arguments about
narrative and consciousness, and saw that he took the epics
attributed to 'Homer' very seriously indeed. More specifically,
Jaynes is astounded by the difference between *The Iliad* and *The
Odyssey*. He suggests that the latter poem took shape at least a
century after the first, and did so in the same way, through
anonymous oral transmissions and transmutations. *The Odyssey*,
however, exhibits, to the alert reader, a totally different worldview

from *The Iliad*. Ostensibly, Jaynes wishes to use the latter epic as evidence of the breakdown of the 'bicameral mind' and the advent of a new form of consciousness. Whether this is still a convincing argument in itself is a matter for neuroscientists and lies beyond the scope of the present discussion. However, Jaynes assembles evidence which suggests that

> *The Odyssey* describes a new and different world inhabited by new and different beings. ... The gods have less to do, and like receding ghosts talk more to each other – and that so tediously! The initiatives move from them, even against them, towards the work of the more conscious human characters, though overseen by a Zeus who in losing his power has acquired a Lear-like interest in justice.
>
> (Jaynes 1990: 273)

In addition, Jaynes finds in *The Odyssey* some developments which are important for our consideration of the Western narrative tradition as a whole, and which are consonant with the centrality of human action in the oral origins of narrative form. Unlike *The Iliad*, the later poem contains a repeated emphasis on the value of cunning, guile and deceit in social relations. There is an increased ratio of abstract terms to concrete ones, far more reference to qualities than to simple existing facts. Crucially, though, there seems to be an increased awareness of self on the part of characters in their interactions, one symptom of which is the guile of Odysseus. And there is a much greater sense of spatial and temporal co-ordinates than in *The Iliad*, with Odysseus and others maintaining a time-frame for Odysseus' journey home as well as a perception of the land, sea and islands that he has to cover.

In short, for Jaynes, *The Odyssey* marks a most significant departure in epic poetry because it is "a story of identity, of a voyage to the self" (1990: 276). If indeed this does represent a pivotal moment in the pantheon of epics, then there is a strong case for *The Odyssey*'s location at the very beginnings of the Western tradition of narrative. As we will argue, such a tradition has at its very centre a concern with character, identity and consciousness; an acute desire to render the vicissitudes of time and space; and, perhaps above all, an obsession with signs, appearances and reality.

# 3

# THE RISE AND RISE
# OF THE NOVEL

The precise moment of transmutation from oral narrative to written narrative is almost impossible to identify. However, the work of Havelock (1963, 1986) draws attention to a pivotal event. For him, the teachings of the ancient Greek philosopher Plato constitute a clarion call of commitment to a new, *literate* form of consciousness. As Havelock and Lord (2000) argue, oral discourse, and especially oral narrative, did not simply disappear with the advent of writing. To be sure, the chief distinction between the two remained: as Lord shows at some length (2000: 30–67), oral narrative relies heavily on set formulas and repetition; written and printed narrative, on the other hand, allows a greater freedom of expression. Neither the teller of print narrative nor the reader of it require the formulaic aids to memory which were necessary in the oral medium: events in previous stages of a narrative remain preserved in material form on the page. Nevertheless, the residues of oral narrative lingered on in the new written forms.

Considering the transition, it is that part of Plato's philosophy concerned with modes of depiction which, for Havelock, addresses precisely the interface between the old and new, telling us a great deal about the imperatives that underlie modes of depiction which have survived through to the present. What is well known about Plato's teaching, in particular the work entitled *The Republic*, is that the vicissitudes of representation are central to it. Ostensibly, *The Republic* is a series of dialogues about the principles necessary for an ideal political state; but, as Havelock points out, only a third of this work actually deals with statecraft (1963: 3). What *The Republic* is most frequently concerned with is the concept of 'mimesis', a term which is so nebulous in Plato's teachings that it has provoked debate and confusion among scholars for centuries (Havelock 1963: 24).

## MIMESIS

Halliwell suggests the following possible meanings for the term in Plato's work. First, mimesis is a linguistic, philosophical or cosmic phenomenon. As such, mimesis is considered to be a reflection of an 'eternal model' of the world in language, in the thought of the philosopher, and in material things respectively. Second, mimesis can be visual, mimicry, behavioural or impersonatory. According to this interpretation, the painter depicts the appearance of things, the voice and body reproduce certain properties of the animal and natural world, straightforward emulation takes place, or there is the acting out of a specific role. Third, mimesis consists of poetic, musical and choreographic modes. Here, the mimesis is based on the verbal 'image-making' to be found in the structures of poetry, the expression of certain human experiences through the medium of music, and the representation of human life that takes place in the movement within dance (Halliwell 1998: 121).

It should be clear from this that 'mimesis' does not simply entail artistic or poetic modes of imitation but, instead, refers to a very general act of depiction. It is true that Plato makes reference to pre-existing uses of the term which seem to be exclusively connected with artistic modes. Furthermore, there have been similar uses of 'mimesis' since Plato which have been concerned with narrative aesthetics. Frequently, mimesis has been considered to be a dramatic *imitation* of events and characters, which simply 'shows' to readers or spectators what goes on in a narrative; this has been opposed to *reporting* of events and characters, which 'tells' what goes on in narrative and is prone to the charge of didacticism (see, especially, Lubbock 1926 and Booth 1961).

Nevertheless, Halliwell insists that there is a need to be flexible when approaching Platonic mimesis (1998: 109, 116). The reason for this is related to narrative and its origins. Havelock reminds us of the social function of early narrative when he argues that

> Plato writes as though he had never heard of aesthetics, or even of art. Instead, he insists on discussing the poets as though their job was to supply metrical encyclopedias. The poet is a source on the one hand of essential information and on the other of essential moral training.
>
> (Havelock 1963: 29)

Scholars have rightly been concerned by Plato's discussion of mimesis, especially the way he seems to confuse poet, actor and the student in the class in their uses of the mode. But such conflations, argues Havelock, are faithful to the facts of the situation because Plato is describing a "total technology of the preserved word" (1963: 44), where the word was orally transmitted and where it would be embedded in a narrative of human actions for the purposes of memory.

However, the social status of mimesis which concerned Plato has tended to become buried, retrospectively, by the aesthetic orientation which Havelock argues is embodied in literate culture. In the following famous passage of *The Republic* it is reasonably easy to see how the aesthetic orientation or concentration on a specific technique of depiction might be extrapolated from the dialogue:

Let me put it in this way. Any story in prose or verse is always a setting forth of events, past, present or future, isn't it?

Yes.

And that can be done either in pure narrative or by means of representation or in both ways.

I am still rather in the dark.

I seem to be a poor hand at explaining; I had better give a particular illustration. You remember the beginning of the *Iliad*, which describes how Chryses begged Agamemnon to release his daughter and Agamemnon was angry, and Chryses called on his god to avenge the refusal on the Greeks. So far, the poet speaks in his own person, but later on he speaks in the character of Chryses and tries to make us feel that the words come, not from Homer, but from an aged priest. Throughout the *Iliad* and *Odyssey* events are set forth in these two different forms. All the time, both in the speeches and in the narrative parts in between, he is telling his story; but where he is delivering a speech in character, he tries to make his manner resemble that of the person he has introduced as speaker. Any poet who does that by means of voice and gesture, is telling his story by way of dramatic representation; whereas, if he makes no such attempt to suppress his own personality, the events are set forth in simple narrative.

Now I understand.

Observe, then, that if you omit the intervening narrative and leave only the dialogue, you get the opposite form.

(Cornford 1945: 81)

As such, mimesis seems to be the imitation of the exact words a fictional character speaks, which is precisely the mode of drama, the mimetic art *par excellence*. Everything that is not mimesis, on the other hand, is associated with the poet's voice or person.

This separation is one which is now familiar to any twenty-first century reader of written representations and it is one that is couched in largely artistic terms. The resultant implication might be that Plato was a believer in the power of single imitative representations to influence individuals. This, however, is not the case: it should be stressed instead that, for Plato, mimesis was a widespread phenomenon thoroughly rooted in socio-cultural imperatives and extending well beyond purely artistic matters. Plato's teachings took place in an environment in which the *explicitly* social function of narrative was omnipresent and the poetic effect of mimesis was redolent of the recent sovereignty of oral culture in which narrative had played such a key role. Havelock writes,

> Greek literature had been poetic because the poetry had performed a social function, that of preserving the tradition by which the Greeks lived and instructing them in it. This could only mean a tradition that was orally taught and memorized. It was precisely this didactic function and the authority that went with it to which Plato objected. What could have been his motive, unless he intended that his own teachings should supplant it? What was the difference? The obvious one ... was that his own teaching was formally non-poetic. It was composed in prose.
>
> (Havelock 1986: 8)

In sum, Plato's comments on mimesis can be read as a demand that the Greek mind break with the poetic inheritance in favour of the syntax of written scientific discourse (Havelock 1963: 182).

The consequences of such an understanding of mimesis are important for the analysis of both ancient and modern narratives. Plato's perspective demonstrates that, underlying all poetic representation, there lurks a didactic or instructive intent. This is the case whether imitative mimesis is mixed with a discourse in which the poet 'speaks in his own person', whether there is imitation or whether the discourse is philosophical in orientation. Yet, where Plato wrote of mimesis as a means of both image-making and philosophizing (Halliwell 1998: 120), Aristotle, in his *Poetics* (*c.*330 BCE), formulated a perspective which became more narrowly focused on artistic concerns and, arguably, forged a new role for the aesthetic dimension of mimesis while further burying its more explicitly social one.

## ARISTOTELIAN MIMESIS

Both Plato and Aristotle considered drama a 'mimetic' art, while lyric poetry such as the dithyramb was seen as a representative art narrated in the poet's own voice (Cornford 1945: 82). However, both also mention epic, a form which is best exemplified in *The Republic* by the works of Homer. Here the putative, describing voice of the poet can be discerned, but it is accompanied by the mimetic presentation of characters' speech in the kind of opposition which we have seen demonstrated by Plato and which is fairly standard in modern narrative. Indeed, it is well known that Aristotle states, in the fragmentary set of "suggestive *aperçus* and laconic observations" (Halliwell 1998: 122) which make up the *Poetics*, that Homer is a pivotal figure in the history of epic for the way in which, unlike other poets, he utilizes imitative mimesis in addition to his own voice (see Aristotle 1996: 40 [10.4 or Chap. 24, 60a]; cf. Halliwell 1998: 126–8).

This is significant information in favour of the important role of Homer in early narrative. Yet Aristotle's formulations about mimesis in general are even more crucial to narrative analysis. Halliwell argues that, contra Plato, Aristotle insists on treating mimesis largely as an artistic issue rather than a socio-cultural and philosophical one; he writes,

> Aristotle is arguing for the independence of art from straight-
> forward subjection to standards and criteria of truth-telling
> and virtue (Plato's expectations of it) and that, against the
> Platonic castigation of mimesis as falsehood, he is adumbrat-
> ing a concept of *fiction* which allows the poet's stance towards
> reality to be more oblique.
>
> (Halliwell 1998: 133)

What is more, Aristotle, in ignoring the distinction between
mimesis as philosophical falsehood and mimesis as artistic imitation, choosing instead to focus on the latter, actually brings the
two conceptions together by suggesting that the poet can get at a
different kind of view of the world, one that is not necessarily
based on falsehood. For Halliwell, Aristotle's interpretation of
mimesis "perhaps restores to the poet at least something of the
possibility of the knowledge and wisdom which Greek tradition
had always claimed for him, but which Plato had been impelled
to deny" (1998: 137).

As such, the mixture of imitative mimesis and the poet's voice
which is to be found so prominently in epic, especially as it is
promulgated through the name of Homer, has noteworthy properties. Not only are Homer's epics demonstrably accounts of
human action embodied in a narrative form; they also proceed
through a mimetic mode that allows for a kind of 'poetic truth'
which is different from the truth of abstract scientific categories.
The mix of imitation and the poet's voice in this formulation constitutes a powerful means of representing the world, and,
undoubtedly, its foremost manifestation is narrative. While the
purest form of mimesis for Aristotle is the imitation of human
action in drama, narrative, especially in its implementation of
imitative mimesis after Homer, *records* and *re-enacts* human action.
To be sure, there have been narratives from the ancient period to
the present which have eschewed imitative mimesis; however, the
imitative orientation can lend an enormous amount of power to

re-presentations of fictional events through the direct depiction of dialogue.

## IMITATION, QUOTATION AND IDENTITY

The mixed mode of depiction provides the spinal column for the whole of the novel tradition in the West and has been the source of debate down the years about the relative efficacies of 'showing' (imitative mimesis as envisaged by Aristotle) and 'telling' (supposedly, the 'poet's voice') in narrative. As an example of such arguments about mimesis as an imitative artistic device, the novelist David Lodge's (1992) discussion of 'summary' and 'scene' is admirably clear. Summary, he explains, is a form of prose in a narrative which *tells* about events or people without imitating them and, in Aristotle's and Plato's terms, it takes place through the 'poet's voice'. A narrative might move, by way of summary, to a later point in time, passing over quickly what happens in between; alternatively, by the same means, it can move from one place to another, more distant one. Summary has the benefit of "hurrying us through events which would be uninteresting, or *too* interesting – therefore distracting, if lingered over" (Lodge 1992: 122). Alternatively, scene is like drama or Aristotelian mimesis: it *shows* the events and, more often than not, such events will contain speech which scene is able to imitate through the use of quotation marks.

Such departures from the original variegated Platonic conception of mimesis as those described by Lodge have probably been hastened by the development of certain kinds of punctuation in writing. Punctuation provided a crucial differentiating device for separating and recognizing the imitative voice as distinct from the poet's voice in written narrative. For readers in an age of print and word-processing it is startling to consider that Ancient Greek and Roman texts consisted only of unbroken rows of letters. It was only after the fourth century that such innovations in written script as gaps between words and new lines for para-graphs were introduced. Later, the spread of printing in the six-teenth century led, especially in France, to the use of the 'diple' (>) to mark out passages of quotation, a practice which English printers followed by elevating the distinguishing marks into inverted commas (') (Parkes 1992; Rée 2000: 369–70). The dif-ference between mimesis and the frame for mimesis was now a visual event and there hence arose a manifest difference in the dis-course within quotation marks and that outside.

Nevertheless, the understanding of the distinction between imitative mimesis and 'the poet's voice' by reference to 'summary' and 'scene' also relates to other definite factors within narrative that we have discussed: space and time. Scene clearly attempts to imitate the space and time inhabited by events and characters. Unless the speech of characters is read very slowly or absurdly fast, scene should give a reasonable approximation of the time-scale in which a character makes the utterance. This is fairly obvi-ous. It is less often considered, however, that some narratives use scene to invoke space. A drama does this within the confines of a given stage set, but a verbal narrative might also do it: Umberto Eco, for example, explains that his novel set in a monastery, *The Name of the Rose* (1980), was filled with dialogue which began and concluded in time-frames and, by association, space-frames, which exactly matched the characters walking from, say, the refectory to the cloister while in conversation (Eco 1985: 25). In contrast to these aspects of scene, summary does not imitate straightforward understandings of time and space; instead, it pos-sesses the ability to subvert them, delivering the narrative through events in different locations while also shifting back and forth in time.

The separation between the 'poet's voice', which summarizes and tells of the action, and the other voices in a narrative which are enacted through mimesis is undoubtedly important, espe-cially in relation to the rendering of time and space. However, the distinction should be treated circumspectly. When a description of characters is given, for example, this too is an example of mimesis as it is understood by Plato, because it is a verbal image-making. Not only is it a *narration*, in the sense of having the function of simply getting readers through the narrative, it is also a *description*, having a function consonant with that of mimesis and scene of directly *re-presenting* features of the fictional or real world (cf. Ronen 1997: 283). Similarly, imitative mimesis of the kind envisaged by Aristotle is not always clear-cut: in audio-visual narratives such as those on film, television or DVD, it is especially difficult to ascertain whether a scene which is depicted on screen appears as a result of the control of someone absent from the scene such as a director or, even more remotely, at the behest of the economic concern of individuals such as the owners of independent broadcasting companies.

The fate in Britain of the Australian film *Romper Stomper* (1992) provides a straightforward illustration of the refusal of the voice of characters and the voice of the producer of the narrative to remain absolutely distinct. The film's narrative consists of a chronicle of the exploits of a group of Melbourne skinheads whose leader (Russell Crowe) attempts intellectually to justify their racism and violence. For reasons more to do with the mode of representation than with the content of the narrative, the film came close to being banned and, indeed, its video release was much delayed. The controversy that the film provoked in Britain centred not around the explicit nature of the depiction of the violence *per se*, but on its mode: imitative mimesis. The British Board of Film Classification was concerned that the film presented the violence of racist attacks so graphically, and in such a detached way, without explicitly showing the immorality of such crimes, that audiences might fail to register how repellent the skinheads' actions were, or, worse, might find them attractive. What audiences do with narratives is, of course, a matter of great debate; but, clearly, this example demonstrates that the British

Board of Film Classification, and perhaps others, believed that an apparently imitative mode such as cinematic narration can and should be as didactic as the 'poet's voice'. The film-makers were thought to be guilty of failing to organize imitation in a persuasive, instructive and morally proper fashion. Famously, Plato sought to banish poets from his republic and the example of *Romper Stomper* illustrates why: even when the poet is engaged in imitation, rather than his/her own voice, s/he still possesses powers of persuasion, influence or, in extreme cases, even manipulation which may be detrimental to the running of a state based on scientific principles.

Nevertheless, the separation of the voices in Aristotelian imitative mimesis and the voices which frame mimesis remains a crucial analytic distinction, even if its implementation does not constitute an ultimate resolution of the problem of accurate representation. Aristotle suggested that the mixture of modes was an important way of getting at a version of truth through fiction and, clearly, it is necessary to render a multi-faceted world in more than just one voice. But, during the Middle Ages, when Aristotle was rediscovered and became the most important philosopher, the purveyors of narrative continued to agonize over the role of mimesis and the poet's discourse.

Two fundamental reasons for this can be stated quite plainly. First, the Western narrative tradition continued to be very much concerned with the recording of factors, moments and events involved in defining identity. Narrative devices which might assist in providing a stable depiction of identity were therefore crucial. Yet, second, not only was the separation of the imitative voice and the poet's voice realized in narrative, there grew an increased awareness of the potential difficulties involved in maintaining a unitary, stable version of the latter. If narrative was bound up with the establishment of identity, who was the narrative voice of that identity: the 'poet', the character or, even, the 'narrator'? The visual marking of speech further buried the oral heritage of narrative. It provided further distinguishing marks for the character's voice, aestheticized the issue of mimesis and foregrounded the question of identity in narrative; as Rée states, punctuation was useful but

> the marking of quotations could also be an annoyance, since it forced writers to give a definite attribution to each word in their story: if it was in quotation marks, it belonged to a character, otherwise it belonged to the narrator, and the indeterminate middle-ground occupied by oral story-tellers was thus ruled out of bounds.
>
> (Rée 2000: 170–1)

These problems were to be carried over into a form which used the mixed mode more than any other: the novel.

## EPIC, IDENTITY AND THE MIXED MODE

Although the term 'novel' only came into use in the eighteenth century it is easy to see why theorists have projected an idea of the novel form onto the epic tradition in the West. First and foremost, the major epics which have been canonized and kept alive have shared with Homer's narratives the function of recording defining moments of identity. Virgil's *Aeneid* (*c.*19 BCE), for example, like *The Odyssey*, deals with a warrior in the aftermath of Troy. The protagonist Aeneas, escaping from the ruins of the city, carrying his father on his shoulders and pulling his son by the hand, experiences the burden of the past and the demands of the future. Aeneas is even more explicitly representative of a new age and identity than Odysseus in that he is instrumental in establishing what will later become the Roman Empire. The resonance of this theme alone is frequently argued to have been sufficient for the poem to have survived and been ranked very highly, especially in the Middle Ages (Lewis 1960; Scott 1984: 251). Certainly, it is well known that the *Aeneid*, in turn, haunts the major epic of the Middle Ages, *The Divine Comedy* (1321) of Florentine poet, Dante Alighieri (1265–1321).

Like the *Aeneid*, a great deal of the power of *The Divine Comedy* consists in its mix of the poet's voice and the very strong voices of the characters. *The Divine Comedy* charts the author's odyssey through Inferno, Purgatory and, ultimately, to Paradise, and does so through a narrative which is rich in allusion of a religious and political nature, and allegorical in highly particular ways. The specificities of Dante's religious and political philosophy, as well as the correspondence of his characters to political and local contemporary figures in the real world have kept scholars busy for hundreds of years. Unsurprisingly, however, Dante's vision is projected through a narrative of human actions: the poet's and the characters'.

In one way, the narrative is overwhelmed by the voice of Dante, who is a character in the action of the story and who narrates it. Indeed, if Dante's voice is not authoritative enough, it is surely enhanced by the fact that the *Comedy* enlists Virgil as Dante's guide through Inferno. Not only was Virgil considered an important pre-Christian prophet by Dante, but the *Aeneid* was also seen as a narrative of the soul's journey to spiritual fulfilment. The *Comedy* appears, too, at "the beginning of a great tradition in European culture, which came to look upon poets as repositories of wisdom and essential knowledge" (Scott 1984: 252).

Yet, if *The Divine Comedy* was to be anything other than a political tract, something more would be needed. Central to the narrative is the form of allegory employed by Dante and others in the Middle Ages. This was one version of the same exegetical method which was applied to the reading of Christian scriptures for the purposes of spiritual revelation. Particularly important to Dante, however, was the device of personification. Any reader of Dante's *Comedy* will quickly realize that many of the *dramatis personae* are given very specific characteristics and/or punishments in

Inferno, and that each character and his/her punishment represent a moral point. Referring to this method, Lewis suggests that "what looks like a platitude when it is set out in the abstract may become a different sort of thing when it puts on flesh and blood" (1998: 138).

Not only does the moral point become a narrative of human action, but it has also been assumed that the reader can become involved in the humanity and identity of the characters. Josipovici argues that the universe of the *Comedy* and other works of the time proceeds from

> the assumption that each reader can substitute himself [sic] for the hero, the 'I' figure. This is the essential condition of the allegory, and it rests on the medieval analogical view of human character: the 'I' is not so much a 'rounded figure' (though we are given some details about him) as a pair of eyes and an affective system no different from our own. Like us he is lost to begin with, but if we stay with him (in him?) we too will be led to vision and understanding.
>
> (Josipovici 1979: 78)

Indeed, for commentators such as Auerbach, the medieval reader would not only 'inhabit' these relations (1984: 98) by convention, s/he would also be compelled to do so by the consistent detail in the portrait of an individual's inner growth.

Dante, along with Virgil, is obviously the controlling moral figure in *The Divine Comedy*; but there are powerful characters other than the main one who also contribute to vision and understanding. In Canto V, for example, there appears Francesca, a woman who has been the object of much commentary, partly because of the way that she is so economically drawn as well as for her tragic condemnation to Inferno for the all-too-human sin of lust. The characters in the *Comedy* might be said to embody traits, but they also have a grounding in 'reality' for the interpreter of the text. Put another way, the religious or allegorical message, in order to be in any way convincing to the reader, needed to be 'realistic', conveyed through imitative mimesis and the poet's voice, to reach the heights of poetic truth envisaged by Aristotle.

## QUESTIONING THE VOICE IN THE MIDDLE AGES

Dante's was not the only perspective on rendering the real in the Middle Ages, though. The culture of the period was an eclectic one, comprising a selection of influences, many from the classical world. One commentator portrays the Middle Ages as a period of constant 'rewriting' of past works, as if the inhabitants were a shipwrecked people on a desert island, "depending on the odd collection of books which happened to be on board their ship" (Lewis 1998: 43). The fragmentary nature of memory in this period, resulting from a past during which the church and individual monasteries had had to preserve classical works in the midst of invasions from Vandals, Goths and, later, Norsemen, probably contributed to the survival of some narrative traditions and the death of others; but it is also likely that the reliance on writing and the kinds of identity accruing to characters, narrators and authors within this medium enabled different means of rendering narrative identity to flourish.

The period witnessed narrative developments which extended the common understanding of what constituted the 'poet's voice'. Noteworthy and exemplary figures in this respect are the poets Chaucer (Britain, c.1343–1400), Boccaccio (Italy, 1313–75) and, in the late Middle Ages and into the period of Renaissance, Rabelais (France, c.1494–1553). Each wrote works which seemed to undermine the Dantesque allegorical relationship between reader and character in narrative. Each was concerned to convey truth but equally concerned that narrative representation of the kind used by Dante was artificial. These poets believed that they had found one means of escaping the dilemma of artifice.

In the case of Chaucer, Josipovici suggests that "we find an 'I' figure who appears as naïve, well-meaning and obtuse, the joke depending on our grasping the *discrepancy* between the figure and his witty creator" (1979: 78). The *Canterbury Tales* (*c*.1386), a series of stories told by pilgrims on the way from London to the tomb of Thomas à Becket, possesses a structure which lends itself nicely to this goal. It comprises a series of tales, each told by a pilgrim whom the main narrator, equated with Chaucer himself, has met in The Tabard, a Southwark inn. Each of the stories is recognizably a morality tale and the didactic intent is evident. The tales of the pilgrims are each preceded by a prologue and there is a general prologue placed at the beginning of the collection which describes the meeting at The Tabard and offers vignettes of the Miller, the Wife of Bath, the Clerk and other subsequent raconteurs in the work.

While the tales told by the pilgrims contain quotation, it is also correct to say that the tales themselves are 'quotes' framed by the general prologue which explicitly apologizes for the vulgar tones which are to follow:

> Whoso shal telle a tale after a man,
> He moot reherce as ny as evere he kan
> Everich a word, if it be in his charge,
> Al speke he never so rudeliche and large
> (Chaucer 1966: 74, ll. 733–6)

This constitutes a significant disclaimer. What Chaucer meant, intended and thought is not, therefore, to be gleaned from a straightforward reading of the narratives or from an equation of the poet with the narrator of the prologue. As Pearsall puts it, "Whoever is telling the tales, we can be sure that it is not Chaucer. In this way, Chaucer gained for himself the freedom of manoeuvre which he needed in order to experiment with confidence" (1970: 175).

The narrative of Boccaccio's *Decameron* (1349–51) operates in a similar fashion. A hundred tales are presented as they have been narrated over ten days by seven women and three men. These are framed by a 'Pröem' and a 'Conclusion' by a narrator who anticipates and responds to criticisms of the vulgarity, length and unlikeliness of the stories by proclaiming, simply, that he has no real control over them and that this was how they were told. If Chaucer and Boccaccio problematized the 'poet's voice' by presenting tales framed by a narrator who comments on them, often ironically, Rabelais, on the other hand, in the later Middle Ages, preferred to distance author and character by drawing attention to the artificial acts of the former. In Rabelais' outlandish tales of the exploits and meetings of two giants, *Gargantua and Pantagruel* (1532–4), each of the five books is preceded by an 'author's prologue' in which the author proclaims himself a 'boozer' and assumes that his readers are equally afflicted with gout and a devotion to alcohol. The author also announces that he is sloppy about his writing, that his books are important and definitely true, that he cannot see his readers without wearing his spectacles even though he has referred to the book as a printed commodity and, later, that the printers have done such a bad job on the initial books in the series of five that he has been sorely misrepresented. In the first prologue he also tells the readers to be cautious about allegory, asking whether they believe the allegories that have been drawn out of the works of Homer by Plutarch, Eustathius and others:

> If you do not believe those arguments, what reason is there that you should treat these new and jolly chronicles of mine with the same reserve, seeing that as I dictated them I gave no more thought to the matter than you, who was probably drinking at the time, as I was?
>
> (Rabelais 1955: 39).

As Josipovici suggests, "Again and again he brings before the reader the image of himself sitting at his desk, writing down the words which we are now reading, explicitly focusing on the private and subjective nature of his fiction" (1979: 114). The 'poet's voice' is often so ridiculous in the Rabelaisian prologues that the only alternative is to imagine that there exists a narrator distinct from the author.

We have witnessed two broad approaches to rendering the real which were to become important parts of the novel's narrative armoury. There was the tradition, valorized in extant epics, which interspersed imitative mimesis with the poet's voice and which, in Dante's case, attempted to draw reader and character closer together by means of allegory. Novels would later employ this device at length, although it is palpable in relatively minor details such as the peopling of narratives with characters whose names would reveal their attributes: Allworthy (Fielding's *Tom Jones*, 1749), Lovelace (Richardson's *Clarissa*, 1747–8), Gradgrind (Dickens' *Hard Times*, 1854), for example. There was also a medieval tradition of drawing attention to the 'constructedness' of narrative by distancing the author from the imitative mimesis and even the descriptive prose which had previously been assumed to represent the poet's voice. Helped by punctuation and printing, characters came to say things in narrative which were not necessarily a representation of the author or poet's views. Indeed, *narrators* describing events and characters without resort to imitative mimesis were becoming recognizably different in *their* utterance from authors.

The existence of the narrator, of course, was a fact that was recognized at the very outset of Homer's *Odyssey*. The oral narrative tradition, in which poet-singers recited narratives whose origins were not always known, required a means to commence recitation. The usual devices such as 'Once upon a time ...' or 'Tell me, Muse ...' presupposed both a formula for the procedure and that the words of the story were not necessarily those of the poet-singer but, instead, those of the narrator of the story that had been passed on to him (Lord 2000). In the Middle Ages, it was much more possible to identify the poet or author of a contemporary written work in the real world; yet some poets chose to narrate their stories in voices very different from their own and their characters'. In such cases, it is frequently difficult to say definitively which 'voices' are privileged, the most important or taken most seriously by readers. In fact, Bakhtin (1981) argues that this 'polyphonic', or multiple-voiced, effect in narrative is the defining feature of the novel.

## THE LOW FORM OF THE ROMANCE AND THE RISE OF THE NOVEL

Prior to the rise of the novel in the eighteenth century, the separation of voices did not just take place within the confines of the epic; another major European narrative tradition partook of the same mixed mode. This was the 'romance', a narrative form that developed in the twelfth and thirteenth centuries, as opposed to the contemporary 'romance' genre that is well known in films such as *Titanic* (1998) or the work of the late Barbara Cartland. Romances were stories which depicted chivalry and the rules of 'courtly' life rather than the sublime elements which were so much a part of the epic tradition. Issues of personal loyalty, integrity or love were foregrounded in narratives of the search for spiritual truth. Under this heading such works as *Sir Gawain and the Green Knight* (late fourteenth century) and Malory's *La Morte d'Arthur* (1470), both of which deal with the Arthurian legend, might be included. Many romance narratives in English were frequently derived from models provided in France and Germany by Chrétien de Troyes, Benoît de Sainte-Maure, and Gottfried von Strassburg. Later romances such as Sir Philip Sidney's *Arcadia* (1580, 1590) and the celebrated narrative which first appeared in Spain in 1605, Cervantes' *Don Quixote de la Mancha*, began to break from this mould (Brink 1998: 20–45). Alternatively, it is sometimes possible to recognize the mixture of both 'epic' and 'romance' in such works as *The Faerie Queene* (1590–6) by the English poet, Edmund Spenser.

One reason for the spread of romance was the technology of printing. Probably the most famous English romance, *La Morte d'Arthur*, completed by Sir Thomas Malory in 1469–70, was adapted and translated from French works but disseminated most successfully when it was printed in 1485 by William Caxton. Another reason for the popularity of romance was that such narratives were written not in Latin as were epics and sacred texts, but in vernacular language, hence making them available to readers who were literate but did not possess the language of the church. Indeed, the Latin term *Romanice*, meaning 'written in the vernacular', not only spawned the name for the romance but also played a part in the etymology of 'novel'. In English-speaking countries it is easy to forget that the term 'novel' is derived from the Old Italian 'novella', which referred to a reasonably short narrative, the kind that would probably be called today *un racconto*. The books which make up Boccaccio's *Decameron*, for example, would have been called *novelle* rather than *racconti*. Elsewhere in Europe the longer, novel-length narratives derive their name from the romance (*le roman* in France, *il romanzo* in Italy).

Many commentators emphasize the survival of aspects of the romance in later narrative forms, pointing out "the continuity of narrative technique that runs from sixteenth- and seventeenth-century narrative (Sidney, Spenser, Cervantes) through the eighteenth- and nineteenth-century novel to the modern period" (Keen 1998: 180). Certainly, the vernacular language tended to invite assessments of romance as a 'low' form. Moreover, this was exacerbated in later romance narratives which, in preference to the perfect knights of the twelfth and thirteenth centuries, featured characters of lower status or characters who fitted the ideals of the times. Castiglione in his Renaissance romance, *Il Cortegiano*

(1528), for example, presents his hero as a humanist scholar-courtier. The 'low' status of such narratives was passed on to the novel, despite the fact that early novelists were keen to distinguish their product from epics and romances and frequently sought to do so to the detriment of the two preceding forms (see Roberts 1993; cf. McKeon 1987).

Subject matter was often the moot point in these distinctions and the issue is crucial in understanding the orientation to everyday reality of the novel form. Early commentators on the novel in the eighteenth century, such as Chesterfield and Congreve, welcomed a more down-to-earth set of themes than those which had traditionally appeared in epics and romances (Hawthorn 1997; Roberts 1993). The novel facilitated depictions of everyday life and its tribulations rather than the sublime world of gods which was so much a part of the epic. It promoted the depiction of a world which was relatively stable and certainly not prone to the supernatural elements which so frequently intruded into the elaborate rituals of the court as described in the romance. Some early English novelists such as Henry Fielding (1707–54) wished specifically to distance themselves from romances and see their work in the epic tradition. Others eschewed both romance and epic, a well-known example being Samuel Richardson (1689–1761).

The novel, however, was not a simple outgrowth or 'technical' response to the epic and the romance, even though these last two were important forms of narrative. Indeed, the novel had existed in embryonic form as a long and highly organized fictional narrative focusing on multiple characters even in the first century (see Doody 1998: 15–172). Its major resurgence in the eighteenth century coincided with the growth of a milieu in which those who did read consumed a variety of reading matter: the Bible, religious tracts and sermons, ballads, Newgate confessionals (accounts of criminals' lives), 'picaresque' tales (narratives which first developed in Picardie and which dealt with the exploits of rogues), 'chapbooks' (collections which included ballads and romances), histories and chronicles, biographies, accounts of travel, magazines, periodicals and journalism of all kinds (Hunter 1990; Barron and Nokes 1993).

Eighteenth-century novels such as *Tom Jones* (1749) clearly contain elements from other forms such as the epic, the 'picaresque', the biography and the ballad. Yet, there is a strong argument to suggest that the novel is, "in the pseudo-referential character of the language of the earliest English novelist", perhaps dominated, but certainly bound "in a peculiar and complex way, to the world of 'facts'" (Lodge 1997: 25). Davis (1983: 40–2), for example, holds that eighteenth-century novels most frequently imitated existing forms of non-fictional discourse such as journalism (cf. Williams 1985). This seems to suggest that the rise of the novel as a narrative form is not just an 'artistic' matter, but is determined by developments in the social world and the problem of their representation. If journalism was so esteemed in the period, why was there a desire for fictional novelistic narratives at all? One answer to this lies in the continuing Aristotelian faith in the special kind of truth which the mixed mode could yield.

## THE TRIPLE RISE THESIS AND BEYOND

As we have already indicated, the novel was read by *literate* citizens in the West. Essentially, the novel is a *written* form of narrative and is usually consumed as such, although public readings in the nineteenth century and 'audiobooks' in the early twenty-first century do provide a couple of exceptions to the rule. The precondition for the growth of a novel-reading public, then, was a growth in literacy in Western culture. The general growth of the population in the seventeenth and eighteenth centuries encompassed the significant growth of a new, non-servant, bourgeois, middle class. Made up of merchants, manufacturers, artisans and others, this relatively wealthy class differed from the landed gentry who made up the dominant social stratum in previous centuries.

In order for this new class to survive, however, it needed to reproduce the conditions which allowed its burgeoning in the first
place; this entailed not simply the maintenance of existing business interests but also their expansion. The appropriate education
of the offspring of this class was therefore necessary; consequently,
the eighteenth-century witnessed an exponential growth of
schooling of all different kinds: home tutoring, autodidacticism,
religious schools, boarding schools, Dissenting Academies, char-
ity schools, and, in England, the major 'public' schools: Eton,
Harrow, Rugby, Westminster and Charterhouse. All of these contributed to a growth in literacy among the bourgeois population
while schooling the class' children in pursuits which were
thought appropriate to the station of contemporary gentlemen
(and, in some cases, women) (Stone 1969; Lawson and Silver
1973: 164–225; Porter 1990: 162–9).

The acquisition of literacy was also facilitated by technology.
The printing press had been in use for over three hundred years
before 1800. But in England from 1695, with the lapsing of the
Licensing Act, a new era was opened. The Act had severely regu-
lated and censored printed publications of all sorts until this
time. Now that a range of printed artefacts could be produced for
prospective markets, access to printing technology was sought by
entrepreneurs (Williams 1965: 203–6; Hunter 1990: 193).
Booksellers grew in number. The subsequent growth of magazines, periodicals, newspapers and other printed materials also
aided literacy, whether in schools or when taken up privately by
the self-taught citizen.

It must also be mentioned, however, that the market for
printed works did not stand alone. The mere fact that a 'market-
economy' came into existence at this time is crucial for contextu-
alizing the growth of narratives in novel form. Not only was the
new bourgeois class purchasing printed materials, it was doing so
within a larger context of purchasing consumer goods in general,
a phenomenon which had been far from widespread in Europe

hitherto. These conditions have informed one of the most well known and, indeed, powerful, theses about the rise of the novel. The core of Ian Watt's work (1963) is an analysis of the way in which the mushrooming of the middle class entailed an upsurge in literacy, which, in turn, led directly to the widespread readership for the novel form of narrative. In this way, the novel is, for Watt, a quintessentially middle-class form.

One major adjunct of this "triple rise" thesis (Hunter 1990: 66) is the embedding of 'individualism' in the very form of the novel. The notion of the 'sovereign rights of the individual' is a central product of both the Enlightenment and the middle-class capitalism which succeeded the feudal system of social stratification. It was part and parcel of the new middle class whose mercantile interests were to be furthered in a system which, at least in theory, favoured individual industry over inherited wealth. It was also integral to the revolutionary movements in France and America which would have such an explosive impact later in the century. Yet, more broadly still, the sense of the individual was an important product of literate culture. Writing, "by objectifying words, and by making them and their meaning available for much more prolonged scrutiny than is possible orally, encourages private thought" (Goody and Watt 1968: 62). Furthermore, where written texts in ancient cultures were difficult to reproduce, they were often read aloud, publicly, to groups; in spite of their written nature, then, for such texts there would be a strong demand to promote recall. This is one reason why narrative persisted into the new technology of literacy. Easily reproducible *printed* texts, on the other hand, could be pored over by individuals, often in solitary circumstances. Writing even encouraged inner contemplation through the medium of the 'diary' or the 'confession', an inner dialogue in which the individual could place on record, objectify and even narrativize his/her own private experience. If circulated, this could be read by other individuals, offering the opportunity to reflect on or narrativize *their* private experiences, as opposed to simply embracing the orally transmitted common public identity and traditions of a larger group (Goody and Watt 1968: 42, 62).

The way in which early novels wholeheartedly put a case for individualism, and did so in a sometimes problematic fashion, is widely acknowledged by commentators (see, for example, Ray 1990: 93–104, 188–96 and Lovell 1987: 15–17; 153–5). Individual characters in novel narratives take on a shape which would have been largely unthinkable within the rubric of the romance or epic. Characters' psychological depth and existence in a world determined by their individual will were to become the *sine qua non* of the novel and this, of course, was facilitated from the very start by the fact that narrative enshrines from its originary moment the recording of human actions. Thus Defoe's 1719 novel, *Robinson Crusoe*, records the endeavours of its eponymous character, a man who, in acts of apparently sheer individual will and industry, resourcefully carves out a place for himself on the island where he is marooned (Watt 1963: 66–103). Yet, while it is worth taking seriously the idea that the novel is an allegory of bourgeois economic man, it is possible to question the extent to which Crusoe's resources are actually the result of individual commitment rather than the good fortune of having the riches of the shipwrecked vessel delivered to him intact (see Macherey 1978: 240–8).

Nevertheless, it is clear that the individual has a crucial role to play in the development of the novel form of narrative. One need only consider Lemuel Gulliver, Roderick Random, Clarissa Harlowe and, in the following century, the heroines of Jane Austen's novels, plus Becky Sharpe, David Copperfield, Maggie Tulliver, Isabel Archer and many others from the English novel tradition. In fact, there is a German term for those kinds of novel that focus specifically on the development of an individual character, especially in their youthful years: *Bildungsroman*. Furthermore, the psychological attributes of individuals are emphasized in general in the novel form, and in a way that recalls the arguments of Auerbach (1968) about the Old Testament. Yet novel narratives are not simply a matter of individual psychology: convincing depiction of the individual required the appropriate narrative mode.

## INSTRUCTION, TELLING AND NARRATIVE MODE

In addition to the accurate depiction of individual psychology there was another reason that the period demanded an appropriate narrative mode. In 1731, one of the major periodicals of the eighteenth century, the *Gentleman's Magazine*, was launched. From the outset it claimed to be a combination of "practical information about domestic life and a combination of improvement with entertainment" (Watt 1963: 57). This mission statement reveals a great deal about the expectations of the English reading public in the period. It would be all too easy to dismiss the reading matter of the time as so many entertaining trifles indulged in by a populace which had no access to electronic media such as TV, radio, video and cinema. Clearly, however, the didactic aspect of narrative which Plato had identified in mimesis, and which continued in the mixed mode within narrative, remained as active as ever.

In the preface to his novel, *Clarissa* (1747–8), Samuel Richardson explains that the narrative is made up of a collection of letters. Yet, the aim of these letters is not simply to provide a little diversion for the reader. "[I]n the great variety of subjects which this collection contains", he writes,

> it is one of the principal views of the publication: to caution parents against the undue exertion of their natural authority over their children in the great article of marriage: and children against preferring a man of pleasure to a man of probity, upon that dangerous but too commonly received notion, *that a reformed rake makes the best husband.*
>
> (Richardson 1985: 36)

Reading this passage almost makes it seem as though entertainment is a side-issue, so prominent is the function of instruction. Even more notable, though, is that *Clarissa* is an epistolary novel: it is made up of a series of letters between characters without the intrusion of a narratorial voice. The author sees fit to write this preface emphasizing the importance of instruction, but his view of mimesis matches Plato's in that he feels the voices of the characters will be sufficient to carry out his intentions.

If instruction is so important to novelists, then, arguments about modes of depiction become crucial. For instruction to be credible, novelists were required to maintain a mode which would not only 'tell' their readers about the world but would also do so convincingly. The world depicted had to be thought to be closely related to the world outside the novel which people inhabited. The voice of the narrator or even the voice of the author was obviously important to novelists: this was the means to *tell* the public about moral imperatives or issues of the day. But imitative mimesis was indispensable: the novel audience increasingly wanted narratives which were neither mere parables nor allegories whose outlandish nature was to be decoded into everyday terms. Instead, the novel was to be 'realistic', in a general sense, with characters broadly imitating the speech of people, with situations broadly resembling real situations in the world and with events tending to follow the logic that they would in life. A depiction can *never be* that which it depicts, of course; it follows, then, that the 'realism' which readers might demand of narrative is always an approximation or a compromise.

One of the earliest warnings of the effects of such compromises was offered, curiously, in a *novel* by the Irish writer, Laurence Sterne (1713–68). The narrative of *The Life and Opinions of Tristram Shandy* (1760–7) constantly confounds the reader's expectations that there will be an unspoken relation of 'realism' between the world and its depiction. Tristram, as narrator, is seriously prone to digression; he wishes to give every detail of his life that he can but, in so doing, he only announces that he will speak about the circumstances of his birth by Chapter IV and he only narrates his entry into the world in Book IV, almost 250 pages later. One reason for this is that he recounts at length the often nonsensical conversations of others. Put bluntly, Tristram is over-committed to the notion of a thoroughly realistic and imitative depiction: when his character Yorick dies and closes his eyes never to open them again, the next page is entirely filled with a black rectangle. At the end of Book VI, Tristram starts to present diagrams of the narrative path he has taken in previous books.

Ultimately, Tristram is grappling with the problem that the more he writes about his life mimetically, the more he will need to write. If he is to try to include everything about himself then he will need to carry on writing indefinitely, and even then he will never catch up with life. This dilemma is the product of the 'realist' reliance on the balance of mimesis and the narrator's voice, particularly the overlap of the two which we have mentioned in relation to 'description'. In order to maintain felicity to the real world rather than simply laying out a series of unembroidered events, a narrative must engage in a quasi-mimetic presentation which accurately *describes* details such as the interior of rooms, the physical appearances of minor characters, the weather and background sounds, even if the details pertain to circumstances which are fictional. Roland Barthes (1992: 133–41) calls the results of this imperative "the reality effect". But description of details cannot be maintained for too long. In Richardson's *Pamela* (1740), for example, the heroine's account of her wedding day, purportedly written on her wedding night, proceeds at what seems interminable length for the modern reader. Entries in her journal at six o'clock in the morning, just after half past eight, at three o'clock and at ten o'clock in the evening, give page after page about the day's events (Richardson 1980: 370–80). This amount of detail is not uncharacteristic for a bride, particularly one writing for her parents as Pamela is; however, it strains the belief and patience of the general reader to imagine that she wrote the journal entry on the same day as the events and sees the need to recount so much.

Once more, this is an example of the way that narrative is necessarily bound up with *re*-presentation. In order for detailed description to have any kind of purchase in narrative it must leave some things out in favour of others. Auerbach (1968: 473–80) outlines the importance of the selection process in the work of the French novelist, Balzac, whose detailed descriptions of characters arise out of a concern with the interconnectedness of different features of the milieux that they inhabit. The selection process enables a great deal of description, but this will not be constrained simply by correspondence to the real world. Pamela's account of her wedding day may not be 'untrue', but one is led to question whether she had time to write it and whether the details are not too numerous or too disparate. If they are found to be *too* disparate, and therefore unrelated, then they will not be consistent. Such consistency is crucial because it is one feature of 'verisimilitude' in narrative, a logical and meaningful connection between described objects as opposed to a completely detailed analogue of them. 'Pure' mimesis and overly detailed description without narration run the risk of mitigating verisimilitude and, effectively, becoming too 'realistic' for their own good.

Yet there is also an approach within narrative which retains the didactic intent of mimesis in general and is to be found in the work of one of the key names in the early history of the novel's resurgence. It can be argued that Jane Austen's narratives leave little doubt about their moral structure. The question of who is a worthy character and who is an unworthy one is usually settled by the framing voice of the narrator, who may hold the character in disdain or esteem, as well as by the actual utterances of the character, which the reader is invited to judge. Nevertheless, Austen's narratives often rely on a further development of the mixed mode which, in Anglophone circles, is sometimes known as 'free indirect discourse' (Lubbock 1926: 256–7; Friedman 1955: 1178; cf. Cohn 1966; Rimmon-Kenan 1983: 106–16) or as *skaz*, the phenomenon identified by Bakhtin as an "orientation towards *someone else's speech*" (1984: 191).

In *Persuasion* (1818), Mr. Shepherd recommends to Sir Walter, enthusiastically and at some length, a group of tenants who might rent the latter's erstwhile home:

> Mr. Shepherd hastened to assure him, that Admiral Croft was a very hale, hearty, well-looking man; a little weather-beaten, to be sure, but not much; and quite the gentleman in all his notions and behaviour; – not likely to make the smallest difficulty about terms; – only wanted a comfortable home, and to get into it as soon as possible; – knew he must pay for his convenience; – knew what rent a ready-furnished house of that consequence might fetch; – should not have been surprised if Sir Walter had asked more; – had enquired about the manor; – would be glad of the deputation, certainly, but made no great point of it; – said he sometimes took out a gun but never killed; – quite the gentleman.
>
> (Austen 1985: 51)

This passage is an example of 'free indirect discourse': the character's habit of speech is present, but direct imitation and quotation marks are not. In terms of the plot of the novel, this moment is crucial because among the party who will be associated with the house is Captain Wentworth, whose re-entry into the life of the heroine, Anne Elliot, constitutes the main story. Furthermore, the plot turn is hastened by Mr Shepherd's eagerness which, itself, is arguably more convincing due to the economical way in which it is conveyed. Rather than placing Mr Shepherd's words in inverted commas and framing them with an account of his committed demeanour, the staccato pattern of the character's speech is reproduced at second hand and in the past tense. The narrator, in rendering the speech in this way, is demonstrating an awareness of Mr Shepherd's keen discourse and indicating it to the reader, thus eradicating the need to reproduce it verbatim, and making further comment unnecessary.

'Free indirect discourse' has been used copiously in narratives from the work of Austen to that of the contemporary crime novelist, Elmore Leonard (Cobley 2000: 78–98). Potentially, the device blurs the boundaries between character and narrator, so much so that Austen's narratives are often unsure about whether the free indirect discourse should appear between inverted commas or not (Rée 2000: 371). The device also has the potential to restore the freedom of the oral storyteller and liberate narratives from the fidelity to characters' words required by the use of speech punctuation.

In spite of Plato's prescriptions, the oral heritage of narrative was not suddenly eradicated. Nor did it fade away with the advent of such multi-layered and sophisticated means of representation as the novel, itself facilitated by thoroughgoing technologies of writing and printing. It lingered in the background, as Havelock and Lord suggest, with larger social concerns about representation transformed into apparently more localized aesthetic ones. The mixed mode, incorporating imitative mimesis and the author's or narrator's voice, seemed to be the artistic embodiment of the new role for narrative in the literate world. Yet narrative modes steadfastly refused to become simply a question of aesthetics. Epics, romances and novels remained representations of human action; they continued to play out the definitions of identities; and they made narratives crucial vehicles and investment points for cultures which sought to know their past and present. In turn, the mode of depiction within narrative remained a significant means for rendering and stabilizing identity: the relation between the voices of characters, narrators and authors might result in a more rounded picture of the world, in Aristotle's terms, because it did not simply rely on the unitary *telling* of scientific or purely didactic discourse. At the same time, however, the potential disparity of voices within narrative might lead to difficult questions such as 'Who is in control of these signs?' and 'Who is the authority here?'. In the nineteenth century, the novel attempted to contain narrative and head off such questions through a zealous pursuit of realism.

# 4

## REALIST REPRESENTATION

In the nineteenth century, realism and the novel developed into the major narrative form that is so often the focus of attention from critics, historians and narrative theorists. The realist novel has commanded attention because it has been so supremely concerned with social setting (Snow 1978), because it allowed the development of a 'great tradition' which was 'alive' to its time (Leavis 1962), because it embodied the aspirations of the emergent and then dominant bourgeois class (Lukacs 1969), because it rationalized consciousness of time and space (Ermarth 1998) and because it provided domestic pleasures (Showalter 1978). For so many commentators, the novel is a noble attempt to place in narrative form the complexity of the social world and its contemporary flux. Raymond Williams, for example, in an analysis that was to be echoed by Anderson (1991), sees the development of the realist novel in the nineteenth century as concomitant with the rise and fall of a knowable community:

> the novelist offers to show people and their relationships in essentially knowable and communicable ways. Much of the confidence of this method depends on a particular kind of

social confidence and experience. In its simplest form this amounts to saying – though at its most confident it did not have to be said – that the knowable and therefore known relationships compose and are part of a wholly known social structure, and that in and through the relationships the persons themselves can be wholly known.

(Williams 1970: 13)

This formulation points directly to the firmly embedded belief that the novel possesses a special ability to depict the increasingly varied social world which gives rise to it.

## SECRETARIES TO THE NINETEENTH CENTURY

Although purveyors of realism in the nineteenth century were beset by difficulties when describing *what* they were doing, they were, it seemed, reasonably confident in their ability to apprehend the real. In France, as we have mentioned, the novelist Honoré de Balzac (1799–1850), along with Stendhal (Henri Beyle, 1788–1842), pursued realism by paying a great deal of attention to the depiction of milieux. Their attempt to place complex historical and personal relations within a narrative frame constituted a sophisticated technical exercise in novelistic 'description'; however, its main points correspond with those of Williams: a confidence in the ability to know common persons through the web of their relations within a social structure. Both novelists explored further the pre-existing novelistic concern with common characters and the everyday instead of the sublime, and conducted their exploration through the medium of large canvasses, minutely detailed to give a sense of richness, conveying a picture of a definite period in history (Auerbach 1968: 485). Indeed, Balzac understood his role of novelist as akin to being the "secretary to the nineteenth century" (Balzac 1992: 29). With qualification the same might be said of Balzac's English and

American contemporaries, Sir Walter Scott (1771–1832) and James Fenimore Cooper (1789–1851) or, later in the century, Balzac's countryman, Emile Zola (1840–1902).

The emphasis on the psychologies of individuals in the novel form of narrative had begun to shift in favour of a more detailed exploration of individual relationships within a recognizable social structure. The crises of everyday existence, witnessed in the vast majority of nineteenth-century English realist novels from Jane Austen's *Mansfield Park* (1814) through Charlotte Brontë's *Jane Eyre* (1847) and Anthony Trollope's *The Warden* (1855) to Thomas Hardy's *Jude the Obscure* (1895), were crises which could become manifest because of the growing belief in the ability to know social relations. As Williams adds, the relationships that result from urban communities in the early stages of Western industrialization promoted a confidence in the ability of individuals to know each other. However, social relationships do not provide total knowledge of human beings: "some part of the personality precedes and survives – in a way is unaffected by – relationships; [...] in this special sense persons are not knowable, are indeed fundamentally and crucially unknowable" (Williams 1970: 14). The latter point was to be central to early and high modernist developments in narrative; where the realist novel is concerned, though, there is great emphasis on the possibility of social relations manifesting knowledge of individuals and groups.

The emphasis on the large canvas, the breadth of social existence and the historical period in novels as different as Scott's *Waverley* (1814), Cooper's *The Last of the Mohicans* (1926), Disraeli's *Sybil, or the Two Nations* (1845), Elizabeth Gaskell's *Cranford* (1853) and Tolstoy's *War and Peace* (1869) constituted the most obvious coupling of relations between individuals and larger social relations. Yet, most importantly, the vehicle for these explorations of relationships continued to be the interplay of mimesis and narrators' voices. Realist narrative offered verbatim imitations of what characters said but, rather than allowing characters to speak interminably, linked the places and times in which they spoke by way of the narrator's summarizing voice. The realist novel sought to perfect the transition from summary to scene, making it as smooth as possible and taking care to avoid disconcerting jumps and disturbing juxtapositions. The complexity of contemporary industrialized existence was represented within a particular space: for example, drawing rooms where people met or larger spaces such as entire towns. Time was invariably presented as consisting of discrete moments along a straight line; any extended lingering took place in the service of the narrator's exposition or summary rather than as a result of characters' subjective impressions.

Narrative mode, then, was once again demonstrably more than just a matter of accurately depicting the actions of individual characters; it was a matter of time, space, social relations and what was *not* depicted. For very good reason, then, the mode of depiction known as 'realism' has repeatedly been the cause of heated debate (see Adorno et al. 1980; Lovell 1983; Swingewood 1986; Furst 1992; Walder 1995). Indeed, it is easy to see from the outset that such debates harbour a political issue in modern societies. Whoever lays the strongest claim to a method of imitating or representing the real henceforth has the greatest access to 'reality', or what is believed to be 'real'. Additionally, such a party with such a claim can go on to prescribe which methods are appropriate and which inappropriate for the purposes of depicting and describing the world. And if such modes of depiction are so prevalent and widely rehearsed, in schools and early education for example, then they have the potential to become the 'common sense', self-evident, unquestioned means of access to the real.

## BATTLES OVER REALISM

Although debates about realism have been ongoing for some years and have exhibited different levels of complexity, a brief review of just one example from the many possible will serve to illustrate what is at stake. Film and literary theorist Colin MacCabe put forth, in a couple of powerfully argued essays and a full-length book on James Joyce, the notion of the 'classic realist text' (1974, 1977, 1978). Essentially, he argued that, in the present, literate citizens have become so used to the constructed form, 'classic realism', that they often tend to forget both its artifice and the fact that it is at work in all sorts of narratives. Traditionally, in the nineteenth-century novel, which, MacCabe argues, has become a dominant and paradigmatic genre, there exist the discourse of the characters in inverted commas, and the discourse of the narrator outside the inverted commas and in prose form. This description tallies, of course, with parts of the Platonic conception of mimesis and, especially, the Aristotelian conception of 'imitative mimesis' and the 'poet's voice'.

What the 'classic realist text' does, for MacCabe, is to give a false sense of the freedom of the words in the inverted commas. It is almost as if the words that characters speak in narratives seem to be their own, spoken freely and not subject to interference by others; ultimately, however, such imitative mimesis is framed, contextualized and controlled by the prose outside the inverted commas. This is the crux of MacCabe's argument: that the narrative prose outside inverted commas exercises its power in an authoritarian way, controlling readers' access to reality in such an insidious manner that they do not notice its operation. For him the narrator's control indicates that there is a hierarchy in classic realism: the character's voice is heard, but it is subordinate to the voice of the narrator. Furthermore, the 'subjective' nature of the character's voice seemingly offers a contrast to the narrator's voice; the narrator's task of providing summary and detail in narrative, coupled with its distinction from the voice of the character, appears to lend the narrator 'objectivity'. As such, the narrator's description of events in prose, outside the inverted commas, can become the 'objective view' of events, even to the extent where it seems that there is no narrator at all. Obviously, the disappearance of the narrator is an impossibility because, as we have stressed from the outset, the rendering of an object can never be the object itself and a *re*-presentation is always undertaken by some agency. However, MacCabe's point is that readers have become so used to 'classic realism' that they 'forget' that it is there, manipulating, framing and presenting its own version of events.

For MacCabe and others, one of the monuments of the 'classic realist text' is the nineteenth-century novel by George Eliot (neé Mary Anne Evans) entitled *Middlemarch* (1872). Quintessentially, it is an example of classic realism because Eliot, as author, presents the events of people's lives but, at the same time as she is presenting them, she allows the moralistic tone of the narratorial voice to scorn and pass judgement on events and characters. For example, when the idealistic doctor, Lydgate, meets Rosamond for the first time in her father's house, Rosamond plays the piano. She is also a polite conversationalist and Lydgate is captivated. This marks the first step towards a marriage which is in ruins by the end of the narrative. However, the narrator constructs the possibility of a judgement of Rosamond before the playing or conversation even begins by describing Mrs Vincy and then moving to her daughter:

> The tinge of unpretentious, inoffensive vulgarity in Mrs. Vincy gave more effect to Rosamond's refinement, which was beyond what Lydgate had expected.
>
> Certainly, small feet and perfectly turned shoulders aid the impression of refined manners, and the right thing said seems quite astonishingly right when it is accompanied with exquisite curves of lip and eyelid. And Rosamond could say the right thing; for she was clever with that sort of cleverness which catches every tone except the humorous. Happily, she never attempted to joke, and this was perhaps the most decisive mark of her cleverness.
>
> (Eliot 1965: 188)

In the space of a few sentences, the narrator describes the difference between Mrs Vincy and her daughter, but also presents the latter as cunning and sly, hints that Lydgate is a flawed dupe and suggests that the relationship is doomed from the start. The contempt in which Rosamond and, to a slightly lesser extent, Lydgate are held by the narrator is quite clear.

Undoubtedly, this is only a brief passage and it should be emphasized that *Middlemarch* is a vast and ambitious narrative. Indeed, its vastness is typical of realism's predilection for large and detailed canvasses depicting a specified historical period. In order to take the arguments about *Middlemarch* and classic realism in narrative seriously, then, some concentrated discussion of the novel will be necessary.

## *MIDDLEMARCH* AND 'CLASSIC REALISM'

*Middlemarch* seeks to present both psychological insight and a sharply focused picture of the everyday lives of its main characters: Lydgate; Rosamond; Dorothea, the heroine whose unhappy marriage enforces a voyage of discovery; Ladislaw, the young artist whose ideals are later met by political reform; Casaubon, Dorothea's pious, humourless and chauvinist husband; and the troubled banker, Bulstrode. It also carefully assembles multiple storylines in its portrait of a provincial town. Its desire to present as much background for motivation and causality is evident throughout in digressions; one illustration among the many possible is the way in which Lydgate's current position, psychologically and socially, is shown to be at least partly determined by his erstwhile infatuation with a French actress. The account takes up the bulk of Chapter 15 although, as the narrator iterates, it concerns matters which are not known to the inhabitants of Middlemarch and, moreover, are to have no *direct* bearing on the 'events' of the narrative. Although the Lydgate digression seems to have no discernible connection to the main narrative events, let us remember that its 'descriptive' nature or its function as a 'reality effect' is very much of a piece with the character of narrative in general. It comes at a point in the novel where there is a focus on Lydgate, which flashes back to an earlier, pre-*Middlemarch*, defining phase of his life. The details of this digression may or may not augur badly for the future. The main point of the digression, however, seems to be its enactment of the dynamic of 'memory–attention– expectation' which Ricoeur argues is so central to the relationship of narrative and time. Lydgate's scientific bearing has been undermined by superficial emotions in the past; will this happen again in the future?

This depth of description is one factor which, in the view of a number of critics, makes the novel so worthy of note. For one of the most famous commentators on Eliot's work, the novel's subtitle, 'A Study of Provincial Life' is

> no idle pretension. The sheer informedness about society, its mechanism, the ways in which people of different classes live and (if they have to) earn their livelihoods, impresses us with its range, and it is real knowledge; that is, it is knowledge alive with understanding.
>
> (Leavis 1962: 76–7)

The novel is about people in a small town but deals with issues of industrial, agricultural and medical progress; education, knowledge and the clergy; morals, politics, political reform and personal reform. So the novel is indeed about personal tribulations, but it also contains great detail in the way it addresses larger historical and political questions.

The mode of addressing broad political issues in the form of a narrative about people in a highly localized situation had, however, been the focus of controversy even before the classic realist text thesis. Conveying the flavour of the controversy, which has important implications for the analysis of narrative, will require some historical background, and it is worth remembering that 'background', here, actually refers to a particular historical *narrative*.

The novel is set in Britain in the year 1829, amidst the clamour for parliamentary reform which was to reach a seeming climax in the Great Reform Act of 1832. The preceding years, in the wake of the British victory over French forces at Waterloo had been lean for many citizens. There was opposition to automization as machines were being developed to take the place of human employees in urban factories. Machine-breaking in the textile industries of the North and Midlands had been occurring sporadically since the period of Luddism from 1811–12 and, to an extent, this was associated with more overtly political agitation for reform (Dinwiddy 1979).

Similarly, agitation among Lancashire weavers for better pay and conditions also became more closely connected with broader political issues, and the government responded to this in turn. In 1817, a mass march of textile workers from Lancashire to London was planned, with the ultimate aim of presenting a petition to the Prince Regent. Smouldering discontent at factory conditions, particularly among skilled workers, was exacerbated by the workers' distance from the centre of power in London. Before the 'March of the Blanketeers' could gain any significant momentum, not to mention the expected huge numbers, it was intercepted by troops at Stockport. The same year a small rebellion in Derbyshire, known as the Pentridge Rising, was thwarted and its leaders executed. Then, in 1819, a series of mass rallies culminated in a final meeting at St Peter's Field in Manchester. The local yeomanry, agitated by the gathering, used arms to disperse the peaceful crowd and killed eleven people in what was to become known, ironically, as the 'Peterloo' massacre (Read 1958; Thompson 1968: 746ff.; Dinwiddy 1986).

*Middlemarch*, then, is set amidst the popular demand for reform which, in the three years before the Reform Act, seemed as though it could quite easily spill over into revolution. Yet, for one hugely influential critic, *Middlemarch*

> is an historical novel in form with very little substantive histori-cal content. The Reform Bill, the railways, cholera, machine-breaking: these 'real' historical forces do no more than impinge on the novel's margins. The mediation between the text and the 'real' history to which it alludes is notably dense; and the effect of this is to transplant the novel from the 'histor-ical' to the 'ethical'. *Middlemarch* works in terms of egoism and sympathy; 'head' and 'heart', self-fulfilment and self-surrender ...
>
> (Eagleton 1976: 120)

In short, *Middlemarch* makes big political and historical issues into localized, personal problems; and, in so doing, Eagleton believes that it does considerable damage to our chances of under-standing what really goes on in history. Undoubtedly, *Middlemarch* is a *re*-presentation and is therefore *necessarily* differ-ent from the 'truth' of history. Yet in addition, as Eagleton insists, it is frequently the case that Eliot's narrator seems to be arguing that the greater good can be achieved by personal moral reform rather than widespread political reform or a series of con-certed measures against the serious iniquities that exist in capital-ist society.

One reason that Eliot promotes this perspective, according to Eagleton, has to do with the time in which she is writing, the way that she embodies this time, and, crucially, the narrative devices she utilizes to depict social reality. For Eagleton, nineteenth-century British society is itself the subject of a narra-tive to do with the way in which it is sustained by its economy. That is to say, British society is characterized by a mode of pro-ducing goods which is capitalist, relying on the means of produc-tion being held by relatively few individuals who harness the labour force of many individuals at a profit. Eagleton's critical narrative depicts the growth of this industrial capitalism, which was a rapid and new phenomenon at the time, in three phases (Eagleton 1976: 110ff.).

The first is an 'individualist' (Romantic) phase: here, capitalism is promoted by its defenders and supporters largely in terms of the rights and powers of individuals. As we have seen, the notion of individualism is a product of the Enlightenment, and not only is it a strong component of the novel form but it is also a strong current in all kinds of contemporary thought. The second phase of capitalism which Eagleton identifies is the 'corporatist phase', where capitalism consolidates itself. Following the agitation which led to the Great Reform Act and the class struggles after the Act, such as the Anti-Corn Law League, Chartism and trade unionism, capitalism began to embrace disparate elements of its labour force, the working class, and its supporters stressed collective national effort. The third phase is imperialism. In this case, capitalism extends its activities and effectively plunders the raw materials beyond national boundaries (see Chapter 5). In the later part of the century Britain and other countries in the West furthered their explorations and economic exploitation of the resources of 'underdeveloped' countries, especially during what was known as the "scramble for Africa" (Pakenham 1994).

Eliot's narratives were published during the corporatist phase but, as we can see, her stress on the 'personal' very much marks *Middlemarch* as favourable to the individualist phase. The narrative of the novel addresses the 'corporatist' common good of the provincial town, but this is, theoretically at least, at odds with the heavy emphasis on individual self-realization. The contradiction is 'resolved' through the phenomenon of 'classic realism'.

This can be seen, first, in the way that *Middlemarch* thoroughly concerns itself with the issue of how to depict the world most adequately and most realistically, a concern which has also been attributed to George Eliot in writing it. Ladislaw, as an artist who then pursues a political career, is a key figure here; clearly, accurate representation is a fitting preliminary for good politics. When Dorothea encounters Ladislaw's paintings early in the novel, there can be little doubt that her grappling with their mode of depiction is somehow central to her personal development:

> 'I am no judge of these things', said Dorothea, not coldly, but with an eager deprecation of the appeal to her. 'You know, uncle, I never see the beauty of those pictures which you say are so much praised. They are a language I do not understand. I suppose there is some relation between picture and nature which I am too ignorant to feel – just as you see what a Greek sentence stands for which means nothing to me'. Dorothea looked up at Mr. Casaubon, who bowed his head towards her ...
>
> (Eliot 1965: 105)

Also, given the way in which the novel collapses the political into the personal, the following commentary, by the narrator rather than Dorothea, on how depiction should be considered, is noteworthy:

> And here I am naturally led to reflect on the means of elevating a low subject. Historical parallels are remarkably efficient in this way. The chief objection to them is, that the diligent narrator may lack space, or (what is often the same thing) may not be able to think of them with any degree of particularity though he may have a philosophical confidence that if known they would be illustrative. It seems an easier and shorter way to dignity to observe that – since there never was a true story which could not be told in parables where you might put a monkey for a margrave, and *vice versa* – whatever has been or is to be narrated by me about low people, may be ennobled by being considered a parable; so that if any bad habits and ugly consequences are brought into view, the reader may have the relief

of regarding them as not more than figuratively ungenteel, and may feel himself virtually in company with persons of some style.

(Eliot 1965: 375)

Here we encounter the strong narratorial voice which is so characteristic of the novel. All the utterances of the characters, all the historical factors that Eagleton mentions and which are obliquely narrated in the novel, are controlled and manipulated by the voice of the narrator situated at the apex of the hierarchy of voices in the narrative.

In this sense, the 'realism' of *Middlemarch* is not just a matter of showing things as they are in a mimetic fashion; it is also a matter of the *narratorial voice*, of *telling*, often in quite a didactic fashion. Likewise, as MacCabe's argument about 'classic realism' would have it, the narratorial voice not only *tells* the reader what to think about the history and politics, but it actually orders events, choosing to narrate some and omit others. There is thus a specific narratorial device upon which 'classic realism' depends. This device is known as the 'omniscient narrator' and we should consider it briefly here, both in its printed and cinematic forms, as its analysis yields some criticisms of the notion of 'the classic realist text'.

## OMNISCIENT NARRATION

'Omniscient' is defined by the *Oxford English Dictionary* as

1. Knowing all things, all-knowing, infinite in knowledge. **a.** Strictly: esp. of God ... **b.** Hyperbolically: Having universal or very extensive knowledge ... **2.** *absol.* or as *n.* an omniscient being or person: *spec.* (with *the*), the Deity, God ...

(http://dictionary.oed.com/cgi/entry_main/)

In consonance with this, omniscient narration consists both of the narrator's godlike ability to go everywhere and to possess the power and control that derives from unlimited knowledge. If the narrator is omniscient, s/he knows all, but in the act of representation is forced to select areas of knowledge for narration and to deselect others. S/he is able to allow some characters' voices to be heard and not others.

When a *character* in a narrative is the narrator, it is clear that s/he can only narrate certain things. As a rule, s/he cannot narrate directly what goes on in places where s/he is not. S/he cannot narrate what is inside other people's heads, what they think about and what they dream.[1] Sometimes, as in Henry James' story, *The Turn of the Screw* (1898), what is in the narrator's head might be at distinct odds with the 'reality' of the situations in which s/he finds him/herself. An omniscient narrator, on the other hand, who is not a character in the narrative, can go where s/he likes: to some scenes and not others; to different time periods and not others; inside characters' heads; and to Olympian positions, above and beyond the events in the narrative. An omniscient narrator can use a narratorial voice to say what s/he likes without fear of it being out of character. In *Middlemarch*, the narrator is omniscient: s/he takes up a position which is Olympian, pronouncing on events and how they should be told; s/he also delivers the reader so closely to scenes that the impression is almost given that the narrator is in them. The omniscient narrator also tends to know how and where the narrative will end (Rimmon-Kenan 1983: 94ff.).

In print narrative this is a reasonably understandable concept. Print narrative allows narrators easy access into the heads of

---

1   It must be noted that these rules are not steadfast, especially for what are termed 'postmodern narratives'. For example, in a recent novel which does not even bear the hallmark of 'postmodernism', Stephen Dobyns' *The Church of Dead Girls* (1998), the narrator is markedly omniscient, narrating what is in most of the characters' minds. However, the narrator is also a character in the novel himself.

characters. In cinematic narratives, on the other hand, this kind of omniscience is not so easily achieved. It is in the nature of film only to be able to present appearances. Of course, a voice-over narration may be able to provide some psychological insight to supplement that of the dialogue and the images; but, strictly speaking, film does not have the same powers of omniscience in narration that print fiction can choose to implement. Thus, the exact nature of omniscient narration in cinematic texts is by no means settled (Bordwell 1985: 66ff; Branigan 1992: 115; Bordwell and Thompson 1993: 75–8). This fact can be illustrated by the opposition of two fundamental features of cinematic narration: long takes and editing/cutting.

Most films rely on a method of narrating which consists of sequences of individual 'shots' of a relatively short duration. For example, if two people are talking in a scene, a shot of one of them uttering a sentence might be made, followed by a shot of the other person responding; or numerous shots of the first person uttering all his/her sentences in the scene might be made, followed by the same for the second person. In the finished product, after editing, each shot of each person uttering each sentence will appear on screen consecutively until the end of the scene. Then there may be a cut to another scene. The cutting from person to person, from utterance to utterance, and finally to another scene is one example of omniscient narration in that the choices about what is presented are made for the audience by a narrating agency who can, potentially, take us to any scene. As with the realist novel, then, narration is crucial in film because it creates a *logical sequence* in which the audience is delivered from one scene to another consecutively, rather than allowing scenes to run on interminably or to be disconcertingly juxtaposed.

Often there are examples of films which have a comparatively limited narration. In Roman Polanski's *Chinatown* (1973), to take just one instance, there are absolutely no scenes which stray from the immediate proximity of the protagonist, Jake Gittes (Jack

Nicholson). Even so, such films still depend on the ability to cut directly from one scene to another. Some films, however, add something to this fundamental process. Rather than assembling a series of uniformly brief shots, they will institute 'long takes' (Bordwell and Thompson 1993: 197–9). This entails that a whole scene, sometimes ranging over a considerable amount of space, will be shot with one camera, without an interval, without recourse to a second, third or fourth shot. Probably the most famous example of this is the phenomenally long take at the beginning of *Touch of Evil* (1953), whose technique is knowingly reproduced during the opening of *The Player* (1992).

In *Touch of Evil*, the shot begins with a close-up of a hand setting a time-bomb which is then planted in a car. The shot continues, without a break, showing the bomber's departure, then following the car's journey through a small town on the Mexican border, to border control, pausing only to follow the path of a married couple and their conversation. The sequence has been praised for its technical virtuosity but the impression that the long take gives is that the camera can go almost everywhere. In this way, the narration is almost omniscient once more. We might ask ourselves which alternative is closer to omniscience: the searching camera of the long take or the elaborately set up cameras of the short takes? In a way, it does not matter because films with long takes ultimately have to resort to new shots and short takes, as *Touch of Evil* does when the bomb goes off. Yet it is an interesting question because it suggests that both processes are limited in what they can tell us. They seem to show us everything, they seem to be flexible, but, in both cases, there is so much that is left out.

Again, this may be an example of the 'classic realist text' at work or, more broadly, '*re*-presentation', selecting some details and not others, but also facilitating the meaningful relations which will transpire with human input. What the example of film, perhaps more than the example of printed fiction, encourages us to ask is whether viewers/readers really take the act of selection in narratives so seriously that they accept it as an analogue of 'reality'. Certainly, narration organizes events and characters' speech in order to produce only one perspective on narrative contents; it also presents a sequence of events that seem to be motivated by logical cause; but must it be accepted by readers as almost completely 'real' or 'objective'?

## REALISM AND THE VOICES OF NARRATIVE

David Lodge's 1981 essay on *Middlemarch* asks questions such as these in taking to task the concept of the 'classic realist text'. Lodge acknowledges the interplay of imitative mimesis and the voice of the poet or narrator, and takes it very seriously. However, he recasts his understanding of the classical distinctions in terms derived from the work of the Russian theorist Mikhail Bakhtin (1981). For Bakhtin, the novel is an interesting form of narrative because it is 'heteroglossic'. That is to say, for him, novels are made up of many different voices, some of which, sometimes, may be competing. Whereas we have thus far in this chapter considered those perspectives on narrative which hold that the novel is dominated by the voice of the narrator, Bakhtin suggests that such domination is not a foregone conclusion and it is not at all certain that the narratorial voice can control all the characters. Nor is it necessarily the case that the narrator's voice will always be distinct from those of the characters.

The overlapping of voices can sometimes work in favour of the narrator. Any reader of *Middlemarch* would be hard-pressed to overlook the degree of venom that the narrator directs at the character of Rosamond; and this venom obviously bleeds into Rosamond's speech and behaviour: where the narrator's commentary on Rosamond ends and where Rosamond's appalling declarations, the imitative mimesis, begin is sometimes difficult to distinguish. Yet, the same principle works against the dominance of the narrator. Lodge is at pains to point out that there are numerous occasions in *Middlemarch* when imitative mimesis and narratorial voice overlap, and the result of this is that the character's voice, rather than the narrator's, comes out on top. For example, at a pivotal moment in *Middlemarch*, Ladislaw goes to see Dorothea whilst Mr. Casaubon is absent. What is significant about the scene is that the voices of Ladislaw, Dorothea and the narrator are, in a certain way, in conflict:

> 'I have often thought that I should like to talk to you again', she said, immediately. 'It seems strange to me how many things I said to you'.
>
> 'I remember them all', said Will, with the unspeakable content in his soul of feeling that he was in the presence of a creature worthy to be perfectly loved. I think his own feelings at that moment were perfect, for we mortals have our divine moments, when love is satisfied in the completeness of the beloved object.
>
> (Eliot 1965: 398)

The passion in the scene, including the reference to Ladislaw's meeting with Dorothea in Rome during the latter's abortive honeymoon, is suggested by the fact that Ladislaw has deliberately called on Dorothea when her husband is out. Dorothea's words are committed but ambiguous: she depicts her affinity with Ladislaw as a purely intellectual one. However, her words, and certainly Ladislaw's, suggest other depths to the relationship. The narrator, speaking to a nineteenth-century readership, would not like to suggest that adultery is desirable and tries to pass off Ladislaw's thoughts as "perfect". Indeed, the narrator, usually so authoritative in all moral matters, says "I think" rather than "I know". As a result of circumstances and conflicting voices, then, the narrator is undermined in the attempt to control the unfolding scenario.

This perspective on heteroglossia implies something important about novel narratives and about the ways in which they offer themselves to readers. The novel, in this view, is not just a simple narrative which is subject to one reading only. It is full of many voices, the potential contest between which almost inevitably leads to overlaps. Furthermore, as the omnipotence of the narratorial voice is in question partly as a result of overlaps with other voices in the text, there is an interesting consequence for readers. Readers are allowed to find authority where it is most appropriate for them, often in defiance of the narrator's dictates. By challenging the fundamental tenet of 'classic realism', Lodge stresses that meaning, even in narratives which profess to be 'realist', is potentially multiplicitous. The idea of the 'classic realist text' carries with it the assumption that there is basically one authoritative meaning to be derived from a narrative such as *Middlemarch*; and one reason for this is that realism is a mere convention rather than a close apprehension of the real.

Let us be clear about what this might imply for any theory of meaning. For Bakhtin, *dialogue* is the defining feature of the signs passed between humans, and dialogue entails that there is always a *relationship* between sign users no matter how much a sign user may think that s/he is not in dialogue with an *other*. Moreover, as Petrilli and Ponzio point out, this relation among signs is unavoidable:

> For Bakhtin, dialogue is not the result of an initiative we decide to take, but rather it is imposed, something to which one is subjected. Dialogue is not the result of opening towards the other, but of the impossibility of closing.
>
> (Petrilli and Ponzio 1998: 28)

Clearly, the relation between signs in a work of narrative fiction is different from the dialogue that characterizes sign use elsewhere. However, there is nevertheless an intimate relation between *dialogue* and *narrative*. Citing MacIntyre and Segre, Hirschkop points out that a dialogue between two people is seen from outside in terms of a narrative theme such as 'gossip', 'comic misconstrual of each other's motives', a 'tragic misunderstanding', and so on (1999: 226–8). Within the frame of an aesthetic investigation of narrative, this reveals the interplay of voices such as those between narrator and character; yet, for people engaged in dialogue, and this includes fictional people, the signs that pass between them are concrete: they are the very stuff of the social world that people inhabit, giving information on what is true, what is hurtful, what is useful, what is relevant; or, to put it another way, the signs in dialogue are 'historical'.

The multiple voices of narrative, then, are not just a matter of an artistic preference which might be analysed by means of a facile academic exercise. Signs are not to be considered as self-enclosed but as operating in a dialogue which is itself necessarily a site of contest or negotiation. This is a fact which puts the apparent individualist bias of the novel in jeopardy, including such pronounced variants of the genre as the *bildungsroman*. Hirschkop points out that "Novelistic representation is defined in Bakhtin's texts as the dialogue which ensures that the merely private is not cut off from the narratives surrounding it and thereby lost to it" (1999: 248). There can be little doubt that this applies to *Middlemarch* in spite of the apparent attempt at control on the part of the novel's narrator. Indeed, if it is the case that narrative is bound up with the establishment of identities associated with nationality, class, gender, occupation, or even a sense of opinions or one's place in the world in relation to others, then the novel, as a 'dialogic' form, cannot escape an orientation to the 'historical'. It cannot avoid recording the relations of signs to other signs or voices to other voices, rather than simply depicting individuals.

## NARRATIVE WITH DIRT UNDER ITS FINGERNAILS

As we have seen, while arguments about the connection between omniscient narration, 'objectivity' and realism in narrative are quite instructive, they are, ultimately, ill-conceived. That this is the case is revealed further by two additional points. First, the prime narrative examples offered to 'prove' the connection between omniscience and 'objectivity' are themselves frequently ill-chosen. The omniscient narrator, especially in nineteenth-century realism, is usually a textual agent of a much more pro-found stamp than is assumed by arguments about the classic realist text. As Lodge argues (1992: 9–12) in a context slightly different from that of the above-cited essay, the most common kind of narrator is not so much 'omniscient' as 'intrusive'; such a narrator, like his/her forebears in oral narrative, begins with "Once upon a time", or, opens the narrative in the fashion of *The Odyssey*, or, like stand-up comedians, says "I want to tell you a story", thus directly addressing the 'dear reader' in a fashion that was common practice among nineteenth-century novelists, George Eliot included. This recalls Bruner's suggestion (see Chapter 1) that both a sense of human agency and a presence of the narrator's perspective are fundamental to the child's 'readiness' for narrative.

Important facts about narrative are also revealed when one considers examples of narratives which attempt to *efface* dialogue or 'voicedness'. Indeed, attempts specifically to eradicate intru-siveness and, perhaps, enhance 'objectivity' only seem to recapitu-late the role of the narrator. European realism, in work as different as that of Stendhal or George Eliot, not only strove for 'objective' presentation, it also emphasized the role of rational and individual action in social relations. Yet, especially in France, the ideas of Hyppolite Taine (1828–93) influenced a change of emphasis in late nineteenth-century realism. Taine's 'positivist' psychology, history, philosophy and literary theory sought not to stress individual rationality but, rather, revealed the constant play of heredity and environment in human life. The results of Taine's influence are most clearly evident in the movement which became known as 'naturalism', and which is exemplified by the novels and critical writing of Zola. Beginning in 1870, the latter's monumental cycle of novels, *Les Rougon-Macquart*, based on the fortunes of an extended family, demonstrates a desire not only to depict social realities in detail and with great fidelity but also to show how human relations and their enactment within a given environment will determine events. For example, the key novel of the cycle, *Germinal* (1885), shows a mining community riven by the conflicting interests of the bourgeoisie and the proletariat, both groups being caught in the grip of the natural resources essential to industrialized existence which are provided by the mine. Naturalism, in this formulation, embodies the dominance over individual voices of almost unimaginable social and natural forces, seemingly rendering the narratorial voice redundant or reducing it to the role of commentator.

Although 'realism' and 'naturalism' are highly specific terms in the study of narrative and cannot be mapped onto corresponding terms in philosophical discourse (see Pizer 1995: 3), the differences between what they designate are nevertheless important. The development of naturalism out of realism revealed a significant point about narration, especially when naturalism was transposed to the relatively young literary context of the United States. America in the late nineteenth century, particularly through the novels and criticism of William Dean Howells, had witnessed realist currents in narrative which, paralleling developments in Europe (Borus 1989; Lehan 1995), then gave way to a form in narrative which was given the specific name of 'American naturalism' (Åhnebrink 1950; Walcutt 1956; Seltzer 1986; Ammons 1995; Budd 1995). At a time of rapid industrialization and automation, increasing capitalist exploitation and mass immigration, 'American naturalism', in consonance with its European counterpart, sought to do two things. First, it wished to depict the grand passions of common people who often led short and brutish lives determined by factors of heredity and environment of which they were often unaware. This 'revolt against gentility' (Cowley 1959) through the depiction of harsh realities was memorably expressed by the naturalist writer, Frank

Norris, when he declared older styles of realism to be defunct: "Realism is minute; it is the drama of a broken teacup, the tragedy of a walk down the block, the excitement of an afternoon call, the adventure of an invitation to visit" (1903: 216). Second, naturalism sought to render real passions in a detached way, through a prose style that was 'transparent' in that it sought to efface its own artifice, offered no comment and was, indeed, an 'anti-style' or 'non-style'.

It is fairly clear that the naturalists' second aim met with abject failure, especially in the case of Norris, whose call for a transparent style was undermined by sometimes absurdly melodramatic prose in his own fiction (Bell 1993: 115ff.). But this did not stop narratives striving for the long-anticipated goal of presenting the common American voice in literature (Berthoff 1981). In a later, post-naturalist period, from the 1920s onward, the critical consensus regarding the work of the American writer, Ernest Hemingway, was that he wrote in a style that would "neither falsify the world without nor betray the world within" (Bishop 1959: 191). Hemingway's narratives have continued to be appreciated in terms of the way that their prose represents an attempt to convey real and fictional worlds without frills and in the sparest possible way, effacing the intrusive narrative voice (Young 1966; Donaldson 1978; Reynolds 1986; Meyers 1987; Lynn 1989). One influence on this method was the discipline of the journalistic enterprise, a fact worth mentioning if only because Hemingway began his writing career as a journalist and continued to write for newspapers until quite late in his life (Dewberry 1996). But journalism also encouraged a 'tough', no-nonsense style which, through Hemingway, was to have a profound influence on American narrative.

'Tough', or 'hard-boiled' writing was to become associated with a certain type of narrative within an immensely popular genre: the thriller or 'crime fiction'. Although 'hard-boiled crime fiction' is frequently thought to be 'unrealistic' in comparison to the kind of valorized narratives which win literary prizes, it is driven by an uncompromising attempt to depict 'reality', and

Hemingway's writing played a part in the crystallization of a hard-boiled style in crime narratives from the 1920s onwards. His 1928 short story, 'The Killers', for example, features two hired assassins who arrive at a diner in order to kill a customer whom they expect to arrive for dinner. As with the following passage from the opening of the story, the narrative of 'The Killers' is dominated by dialogue, and the actions are minimal:

> The door of Henry's lunch-room opened and two men came in. They sat down at the counter.
>
> 'What's yours?' George asked them.
>
> 'I don't know', one of the men said. 'What do you want to eat, Al?'
>
> 'I don't know', said Al. 'I don't know what I want to eat'.
>
> (Hemingway 1955: 57)

The dialogue at first seems to be amateurish and ridiculously laboured, with Al clumsily repeating the uncertainty and terms of his partner's inquiry. The speech is certainly not polished and literary. When it transpires that the men are contract killers, the stilted conversation makes more sense: the two men are really not interested in the food on offer. However, the credibility of the ungainly dialogue also mounts because of the way it resembles the hesitations and seemingly pointless nature of everyday speech. In this respect, its lack of embellishment and polish constitutes an attempt to *enhance* realism; indeed, the absurd pointlessness and repetitiousness of some of the speech in 'The Killers' is of precisely the kind to be found in such contemporary realist narratives as those produced in print by the novelist George V. Higgins, or in film by the director and screenwriter Quentin Tarantino and his imitators.

That some producers of narrative should elect to focus on crime and the lower depths of society, previously the preserve of fiction denigrated as formulaic and popular, did not necessarily entail an abandonment of fidelity to the real; for many the brutishness of life was eminently suited to realism. Commenting on the early purveyors of hard-boiled narrative, especially Dashiell Hammett, who had initially plied his trade in American 'pulp' magazines of the 1920s, Raymond Chandler famously said that he "gave murder back to the kind of people who commit it for reasons, not just to provide a corpse; and with the means at hand, not with hand-wrought duelling pistols, curare, and tropical fish" (1944: 63). There is an unmistakable echo of the naturalists' 'revolt against gentility' in this statement; the ensuing prose style, however, was frequently far more circumspect than that which had gone before.

The foremost characteristic of tough, hard-boiled style lies in its short sentences. These are often devoid of adjectives and adverbs, and the words that remain are generally those that are more commonly evident in everyday language rather than the 'flowery' terms used in literature. So 'said' will replace 'asserted', 'queried' or 'expostulated', for instance. The nouns used are usually concrete and recognizable while any adjectives that are employed will probably be inexact, such as, 'nice', 'bright' or 'big'. Verbs, too, will be stripped to a minimum with a heavy reliance on the verb 'to be'. A passage from 'Winter Kill', a story by the early hard-boiled pulp magazine writer, Frederick Nebel, gives a flavour of the abrupt, pared-down style:

> The plow had been through and August Schnurll walked in the middle of the street past the fields. He went as far as the dowel factory, looked it over, grunted complacently to himself, and turned to head back down Flemming. He saw a dark object lying on the mound of snow and picking it up found it to be a dark Fedora. He shrugged and was about to toss it away when he saw another object lying where the hat had lain. He tried to pick it up but it resisted. He pulled a little harder and this dislodged some of the snow and then he found that he had hold of an arm. He was a plain, everyday man, and he

shuddered. He let go and the arm dropped back to the snow like a rigid stick. He dropped to his knees and began pawing at the snow with mittened hands. In a few minutes he knew that a man lay buried in the snow. He knew that the man was dead.

(Nebel 1965: 97)

The simplicity of word choice is carried over into the construction of hard-boiled sentences: as here, the sentences elsewhere in hard-boiled fiction will likely be mainly simple declarative ones, or a couple of these joined by a conjunction. Similarly, subordinate clauses will be very infrequent, thus lessening narratorial observation. When these sentences are used to describe events or actions, the sequence, as in this example, remains intact with the events being presented in the order in which they occurred, directly and unmixed with comment. As a result the depiction of violence in hard-boiled fiction, which is frequent, often gives an effect of irony, detachment and understatement; as one critic puts it, "If you describe really outrageous events as though they happen daily in your backyard, you get a critical impact which Woe Woe and Cry Havoc do not impart" (Atkins 1964: 87).

Events are invariably recorded in their 'original' time sequence without external comment. The style also accords almost equal attention to the description of inanimate objects such as tables, guns, walls, antiques, and animate objects, people. Hammett's stories and novels, for example, are likely to give a bald account of a town, its layout and inhabitants, as in, say, 'The Gutting of Couffignal', in which the account is roughly equal in size to the passing references made to the narrative's main characters. In general, hard-boiled prose, even when it is associated with a first-person character/narrator such as Chandler's Philip Marlowe, avoids speculation on the thoughts of characters in preference to describing their actions, and pays special attention to reproducing characters' speech without commenting on it.

Undoubtedly, such features of hard-boiled style constitute an attempt to delimit the intrusiveness of narrative prose by forcing the necessary description in a narrative to 'become more mimetic'. Summary has to become a little more like scene in a manner which, understandably, produces a delay or *detour*. Yet, it would be a mistake to assume, as many critical appreciations of Hemingway have, that hard-boiled narrative represents 'objectivity'. In a powerful critique of the realism of hard-boiled style, Bethany Ogdon has shown how it betrays quite clear interests. The "supposedly realistic character of the genre", she asserts, "implies that the hard-boiled writer (and his detective) are ideologically detached from those they describe" (Ogdon 1992: 75). As with nineteenth-century realism, there is, therefore, an attempt by the narrator simultaneously to create distance from, and control over, characters and events represented in the narrative.

The continuity with the nineteenth-century novel is once more couched in terms of the attempt of the narratorial voice to hide its tyrannous reign over its 'other', a kind of argument which continues to be a standard form of narrative analysis. Using an architectural metaphor, Suzanne Keen, for example, has recently argued that the Victorian novel constructs "narrative annexes" which "allow unexpected characters, impermissible subjects and plot-altering events to appear, in a bounded way, within fictional worlds that might be expected to exclude them" (1998: 1). She adds that

> Fears of disease, of working men, of Popery, of dark-skinned others, of the poor who toil and starve in close proximity to the rectories, homes and clubs, and walled gardens of the Victorian self-image draw us down narrow alleys, through thorny hedges, across desolate heaths into narrative annexes.
>
> (Keen 1998: 41)

The same tendency recurs, for Ogdon, in hard-boiled narratives, although it is far more direct and spatial boundaries have disappeared. Apart from the hero, she argues,

> Those who populate and pollute the universe of the hard-boiled detective story are described in terms of excess: excess smell (stink), excess body fluids (sweat, urine, tears, vomit), and/or excess desire (sexual proclivity, sexual perversion, greed, cunning and so forth).
>
> (Ogdon 1992: 76)

This appears to be pretty damning evidence against hard-boiled narrative and 'realism'.

However, it is not the end of the story. Ogdon assumes an inevitable didacticism, manipulation and marginalization of the 'other' on the part of the genre; yet there are some fundamental features of narrative in general, and the hard-boiled style specifically, which militate against this. The chief issue concerns what readers gain from the necessary delays which take place in narrative. Chandler stated his contention that the reader is not interested in the fact that a man got killed in a story, but that at the moment of his death he was trying unsuccessfully to pick up a paper-clip (1984: 214). Simple narration of events, then, is subordinate here to detailed description. If Chandler is correct, it suggests that there is something about digression in narrative that is potentially pleasurable for readers.

In consonance with this argument, Larzer Ziff (1987: 383) has analysed the following sentence from Hemingway's *The Sun Also Rises*: "There were pigeons out in the square, and the houses were a yellow, sun baked colour, and I did not want to leave the café." Ziff finds that, first, the narrator has conveyed his emotions without making reference to them: he does not say he is happy but it is possible to discern that he is so and that this makes him want to stay. Second, it is very uncertain as to whether his emotions are due to or at all connected with the pigeons or the houses and why they should appear in the sentence. It would be far more economical to simply state "I was happy"; but is this really what the passage is trying to say?

This kind of uncertainty in the connection between elements in descriptive digressions is typical of the deceptive economy of hard-boiled style. At the close of Chapter 25 of Chandler's *The Big Sleep*, Marlowe is in his office pondering the authenticity of some information he has received; the last four sentences of the chapter are as follows: "I thought about it most of the day. Nobody came into the office. Nobody called me on the phone. It kept on raining" (1948: 143). The final sentence, although seemingly not associated with the others, might become associated with them by its very juxtaposition. The comment on the weather indicates, perhaps, that the rain constitutes a metaphor for the desultory stage which Marlowe has reached in his case. But it is the reader who has to make the associative leap to bring the sentences together and such an action can never be a foregone conclusion.

Ultimately, we are left in the same position as we were after considering Lodge's analysis of the concept of the 'classic realist text'. Even if we can demonstrate that hard-boiled narrative is dominated by the voice of the narrator, it is still not possible to assume that the narratorial voice necessarily controls all the characters for all readers, whether the characters are depicted as excessive or whether they are marginalized. It is tempting and in many ways logical to imagine that 'realism' embodies a kind of quasi-conscious authoritarian attempt to impose a standard of narrative representation; but to do so is to pronounce on the stability and unassailable ownership of signs. In short, the signs which make up narrative are constantly open to other signs: no single authority owns them and is able to control their uses. The process of interpreting signs, and the means of gaining access to 'reality' cannot be circumscribed in advance in a foolproof way, either by a moralistic author or by an intrusive narrator. In fact, it is evident that there is some recognition of this in those narratives which purported to move 'beyond' realism.

# 5

## BEYOND REALISM

As we have seen, two of the most important features of narrative are the way in which it has been instrumental in the storage of memory and the contribution to the formation of human identity, and the way in which it is thoroughly selective. Indeed, not only has narrative facilitated the selective identity of groups of people, it has, especially in its written form, provided some of the grounds for the *individual* identities of its characters and even those of its originators. A developed sense of character lends narrative a meaningful anchor; similarly, identifying an author of a text helps to introduce a "principle of thrift in the proliferation of meaning" (Foucault 1986: 118), a stabilizing of signs through individualization.

It is hardly surprising, then, that one of the staples of the analysis of *written* literary narratives has been the biographical account of an author. That 'biography' and 'writing' are so closely linked seems to be demonstrated by the contrast with the case of oral narrative: here, the task of locating the individual creative force behind a narrative is almost impossible. It *is* true that Lord, following the work of Parry, sees in the practice of the oral poet a creativity which is akin to authorship (Lord 2000: 13–29); yet

Havelock's work (1963, 1976, 1986) suggests that the creative seat of oral narrative is the collective tradition of storytelling itself rather than the talent of one individual. Ultimately, both arguments demonstrate the futility of embarking on biographical accounts of named authors in the hope of identifying the absolute originators of oral narratives.

Thus, the biographical approach to analysing narrative is clearly a product of literate culture. Moreover, the status of authors of narratives is tied to the commodification that print allows: where oral narrative involves no claims to the ownership of words, a printed narrative, with its specific configuration of written signs, can be demonstrated to be the result of one individual's labour. Hence there arose a need for copyright laws in the eighteenth century, especially after the Statute of Anne, passed in England in 1710; arising from fifteenth- and sixteenth-century edicts designed to raise government revenue the new laws established that one person was responsible for creating a specific narrative or other printed text (Saunders 1992), and that s/he could receive payment, or even punishment (Foucault 1986: 108–9) on this basis.

Yet analyses based on biographical principles, rather than simply acknowledging the individual authorship of narratives, also make other assumptions. First, they tend to assume that the identity of a text's producer is to be found almost unmediated within the text itself, and that the text's production therefore takes place within a 'transmission model'; that is to say, a model in which an isolated individual author simply encodes in narrative form a message with a strictly limited set of meanings which is subsequently to be decoded, with varying degrees of work, by an intrepid reader in tune with the imperatives of the author. Undoubtedly, this perspective derives from the fact that writing, and print especially, not only allowed the individual production of narratives but also their solitary consumption.

Second, biographical analyses will tend to posit a strong relationship between the psychology of different situations and characters in a narrative, and that of the author. Narrative in this instance is assumed to be a transparent container, vehicle or transmitter of an individual author's consciousness. Plot, story, events and character in this formulation will be the keys to an author's psychology and vice versa. Such a unity of author and narrative is challenged, however, when factors beyond the individual in the process of narrative production are taken into consideration. If the notion of the author as a relatively stable or, at least, recognizably individual, identity is brought into question, then the transmission model begins to fray. Equally, it suffers when narrative is considered as a specific ensemble of signs rather than a simple vehicle.

Interestingly, in the case that follows, the common sense of biography and its perpetuation of the transmission model has floundered partly as a result of considering a biographical author of narratives who has become a stalwart of English literature, Joseph Conrad (1857–1924). In addition to Conrad's fragmented biography, his fictional narratives appeared at a time in history when the narrative of the West as a unitary, rather than a selective, identity was itself under challenge. This chapter will be concerned with the way that the narrative of Western identity and, inseparably, narrative in general, suffered that challenge.

## IDENTITY AND THE ANALYSIS OF *HEART OF DARKNESS*

Invariably, assessments of Conrad's narratives cannot avoid recording the facts that the author was a Pole, Josef Konrad Nalecz Korzeniowski, who was actually born in the Ukraine. They offer the information that growing up in a nineteenth-century Poland bearing strong cultural connections with France, Conrad was educated in Krakow and then Geneva; as a young man he joined the French merchant navy; later, he switched to British ships and eventually became a British subject in 1887; and that English, in which he chose to write when he became a novelist, was his third language (Fleischmann 1967: 3–20; Baines 1971: 13–193; Eagleton 1976: 132–5; Watts 1983; Fothergill 1989: 6–10; Murfin 1989: 3–16; Roberts 1998: 16–17). It is undeniable, then, that, even for analyses which hinge on the identification of a unified creative consciousness, Conrad was the product of diverse, albeit mainly European, cultural forces.

The conflicting influences within Conrad's own identity are significant because his narratives are themselves concerned with moral ambiguity and the fragmentation of the self. But where a traditional biographical critic would extrapolate from this decisive evidence of the psychologically determining relationship of author and text, the problem remains that such a conclusion is vitiated by the discernible themes and techniques of Conrad's narratives. In general, these latter have been given the label 'early modernism' (White 1981; Butler 1994); more pointedly, they consist of narrative themes in which a 'reasonable' self is forced to contend with an 'other', 'unreasonable' self co-existing within human consciousness, as well as the introduction of narrative techniques which complement and exemplify this split (Travers 1998: 116–20). Let us therefore attempt to reveal such crises of identity by analysing what is now probably Conrad's most famous novel, *Heart of Darkness*, which was published in *Blackwood's* magazine in 1899 and then in book form in 1902.

On the one hand, *Heart of Darkness* is the narrative of Kurtz, a refined and civilized man whose work in Africa seems to be more of a missionary nature than an economic one. The novel is the tale of his encounter with, and response to, savagery. On the other hand, the novel is about Marlow, the man who is sent to retrieve Kurtz and finds himself being drawn into the crisis which Kurtz is suffering. Or, third, it might be the story of the narrator, ensconced on a boat which is sailing out of the Thames estuary on its own mission, and being subjected to a chilling and problematic tale, told by Marlow, about the 'otherness' in wait for the passengers when they reach foreign shores. Looking at the novel in this cursory way indicates that the narrative is by no means simple. Furthermore, unlike the vast and historically specific canvasses of nineteenth-century realist novels, many of which focus on corporatist and individualist phases of industrial capitalism, this short, but rich, narrative seems to invite different frameworks for analysis.

Undoubtedly, *Heart of Darkness* can be analysed in terms of its narrative focus on a definite historical period, that of imperialism. According to Eagleton (1976: 110ff.), this is the 'third phase' of nineteenth-century capitalist accumulation, in which capitalism extends its activities and effectively plunders the raw materials beyond national boundaries. At the same time that this material exploitation took place, there was a great deal of activity in the sphere of culture: in practices such as journalism, religion, conversation, and literature, imperialism was treated favourably or unfavourably or ambiguously as part of the ongoing development of Western identity. Most importantly, though, such activity sustained imperialism as a *narrative* of historical events. The narrative theme of Europeans travelling to 'underdeveloped', even 'barbarous', 'savage', 'primitive', 'heathen' and 'uncivilized' countries is clearly central to the events in Conrad's novel (see, especially, Watts 1983; Brantlinger 1985; Achebe 1998; and Loomba 1998: 136; see also Said 1994: 197–203).

Yet *Heart of Darkness* is not just a familiar fictional realist account of an episode within the imperialist adventure. It has also been analysed as a kind of mirror of the process of narrative. If narrative is, at its simplest, a movement from a beginning to an end point which is characterized by necessary *detours*, then this thumbnail account also fits the novel well. Marlow begins his journey in Europe, travels upriver in Africa meeting different characters and contemplating what will greet him at his destination and, ultimately, encounters the man he has been anticipating: Kurtz (Rosmarin 1989; Reilly 1993: 20ff.).

If this is accepted, then Conrad's novel also carries out a

precedent which has been set by the tradition of the epic and romance. In the romance, heroes frequently find themselves undertaking journeys in order to recover sacred objects or to do battle on behalf of other humans or ideals. Even in the more ambivalent romances such as *Don Quixote* (1605) or *The Faerie Queene* (1590–6) this is the case. In the major epics, the central characters take a trip explicitly to an underworld. Odysseus and Aeneas travel to Hades in *The Odyssey* and *The Aeneid*, respectively; Dante plumbs the depths of inferno in *The Divine Comedy*; and Satan actually comes to inhabit Hell in *Paradise Lost*. In the increasingly secular world of early modernism, one could argue that Marlow's expedition to the interior is a latter-day version of the voyages which characterize the epic and romance traditions of narrative (Feder 1955; Evans 1956).

Although it is important to note that *Heart of Darkness* is very much the product of the Western tradition of narrative in which, as Jaynes would put it, "a story of identity, of a voyage to the self" is central (see Chapter 2), there is a great deal more mileage in considering the relationships the narrative invokes between imperialism and repression. The narrative of the 'third phase' of Western capitalism is, like all narratives, one which leaves out a great deal from its account. A powerful argument about the novel which focuses on the process of the narrative as well as the events that are narrated is the psychoanalytic one. It would seem to be no coincidence that Conrad embarked on his career as a novelist around the time that Sigmund Freud abandoned elements of the therapies that he was previously using and developed psychoanalysis (see Jones 1964: 239ff.; Clark 1982: 114ff.; Gay 1989: 103ff.). Viewed in this context, the trip that Marlow makes is one which takes him to the uncharted territory of the human mind: the unconscious. As such, the novel, in its events and in the way it narrates them, constantly attempts to put forth one *conscious* version of 'reality' while at the same time invoking another version which is constituted by the *unconscious* (see Guerard 1966;

Crews 1975; Karl 1989). Imperialism undoubtedly dominates the narrative's proceedings, but the transformation of narrative as a whole which *Heart of Darkness* exemplifies results from the fact that imperialism, like other features of the world which impinge on early modernist narrative, is not simply an economic phenomenon divorced from psychology.

## IMPERIALISM AND REPRESSION

That the project of imperialism was itself a narrative with seemingly contradictory imperatives is suggested by two cases where the imperialist impulse was manifested through the stories of individuals. First, representing the vanguard of European identity, Scottish clergyman Dr David Livingstone (1813–73) was to become immortalized for discovering numerous uncharted territories and unknown rivers, and because of the highly publicized 1871 expedition undertaken by H. M. Stanley to 'find' him. Most accounts of Livingstone's life agree that, from an early stage, Livingstone's missionary work was only a small underlying component of his main thirst for exploring Africa (Ransford 1978; McLynn 1993: 42–51), and it is clear that Western economic considerations were entangled in his 'civilizing' zeal. On his final expedition, to chart the sources of the Nile, before his death in 1873, Livingstone

sounded a call for a worldwide crusade to open up Africa. A new slave trade, organised by Swahili and Arabs in East Africa, was eating out the heart of the continent. Livingstone's answer was the '3 Cs': Commerce, Christianity and Civilization, a triple alliance of mammon, God and social progress. Trade, not the gun, would liberate Africa.

(Pakenham 1994: xxiv)

In a much more direct way than Livingstone, the Belgian King Leopold II (1835–1909) played a key role in the impingement of

European imperialism on Africa in the late nineteenth century, initiating the European 'scramble for Africa'. Seeking to develop Belgian interests in 'L'État Independent du Congo', and to cultivate his own spot on the European stage, he presided, in 1876, over a conference of European leaders. The meeting took place in Brussels and discussion centred on Leopold's plan to "open to civilization the only part of our globe where Christianity has not yet penetrated and to pierce the darkness which envelops the entire population" (Pakenham 1994: 21).

In the case of the narratives of imperialism projected by Livingstone and Leopold, then, the Christian 'civilizing' impulse is clearly manifested and, indeed, foregrounded, as these two quotes show. Lurking nearby at all times, however, is the impulse to capitalist exploitation, profit and appropriation of local resources. The narrative of imperialism therefore operates at more than one level. While there can be no denying that narrative is selective, the narrative of imperialism seems to suggest that it is repressive too. An insight into this 'repressive' aspect of narrative selection is offered, once more, by psychoanalysis.

One of the phenomena of communication that Freud was adept at exposing concerns the saying of one thing and meaning another. Because there are certain troublesome impulses which must be resisted to prevent social existence from being unduly disrupted, some things cannot be said or done. No matter how strong such impulses may seem, they tend to be repressed by way of 'proper behaviour', 'good manners' or straightforward consideration for others. They then inhabit the unconscious, a mental realm whose mode of representation is very different from that of conscious existence (see Chapter 6).

The mechanism of 'repression' is crucial for Freud (see Freud 1984a), but he observes that it can often be intensified if it is denied or 'negated' in certain circumstances. Such 'negation' is common in the therapeutic setting of psychoanalysis, according to Freud, but it can be seen to occur also in more commonplace environments. How many times, he asks, is it possible to hear people say such things as "Now you'll think I mean to say something insulting, but really I've no such intention" (1984b: 437)? It is an occurrence so frequent as to go unnoticed. For Freud, "Negation is a way of taking cognizance of what is repressed; indeed it is already a lifting of the repression, though not, of course, an acceptance of what is repressed" (1984b: 438).

In light of this argument, then, there is a clear parallel between the narrative of imperialism in the late nineteenth century and the kinds of acts and dialogue which are contained in *Heart of Darkness*. Leopold II and Livingstone, as exemplars of African exploration, both carry through projects which foreground their Christian, civilized, egalitarian aspects. Yet, at the same time, what is repressed, and barely repressed at that, is the capitalist impulse: an impulse to commerce, as Livingstone would have it, but also an impulse to exploit and annex territory. Kurtz is a fine embodiment of this tension and the fragmentation of his identity dominates *Heart of Darkness*. Throughout the novel the narrative anticipates a man who exemplifies Western civilization: his "mother was half-English, his father was half-French. All Europe contributed to the making of Kurtz" (Conrad 1973: 71). He is a man of Western culture who reads and writes poetry. Furthermore, Kurtz is on a mission which, apart from trade, also requires that he compile a report for the 'International Society for the Suppression of Savage Customs':

And he had written it, too. I've seen it. I've read it. It was eloquent, vibrating with eloquence, but too high-strung, I think. Seventeen pages of close writing he had found time for! But this must have been before his – let us say – nerves, went wrong, and caused him to preside at certain midnight dances ending with unspeakable rites, which – as far as I reluctantly gathered from what I heard at various times – were offered up to him – do you understand? – to Mr. Kurtz himself. But it was a beautiful piece of writing. The opening paragraph, however, in the light of later information, strikes me now as ominous. He began with the argument that we whites, from the point of development that we had arrived at, 'must necessarily appear to them [savages] in the nature of supernatural beings – we approach them with the might as of a deity', and so on, and so on. 'By the simple exercise of our will we can exert a power for good practically unbounded', etc., etc. From that point he soared and took me with him. The peroration was magnificent, though difficult to remember, you know. It gave me the notion of an exotic Immensity ruled by an august Benevolence. It made me tingle with enthusiasm. This was the unbounded power of eloquence – of words – of burning noble words. There were no practical hints to interrupt the magical current of phrases, unless a kind of note at the foot of the last page, scrawled evidently much later, with an unsteady hand, may be regarded as an exposition of method. It was very simple, and at the end of that moving appeal to every altruistic sentiment it blazed at you, luminous and terrifying, like a flash of lightning in a serene sky: 'Exterminate the brutes!' The curious part was that he had apparently forgotten all about the valuable postscriptum, because, later on, when he in a sense, came to himself, he repeatedly entreated me to take good care of "my pamphlet" (he called it), as it was sure to have in the future a good influence upon his career.

(Conrad 1973: 71–2)

So Kurtz is outwardly benevolent, at least in the sense that there was and is a consensus in the world in general that some of the 'savage' customs perceived by Europeans to be in need of suppression at the time (genocide, slavery, cannibalism) are repugnant. Yet Kurtz has clearly gone beyond the thin veneer of Christian benevolence to a position where he wishes extermination of the natives. It is interesting, too, that Marlow says that Kurtz seems to have forgotten the "valuable postscriptum". As this brief consideration of 'negation' might imply, psychoanalysis is very suspicious of the concept of 'innocent forgetting' (see, especially, Freud 1976a).

## IMPERIALISM AND SEXUALITY

It would be tempting to believe that *Heart of Darkness* is simply a realist expression of the different layers of Western identity implicit in imperialism. The historical facts of the narrative of the imperialist venture are omnipresent in the novel. Yet *Heart of Darkness* not only lays bare the psychological underpinnings of imperialism but also reveals how a sense of unified identity has served to hide narrative mechanisms. A simple point about biography and history indicates that this is the case. Central to Leopold's plan was the need to develop transport routes, and one key component was the relatively unexplored river Congo; this geographical and historical fact coincides with Joseph Conrad's biography, as the Congo river, thinly disguised in *Heart of Darkness*, had reputedly been the object of Conrad's interest since he was a child. Conrad confessed that he used to look at maps and yearn to make the trip to Central Africa some day (Murfin 1989: 8), and, in a passage which replays this desire in *Heart of Darkness*, Marlow tells how his passion as a child for maps and the blank spaces on them ultimately leads him, as a man, to enlist for a mission up a great river (Conrad 1973: 11–2). In actuality, Conrad was employed to make the trip in 1890, five years before he published his first novel, when he was charged with the task of taking a steamer to Stanley Falls to retrieve the body of a trader called Klein. The parallels of the historical and biographical incident with the 1902 novel's descriptions of filling blank spaces on maps could not, it seems, be clearer.

However, the fact that Conrad's real-life expedition was but one small event which was precipitated by this moment in the development of nineteenth-century European capitalism is interesting but not conclusive. What is more important concerns the influences which provoked his deep-seated desire to make the trip, the determinants that made the idea of travelling to the very interior of the continent press itself so fervently on his young imagination, factors which might also be operating on the identity of other Europeans. Undoubtedly, Conrad was curious about the location of the Congo in what was then considered a remote part of the earth, and it is likely that, psychologically and socially in the developed West, the curiosity derived from the way this place represented the unknown.

The psychological mechanism framing the desire to see uncharted territories about which there exists a nagging curiosity is, it might be argued, not that far removed from the human propensity to promote curiosity and interest about the unknown bodies of others, especially those of the opposite sex. When evaluating how modern psychology viewed the sexual life of adult women, Freud was to use precisely the English phrase employed by imperialists to describe Africa: "a dark continent", a phrase which, incidentally, does no justice to Freud's attempt to investigate female sexuality (Freud 1962: 124; see also Gay 1989: 501ff.; Appignanesi and Forrester 1992: 2ff.; see also Freud 1973a, 1977a and Mitchell 1973). This certainly is not irrefutable evidence that the ravishing of a continent is identical to the ravishing of a female by a male. However, it would be difficult to deny that the terms in which the two things take place, such as the 'dark' territory, the interior, the obscure object of curiosity, desire and, ultimately, plunder, are quite congruent. Indeed, there is an echo here of the terms used in the earlier plundering of another continent. Writing for the 'Virgin Queen', Elizabeth I, about his discovery of Guyana, Sir Walter Raleigh asserted that it "is a country that hath yet her maidenhead, never sacked, turned, nor wrought" (Raleigh 2000: 164). For sixteenth-century explorers of the New World this was not an uncommon metaphor; Stephen Greenblatt suggests that the 'wonder' felt by Europeans encountering strange new lands was a malleable concept. Commenting specifically on Jean de Léry's experiences in Brazil, he argues that "Wonder is now not the sign of revulsion but of ravishment and ecstatic joy that can be experienced anew even twenty years later through an act of remembrance" (Greenblatt 1991: 16).

What is being suggested here, then, consists of three parts. First, the narrative of imperialism professes a civilizing tendency but is haunted by the desire to exploit; second, this is consonant with a general psychology in the West which seeks to repress troublesome aspects of existence such as sexuality and the bodies of others; and, third, the narrative of *Heart of Darkness* dramatizes the increasing early-twentieth-century concern that human identity is not unified and coherent. All of these points are recapitulated in the novel's famous description of the French gunboat:

> Once, I remember, we came upon a man-of-war anchored off the coast. There wasn't even a shed there, and she was shelling the bush. It appears the French had one of their wars going on thereabouts. Her ensign dropped limp like a rag; the muzzles of the long six-inch guns stuck out all over the low hull; the greasy, slimy swell swung her up lazily and let her down, swaying her thin masts. In the empty immensity of earth, sky and water, there she was, incomprehensible, firing into a continent. Pop, would go one of the six-inch guns; a small flame would dart and vanish, a little white smoke would disappear, a tiny projectile would give a feeble screech – and nothing happened. Nothing could happen. There was a touch of insanity in the proceeding, a sense of lugubrious drollery in the sight; and it was not dissipated by somebody on board assuring me earnestly there was a camp of natives – he called them enemies! – hidden out of sight somewhere.
>
> (Conrad 1973: 20)

Gunfire here, as elsewhere in the narrative, is referred to in terms of weakness rather than strength and there can be little doubt that what is being invoked through recognizably sexual imagery is impotence rather than omnipotence: the limp rag, the lazy swing, the mere 'pop' of the gun and the 'feeble screech'. It is as though the boat believes that it is all-powerful with supposedly 'big' guns; and, undeniably, any sense of power it possesses is enhanced by the relative ease by which firepower has allowed Europeans to subjugate the so-called 'primitive' indigenous peoples of Africa. However, the passage chiefly seems to imply that local victories over the natives are illusory, like the dream of power the gnat might be said to experience when it bites an elephant.

In doing this the passage nicely exemplifies Bakhtin's perspective on heteroglossia. For Bakhtin, the social world is 'heteroglot', made up of many different voices which are constituted by, and reflect, interests and situations in relation to the voices of others. "When heteroglossia enters the novel", writes Bakhtin, "it is subject to an artistic reworking" (1981: 300), a fact that is clear in this example. The different situations which shape the voices of imperialists and the inhabitants of lands that imperialists attempt to subjugate is largely reworked here by the voice of Marlow. He is incredulous about the difference in the situations of the French gunboat and the natives, and he conveys this to others, his interlocutors on the boat leaving the Thames estuary. The language in which this takes place employs the kind of sexual imagery which was commonly associated with the voice of the imperialist venture, yet it also undermines it, voicing flaccidity in place of tumescence.

It is notable that the very same theme of a unified belief in an *omnipotent* identity undermined by a repressed, but nevertheless sexualized, *impotence* is played out in a number of famous sequences in Francis Ford Coppola's *Apocalypse Now* (1979). The film is based on *Heart of Darkness* but transplants the action of the novel from late-nineteenth-century Africa to Vietnam and

Cambodia in the late 1960s (see Fitzgerald 1996). Above all, one portion of the movie in particular has achieved fame, partly for the technical virtuosity with which it is mounted. In the sequence in question, American troops assault a small Vietnamese coastal village. The reason for this and the reason for the subsequent carnage is that the village is located on an impressive 'break' which will provide some excellent surfing waves. The commander of the troops, Lt Col. Kilgore (Robert Duvall) has decided that the assault should go ahead after discovering that a well-known Californian surfer (Sam Bottoms) is among the group he is charged with transporting upriver. At dawn, an array of armed US helicopters rises above the horizon and, to the tune of Wagner's 'Ride of the Valkyries' transmitted through loudspeakers, wreaks havoc and destruction among the scarcely armed villagers. For our purposes, what is interesting is that the sequence is a cinematic replay of the theme thrown up by the impotent French gunboat scenario narrated above.

However, the action is so well staged and the events depicted so mindless and cruel that many early critics interpreted the scene as a thoroughgoing condemnation of American imperialism and a lack of civilized compassion for innocent lives (cf. Lothe 2000: 187ff.). Clearly, the assault is quite large in scale and achieves the capture of a beach solely for the purpose of recreation. But, more importantly, it is a demonstration of childish bravado and an unquestioned faith in American identity. Referring to the inhabitants of the peninsula Col. Kilgore proclaims "Charlie don't surf", but his expedition, like the American forces in general, is unable to suppress incessant Vietnamese guerrilla activity. In Bakhtin's terms, Kilgore and the Americans are acting in bad faith: the scene cannot take place without the voice of the Vietnamese being present, otherwise there is nothing to subjugate; yet, Kilgore acts as though there is only *one* voice, the American one, engaged in a 'monologue'. The narrative, because it must necessarily show the existence of the Vietnamese villagers, allows them a voice which Kilgore cannot hear or which he intends to destroy before hearing it is possible; as such, the narrative is unavoidably 'dialogic'. Indeed, an earlier scene involving the colonel also makes this point. In the aftermath of a similar assault, Kilgore surveys the field of battle and comes across a wounded Viet Cong soldier who is asking for water. He is furious with those of his men who have not answered the dying man's request and offers the soldier water, saying that anyone who fights with his guts so damaged deserves to drink from the same canteen as himself. As such, Kilgore is hearing the voice of the Vietnamese soldier and, in tending to the dying man, is acknowledging their underlying sameness as warriors in battle. However, it is significant that he almost comically forgets the soldier, snatching away the canteen abruptly when he hears that a famous American surfer is among the group who have just arrived and require transportation upriver. Thus, the American voice asserts itself once more, but not wholly triumphantly.

What these episodes suggest is that, when the aggressors are most certain of their omnipotence, or most assured of the unity of their identity and its superiority over others, they are, paradoxically, at their most impotent. Rather than making their effects felt on a continent and vanquishing different cultures, the imperialists are themselves the 'victims' of those cultures that they come to subjugate. European imperialists did not, of course, experience the physical strife inflicted on the inhabitants of so-called 'primitive' lands; on this level there can be no comparison of the suffering of European imperialists and many African natives. But there were effects in Europe on both consciousness and culture.

## NARRATIVE, IMPERIALISM AND THE CONFLICT OF WESTERN IDENTITY

These effects constitute a context which is crucial for understanding what 'early modernism' revealed about the narrative process.

In the sphere of representation in general, beyond narrative, Europe witnessed decisive developments. For example, 'Les Desmoiselles d'Avignon' (1907), the painting completed by Pablo Picasso (1881–1973) around 1905–7, created a furore not just because of his depiction of prostitutes but also because the figures were strongly evocative of certain African carvings, despite the fact that there is now strong evidence to suggest that they were copied from photographs (see *Picasso and Photography* 1999). Similarly, the brightly coloured paintings of Paul Gauguin (1848–1903), themselves the product of prolonged sojourns in the South Sea islands, directly encouraged the formation of a painting group called Les Fauves, or 'wild beasts', in 1905 (Gombrich 1956: 431). If paintings like 'Les Desmoiselles d'Avignon' promoted a multi-angled view of the human form, comprising more than one perspective at a time, including one view of the angle of the nose, a different view of the angle of an eye, and so on, then they also achieved this through embracing 'primitivism'. On the one hand, this entailed an imitation of artefacts from other continents: sculptures, totem figures, domestic designs. On the other, it incorporated a more psychologically orientated perspective on the nature of those artefacts. The overt sexuality in Picasso's painting is clearly at one with the 'Africanness' of most of the figures.

The image of an African woman, unclothed or clothed, devoid of the excessive modesty of her Victorian counterpart in Europe, has had its effects on travellers to the 'dark continent'. As Loomba argues, "native women and their bodies are described in terms of the promise and fear of the colonial land" (1998: 151; cf. Conrad 1973: 87). They are, as such, a powerful symbol of the 'conquered' place. Yet it must also be said that, for many, they are frightening: Marlow, for instance, describes the terror of the "wild and gorgeous apparition of a woman" (Conrad 1973: 87). 'Primitivism' and 'sexuality' shared in common the fact that the late-nineteenth-century West found them psychologically troublesome. In what constituted a futile attempt to deny that each, far from being irrefutably 'other', was a part of Western life, European imperialism tried to suppress them both, to keep them hidden knowing all the time that they were there.

Ultimately, then, the 'early modernist' investigation of identity reveals a fourth point in addition to the three that we have noted, a point about representation in general but also one especially pertinent to narrative: that it is not the product of a unified authorial, or even narratorial, voice. Indeed, the Western repression of 'primitive' voices, a repression whose lack of success is indicated by a constant *fascination* with the primitive, seems to demonstrate that belief in the power of narrative to create an unassailable authoritative identity is unfounded.

Before we proceed to discuss this, however, one other feature of narrative's relation to politics and the unconscious should be mentioned. Although we have suggested that imperialism is not simply an economic phenomenon divorced from psychology, it should not be forgotten that imperialism can never be understood *solely* in terms of psychological factors. The equation of primitivism and sexuality is clear in the context of modern European art; yet *Heart of Darkness* and *Apocalypse Now* might be understood as performing 'universalizing' functions in terms of Snead's arguments (1990) discussed in Chapter 2. Both narratives can be seen as embodiments of the theme of 'human nature', but it is important to be aware that such a perspective on the texts obliterates geographical and historical specificity. By relocating in the *unconscious* the imperialist ventures that took place originally in Central Africa and Vietnam, these fictional narratives refigure the existing narrative of imperialism and, perhaps, supplant the economically and physically repressive aspects of imperialism in favour of a universal psychology.

## THE READER AND THE NARRATIVE

The fact that the narrative of imperialism in the real world of the nineteenth century and the pronouncements of its proponents are riddled with statements in which manifest intentions belie more deep-rooted impulses is not simply a 'theme' in *Heart of Darkness*. The very first observations which are usually made about the novel concerning whether this is the story of Kurtz, Marlow or the narrator suggest that its very narrative structure renders problematic the task of identifying a central narrative authority. Perhaps unwittingly, one of the most famous commentators on Conrad offers an insight into the consequences of such a narrative structure. F. R. Leavis, in trying to draw Conrad into a 'Great Tradition' of writing in the English novel, objects to the more sensational and 'popular' modes of representation in Conrad's *oeuvre*. In *Heart of Darkness*, particularly, Leavis feels that the continual reference to 'unspeakable rites', 'unspeakable secrets', 'monstrous passions', 'inconceivable mystery', and so on, serves to "cheapen the tone" (1962: 206). Unlike Prickett, for instance, who sees in Conrad a biblical influence marked by his "constantly groping after ineffable mysteries seemingly just beyond the reach of language" (1996: 266), Leavis feels cheated and soiled. For Leavis, Conrad attempts "to impose on his readers and on himself, for thrilled response, a 'significance' that is merely an emotional insistence on the presence of what he can't produce" (1962: 207).

As a humanist, individualist and conservative critic, it is important for Leavis that Conrad be an individual consciousness who is in control of the means of representation, and able, by such means, to produce a profound individualized narrative about the human condition. Yet the fact that the narrative resorts to the implementing of synonyms of the 'unfathomable' is an interesting reminder of the lack of thorough control and authority which narrative in general allows to its producers. Critics *have* suggested that Conrad's use of enigmatic terms is, on closer scrutiny, somewhat excessive (White 1981: 110–20). They have also suggested that they mirror "a situation in which comfortable Europeans who had never witnessed colonial brutality at first hand in Africa were unable to hear the truth spoken by such as Marlow"

(Hawthorn 1997: 165). However, what such terms self-evidently require is the involvement of the reader, a fact that Leavis clearly considers vulgar. It is the reader of the narrative who has to do the work of imagining what the 'unspeakable rites' might involve (cf. Guerard 1966: 59–61 and Toker 1993).

This kind of 'gap' in a narrative account is not unfamiliar to modern readers. One has only to consider a narrative such as E. M. Forster's *A Passage to India* (1926), another novel concerned with the meeting of cultures, which revolves around the very undecidability of what happened to Miss Quested when she visited the Marabar caves. Alternatively, the film *Citizen Kane* (1941) is haunted by the gap designated 'Rosebud': it is the word uttered by the eponymous protagonist on his deathbed and it is the name given to the grand home he builds for himself; but even when the narrative reveals that it is the name of the sledge upon which he was riding immediately prior to the incident in his childhood which would dictate the rest of his life, it is still unclear what the word really signifies. Yet the notion of 'gaps' in narrative is more fundamental and deep-rooted than even these examples suggest. The literary theorist Wolfgang Iser argues that 'indeterminacies' constituted by gaps are absolutely integral to narrative. For him, the literary text is defined by this condition: it is a text's 'indeterminacy', the fact that it is theoretically 'unfinished' or only 'partly written' and shot through with 'gaps', that means the reader must 'fill' what is left unsaid (Iser 1989: 9–10). A simple sentence such as 'The man walked along the road', for example, appears straightforward but actually leaves out a great deal. It presupposes questions of the man: 'How old is he?', 'What colour is his hair?', 'How tall is he?'; of the road: 'How long is it?', 'Is it very busy with traffic?', 'Is it a dirt-track or a major highway?'; of the walking: 'How brisk is the pace?', 'In what direction?', 'Does the man have a limp?' That the 'meaning' of a text is not a foregone conclusion and that the work of the reader is a necessary part of textuality is memorably summed up by Iser's analogy with the process of drawing astronomical constellations: "The 'stars' in a literary text are fixed; the lines that join them are variable" (1974: 282).

If the sentence about the man on the road appears in a narrative, it is possible that, by virtue of signs that have passed before and those which are to follow, such a sentence will have some of its indeterminacies eradicated. However, it is in the nature of textuality that indeterminacy can never be fully abolished; the reader's work can only fill gaps within limits. Nevertheless, a narrative will be conditioned by the fact that it will be enacted by a 'gap-filler'; a collection of such sentences as the one above, when assembled into a fictional work, will therefore have what Iser calls an 'implied reader' (1974: xii, 278). It is important to be clear about this since it would be easy to imagine that an authorial intention somehow *creates* a particular kind of reader or reading by means of a simple 'transmission', through the medium of narrative, from one pole to another, from a sender to a receiver. Iser, however, insists that the signs in narrative constitute a *re*-presentation (see Chapter 1) and that narrative, necessarily, as a result of the reader's gap-filling activity, renders a world which cannot be analysed by reference to a belief in the unitary consciousness of an author and a reader:

> Central to the reading of every literary work is the interaction between its structure and its recipient. Therefore an exclusive concentration on either the author's techniques or the reader's psychology will tell us little about the reading process itself. This is not to deny the vital importance of each of the two poles, yet separate analysis would only be conclusive if the relationship were that of transmitter and receiver, for this would presuppose a common code, ensuring accurate communication since the message would only be travelling one way. In literary works, however, the message is transmitted in two ways, in that the reader 'receives' it by composing it. There

> is no common code; at best one could say that a common
> code may arise in the course of the process.
>
> (Iser 1989: 31)

Narrative structure is not simply a matter of re-presenting the author's voice. As we have stressed from the outset, a *narrator* is also implicated in proceedings. However, what early modernist innovations in narrative make clear is that there is more to narrative structure than just these two entities.

## NARRATIVE LEVELS

*Heart of Darkness* acknowledges and uses different 'narrative levels'. The narrator/Marlow/Kurtz split is a simple demonstration of this and, undoubtedly, the self-consciousness with which the split is enacted constitutes a significant innovation, especially coupled with the early-twentieth-century theme of a 'reasonable' self and an 'unreasonable' other. The device was not a new one in narrative but it does seem to indicate that the hopes of creating an authoritative narrative voice within realism on the part of its purveyors, as well as the critiques of the authoritarian nature of realist narratives which we discussed in the last chapter, are largely futile. While the common-sense view which might be dear to the hearts of novelists such as George Eliot and critics such as F. R. Leavis holds that narratives are produced by industrious and authoritative individuals, and then consumed by avid and painstaking readers, a closer scrutiny reveals that the process is more complex. This complexity applies to all narratives despite the fact that it is especially to the fore in early modernism.

Rimmon-Kenan (1983: 86ff.) identifies the following participants in narrative, each of which might seem to aid the act of transmission but each of which might equally *interfere* with it. Empirical entities named a *Real Author* and a *Real Reader*, both of whom are human beings, appear at each pole of the communication process (sending and receiving, respectively); these are placed in the company of other mediators in a narrative fiction such as a novel as follows: '*Real Author, Implied Author, Narrator, (Narratee), Implied Reader, Real Reader*' (Rimmon-Kenan 1983: 86 [slightly adjusted]; c.f. Gibson 1980).

The *Implied Author* is the organizing principle of the text, the guiding star responsible for the presentation of the text's materials in a specific way: the ordering of scenes, the narration of certain objects and events and the non-narration of others, the structure of the plot and so forth. In a novel such as Bram Stoker's *Dracula* (1897) the narrative is effected by a series of documents such as letters, diary entries and legal communications; it is therefore easy to envisage the *Implied Author* as the agent who brought the documents together, placed them in a particular order but personally kept out of the proceedings. In other novels it might be more difficult to envisage where the work of the *Implied Author* ends and that of the *Narrator* begins. It is well known that many of the stories of M. R. James, for example, were composed and orally transmitted by the author to friends, colleagues and students gathered together on winter nights at King's College, Cambridge. As *Real Author*, James is at pains to stress in the preface to his collected stories that none of the stories has a basis in truth, contradicting the impression that might be given by the fact that they often deal with real, or thinly disguised, places and are narrated in the first person (1992a: ix). The narration of 'The Mezzotint', for example, gives the impression that the university, the group of academics employed by it and the art dealer who is a pivotal figure in the narrative are based on very specific entities in real life. The way that they are disguised by the *Implied Author*, however, merges with the discourse of the *Narrator*. The *Implied Author* represents the university as one which encourages the playing of golf and it is difficult to separate such representations from those of the *Narrator*, who quite clearly allows some things to be narrated and not others, such as that "tea was taken to the accompaniment of a discussion which golfing persons can imagine for themselves, about which the conscientious writer has no right to inflict on any non-golfing persons" (James 1992b: 22). The *Narrator* not only colludes in the *Implied Author*'s representation, therefore, but also collapses the two narrative levels by passing off the collusion as the work of "the conscientious writer" and by anticipating a non-golfing *Narratee* and *Implied Reader*.

Strictly, then, the *Narrator* is a narrative 'voice' which tells the story in the first or third person, sometimes as a character in the story and, on occasion, even omnisciently. The next level is that of the *Narratee*, which appears above in brackets; theoretically, the *Narratee* is that ideal entity to whom the text is narrated, an entity that will accept uncritically all that the text has to offer and the way that it is offered. Yet it is bracketed because, invariably, it is not possible to separate this entity from the *Implied Reader*. In Iser's terms the *Implied Reader* is an anthropomorphization because, rather than being a person, it is a specific process of gap-filling in a text, a set of lines between the text's 'stars' which a *Real Reader* can choose to accept or substitute for his or her own set of lines. In this way, the *Implied Reader* and *Narratee* seem to be identical in the bulk of realist fiction, as the *Narrator* often addresses the reader in an intrusive way or aspires to omniscience. Yet there are many exceptions to the rule. Pooter, the *Narrator* of George and Weedon Grossmith's *Diary of a Nobody* (1892), for instance, obviously has a specifically acquiescent *Narratee* in mind, and someone very like himself, when relating 'hilarious' episodes from his own life. Arguably, it is the *Real Reader*'s detachment from the *Narratee* and the *Real Reader*'s recognition of the *Implied Reader* which will provoke humour at the unfunny Pooter's expense. More pointedly, in an epistolary novel such as *Dracula* the extracts from the clinical diary of Dr Seward, narrated in a reasonably detached manner for those *Narratees* who might be interested in the case of his patient, Renfield, are in contrast to his panic-stricken telegrams to another *Narratee*, Van

Helsing. Indeed, it may be possible that there are *Real Readers* interested in golf who are disappointed by the *Narrator*'s anticipation of non-golfing *Narratees* and *Implied Readers* in 'The Mezzotint'.

This set of relationships maps out the general co-ordinates, with minor variations, in most narratives produced in the Western tradition. In *Heart of Darkness* the *Implied Author* is responsible for bringing together the stories of the narrator, Marlow and Kurtz. The *Narrator*, for the bulk of the novel, is Marlow, but his narrative is, of course, related by a main, unnamed, narrator. In turn, this latter is also the *Narratee* for he is also the person on the *Nellie*, listening to Marlow along with fellow *Narratees*. Yet, given the way that Marlow's narrative makes up the majority of the novel, and the way that it is framed as convincing and true by the main narrator, it is easy to conflate the *Narratee* with a reading of the narrative, the *Implied Reader*. Furthermore, it is possible to imagine that the position of the *Implied Reader* may, at certain times, correspond with that of a *Real Reader*. It is for this reason that the gap-filling procedure in narrative needs to be taken very seriously.

Iser's analysis of narrative insists that, although there may be an element of choice in the way that *Real Readers* read, there is ultimately a pre-ordained, 'given' manner in which a text's most important gaps are to be filled. For this reason Holub suggests that there is a problem at the heart of Iser's enterprise constituted by

> the fact that here and elsewhere freedom is granted to the reader only when it doesn't really count very much at all. If Tom Jones is a pound or two lighter, an inch or two taller, or if his eyes are a darker shade of blue are matters left to the reader. In these areas we are permitted to exercise a certain liberty in filling in the blanks. But when it comes to the meaning of sections of the novel or the work in its entirety, Iser leaves no room for deviating from 'the message'. The indeterminate often seems to involve only the trivial and non-essential

details; where meaning is produced, however, the reader either
travels the predetermined path or misunderstands the text.

(Holub 1984: 105–6)

More forcefully still, Stanley Fish has completely inverted Iser's
argument by asserting that "the stars in a text are not fixed; they
are just as variable as the lines that join them" (Fish 1981: 7). In
Fish's view, the reader's work in filling the gaps in a narrative is
not entirely dissimilar to the work s/he carries out in apprehend-
ing the real world. "Mediated access to the world is the only
access we ever have", he suggests (1981: 10), arguing that experience of the world does not constitute direct, untrammelled
knowledge but is always pre-structured. The fact that a text supplies the name 'Allworthy' is no different from the fact that the
world supplies a real apple: the apprehension of it will always be
caught up in the matrix of interpretations; text and apple come
to him/her as, in a sense, already partly determinate in their
meaning (cf. Iser 1981: 85).

The debate about what happens when we engage in the act of
perception is a massive inter-disciplinary one, and both Fish and
Iser manage only to scrape its surface. Yet, given what has been
argued in this book about the role of narrative in such complicated, but fundamental, mental acts as memorizing, it is clear
that Fish's perspective on humans' *pre-structured* interaction with
the world is pertinent. Moreover, the work of Fish is dedicated to
showing how the interpretation of narratives is invariably tied to
'interpretative communities' which sanction some interpretations
and not others (see Fish 1980). What this suggests is that the
gap-filling required by narrative takes place in specific ways as a
result of certain imperatives both formal and social.

As an example of what is at stake in understanding the gap-
filling process in narrative, consider the well-known film *E. T.: The
Extra-Terrestrial* (1982). It seems clear that the film contains a
story about a benevolent, and even loveable, alien creature who is

trapped on earth and given shelter by an American child, Elliott (Henry Thomas). Elliott takes care of the creature and ultimately enables it to return to the alien mothership; but his task is fraught with danger as various personnel from US government agencies are also keen to catch up with the extra-terrestrial. The narrative is very traditional in the way that it consists of a personal quest and a journey, numerous *detours*, a strong sense of 'innocent' identity, and the trials, tribulations and, in this case, triumph of an individual.

Iser's somewhat problematic comments on indeterminacy in films (1974: 283) suggest that cinematic narration in a film like *E. T.* allows for fewer gaps than written texts. However, even if this were true, it is difficult to deny that there are some major and obvious gaps in this film arising from the fact that the government personnel remain faceless throughout the narrative. Within the context of a 'traditional' reading of the narrative this makes sense, as the facelessness of the bureaucratic forces are in distinct contrast to the human individuality of Elliott and the other children in the film. However, it is not inconceivable that the gaps might be filled in other ways. If one asks such questions as 'Why are the government agents chasing the creature?', 'Might it not be beneficial to humankind if the alien could be approached and persuaded to advise the government?' and 'Why are the complexities of the adult world depicted in a harsh light compared with the simplicity of childhood?', then the faces of the agents will be filled in a very different fashion to that of the traditional or 'implied' reading.

Undoubtedly, such 'dissident' gap-filling will be the result of interpretations relying on imperatives which the narrative does not explicitly activate. It will be a case of the *Real Reader* entering into conflict with the *Implied Reader*. Furthermore, the imperative involved in such a reading will derive from features outside the narrative structure: general attitudes, values and experiences. However, this also reveals something significant about narrative itself. As Fish would argue, specific readings of narratives will arise from the attitudes, values and experiences of groups of people who will have sociological factors in common, that is to say, an interpretive community. Such readers bring aspects of their social lives to the interaction with a narrative. In addition, though, an interpretive community will share reading *practices*, will have common ways of filling the gaps in narrative (see, for example, Radway 1984). It should be clear from this, then, that tracing the history of narrative is crucial for understanding the way that readers might frequently apprehend narrative signs without necessarily realizing that the practice can also involve an engagement with the forging or re-affirmation of identity, myths of individualism, and a sense of unified human consciousness.

Frequently, it seems that narratives straightforwardly show or tell events and that they do so by an act of transmission from one fixed place to another. In *Heart of Darkness*, it is true that mimesis is employed in a familiar way and, indeed, that the narrative is almost entirely a mimetic rendering of Marlow's speech by the narrator on the *Nellie*. Nevertheless, this prompts questions about *re*-presentation; we have approached these through a discussion of narrative levels and gap-filling, but it is easy to see how a different analysis might come to the conclusion that the novel raises such questions as 'Which is the true version of events?', 'Whose truth is it?', and even 'What is truth?' The conscious play with relationships between narrative levels heralds the arrival of what cultural theorists call 'modernism', although this is not to say that narrative levels had remained unnoticed before the late nineteenth century. Producers of narrative in the Middle Ages, such as Chaucer, were certainly aware of these relationships; arguably, the awareness goes back all the way to Homer. What is clear, however, is that the demonstrable existence of different narrative levels makes untenable, in all forms of narrative, the common transmission model. *Heart of Darkness* is just one among many narratives of the period which seem to problematize the notion of transmission by introducing innovations in narrative structure. Issues of consciousness and narrative levels were to become further intensified in the early decades of the twentieth century with the introduction of new narrative technologies.

# 6

---

# MODERNISM AND THE CINEMA

*A Portrait of the Artist as a Young Man*, a novel by James Joyce published in 1916, is about the early years and youth of the character, Stephen Dedalus. It begins as follows:

> Once upon a time and a very good time it was there was a moocow coming down along the road and this moocow met a nicens little boy named baby tuckoo ...

> His father told him that story: his father looked at him through a glass: he had a hairy face.

> He was baby tuckoo. The moocow came down the road where Betty Byrne lived: she sold lemon platt.

> *O, the wild rose blossoms*
> *On the little green place*

> He sang that song. That was his song.

> *O, the green wothe botheth.*

When you wet the bed first it is warm then it gets cold. His mother put on the oil sheet. That had the queer smell.

His mother had a nicer smell than his father. She played on the piano the sailor's hornpipe for him to dance. He danced:

> *Tralala lala*
> *Tralala lala*
> *Tralala tralaladdy*
> *Tralala lala.*

Uncle Charles and Dante clapped.

(Joyce 1964: 3)

At first sight this seems like pure nonsense. The sentences and clauses have no logical connection; the first sentence is unpunctuated and rambling; and there are words unknown to the English lexicon such as "nicens" or "botheth". However, in spite of these linguistic and logical contraventions, it is possible to make some sense out of the passage. It should become clear reasonably quickly that the sequence is narrated from the point of view of a small child, who, rather than trying to make order out of the world, presents the way he is besieged by numerous sensations and impulses. Thus, the first page of the novel is an attempt to reproduce faithfully a child's experience.

Joyce's narrative reveals its purpose immediately by commencing at the level of the character's thoughts. In an analysis of a sequence from Virginia Woolf's novel, *To the Lighthouse* (1927), Auerbach describes the same kind of process in which there is a close approach to objective reality by means of numerous subjective impressions received by various individuals at various times (1968: 536). Commenting on the way that the characters' voices seem to dominate and obscure any narratorial voice he suggests that

> there actually seems to be no viewpoint at all outside the novel
> from which the people and events within it are observed, any
> more than there seems to be an objective reality apart from
> what is in the consciousness of characters.
>
> (Auerbach 1968: 534)

Clearly, Auerbach is indicating the absence of the omniscient narrator favoured by nineteenth-century novelists, although this is not to say that the voice of the narrator has disappeared. The example from *Heart of Darkness* involving the French gunboat that we discussed in Chapter 5 shows that the voices of the natives and the voices of the French are distinct because of the different *situations* from which they operate. Marlow's almost incredulous voice, however, is the one that allows the incident to be narrated. He 'reworks' the incident even though, as a character/narrator witnessing the surface of events, he can never be omniscient.

Bakhtin saw the novel as the genre in which a proliferation of voices is of vital importance and, indeed, unavoidable; however, a voice can only appear given that there is a 'second' voice available, such as that of a narrator or another character, to distance it and lend it identity (see Hirschkop 1999: 93). The example from *A Portrait of the Artist as a Young Man* certainly presents a young child's idiom and, as such, allows a socially *situated* voice to be heard. However, that idiom is embedded in the voice of the narrator who implements a more mature idiom in the course of narrating; as such, the character of Stephen therefore assumes different voices in relation to the narrator and according to the different situations in which he finds himself at different stages of his life. This does not mean that the narrator is omniscient; instead, because Stephen's voice is always located in specific situations, there is a constant tension between the narrator's and characters' voice as a result of their mutual inability to know the entirety of each other's social situations.

*A Portrait of the Artist as a Young Man* exemplifies the 'modernist' recognition that human consciousness is determined by a number of forces and is far from being unified by absolute self-knowledge. Given that even complete knowledge of the self came to be considered impossible, it is hardly surprising that the idea of an all-knowing subject fell into disrepute. Bruner argues that the banishing of the omniscient narrator in the modern novel "sharpened contemporary sensibility to the conflict inherent in two people trying to know the 'outer' world from different perspectives" (1990: 51). While the 'subjective' narrative technique as described by Auerbach seems both to imply an acceptance of the proliferation of consciousnesses and to undermine any belief in the possibility of participation in a unitary, stable public life, two points should therefore be remembered. First, that the consciousnesses of characters as instanced by their situated voices will always be related to an 'other' voice such that their voices cannot be 'monologic'. Second, in narrative, while 'other' voices will frequently be those of other characters, a constant other voice will be that of a narrator who is not necessarily omniscient and by no means in control of the other voices.

The attempt to acknowledge the multi-faceted nature of human consciousness and experience which is evidenced in the narratives of Joyce and Woolf is one feature of 'modernism'. Yet modernism in both narrative and the larger context is a contradictory phenomenon which is difficult to unravel. On the one hand, it consists of a backlash against previous trains of thought, especially those of the nineteenth century. Peter Nicholls argues that there was a strain of modernism embodied by poets such as Ezra Pound and T. S. Eliot and novelists such as Wyndham Lewis whose remit was to attack modernity especially for the way in which it represented democracy, the rise of the working class and the 'life of the crowd'. This went hand in hand with a disdain for nineteenth-century attempts to present the connectedness of social life by means of mimesis (Nicholls 1995: 251). For such modernists as Nicholls describes, the individual self needed to be seen as "closed, autonomous, and antagonistic", divorced from the vulgarity of public life as presented in realist representation. At the same time, though, these thinkers considered romantic individualist notions of the self as 'authentic' to be equally outdated: the self was the product of a complex cultural tradition.

On the other hand, there is a strong sense in modernism of the way in which the recent apprehension of identity as complex, constructed and lacking unity constitutes a major leap forward in the concept of self-knowledge. Bradbury and McFarlane briefly list the characteristics of modernity arising from science, philosophy and recent events in history and culture, suggesting that modernism is

> consequent on Heisenberg's 'Uncertainty principle', of the destruction of civilization and rationalism in the First World War, of the world changed and reinterpreted by Marx, Freud and Darwin, of capitalism and constant industrial acceleration, of existential exposure to meaninglessness and absurdity. It is the literature of technology. It is the art consequent on the disestablishing of communal reality and conventional notions of causality, on the destruction of traditional notions of the wholeness of individual character, on the linguistic chaos that ensues when public notions of language have been discredited and when all realities have become subjective fictions.
>
> (Bradbury and McFarlane 1976: 27)

The description speaks of all manner of assaults on previous understandings of reality. Yet, like the seemingly illogical prose of *A Portrait of the Artist as a Young Man*, implicit in each assault is the presentation of an *enhanced* view of the world.

The example from Joyce's novel which opens this chapter carries with it the assumption that it is worth presenting the disordered thoughts of a small child in order to gain a fuller sense of how the child develops into an adult. This was not a new conception;

however, Joyce's evocation of the theme in a narrative is indicative of a new faith in the ability to explore human identity. As such, it bears affinities with psychoanalysis, whose appearance at a time of self-questioning of identity in the West cannot be coincidental.

Those with only a scant knowledge of Freud's work are likely to know that he sought the answers to human adult psychology through an investigation of the events of childhood. Freud believed that such events, when they could be remembered at all, were retrospectively given a logic or coherence by the ordered experience of adulthood. This may not seem quite so significant to inhabitants of the early twenty-first century: particular mental states are now thought to be self-evidently tied up with a person's development as a human being. Similarly, the work of psychotherapy, stemming from Freud's inauguration of psychoanalysis and his arguments about human development, has had such a profound impact on the methods for the treatment of pathological mental states that it is now part of the social landscape of consumer choice (see Knight 1986 and Kovel 1990). Nevertheless, in the early years of the twentieth century, Freud's insights were quintessentially 'modern'.

This 'modern' quality of psychoanalysis is important for understanding the kinds of shift from an omniscient narrator to the voices of many selves which Auerbach described in his comments on Woolf. Before the mid- to late nineteenth century, mental illness had most frequently been treated, especially in its more severe forms, by incarceration (Foucault 1971). For many years the idea had persisted that the mentally ill were possessed by demons. In fact, there is an echo of 'exorcism' in the term given so frequently to early psychiatry: a "dark science" (Masson 1986). Under the yoke of industrial capitalism, science might progress sufficiently to enable the introduction of the steam engine and heavily automated factories, and even the physical sciences such as medicine might discover the efficacy of different vaccines. But the workings of the mind and the means of understanding and treating them remained one major symbolic obstacle to the march of knowledge. Advances in the area of mental life would, understandably, promote even greater confidence in the technologies that everywhere in the Western world were being introduced for the purposes of conquering nature.

As psychoanalysis developed and discovered crucial evidence in dreams as well as waking life which pointed to the existence of a fertile realm known as 'the unconscious' (Freud 1976b), Freud and those sympathetic to his work grew increasingly confident about the new epoch dawning. In his *Introductory Lectures* of 1916 Freud identified humankind's suffering of "two major blows at the hands of science". The first was the realization, partly as a result of the Copernican revolution of the seventeenth century, that the earth was not the centre of the universe but only a tiny fragment of a cosmic system of scarcely imaginable vastness; the second was when biological research associated with Darwin demonstrated the animal ancestry of humans. A third "and most wounding blow" would result from contemporary psychological and psychoanalytic research which sought to show that the human ego is not even master in its own house (Freud 1973b: 326). Psychoanalysis, then, represents a major step forward in human self-knowledge as opposed to human 'self-love'. One of the keys to this self-knowledge is an understanding of childhood and, especially, the role of sexuality in the formation of human beings.

Psychoanalysis, in this formulation, is, of course, itself a retrospective narrative of the making of the adult by the child, yet the hubris embedded in its confidence in its own narrative is not unique during this period. Science in general, especially the achievements which it manifested through the developments of new technology, fulfilled a narrative of human progress and knowledge. Indeed, it was in the field of communications where the most tangible leaps forward were made by technology in the late years of the nineteenth century and the early years of the twentieth. The telegraph (1837), photography (1839) and the typewriter (1873) were to be followed by the telephone (1876), the phonograph (1878), wireless (1895) and, after 1895, what was arguably to become the major technology of narrative in the twentieth century: film.

## WRITING IN LIGHT

The consideration of narrative in film is not as straightforward a task as it might at first seem. Undoubtedly, film is a form of representation, a fact that it shares with oral and printed narrative. Yet it is mainly *visual*, a fact which tends to suggest that it should be grouped with theatre, photography and painting, all of which are themselves capable of embodying narrative. In the light of Bruner's criteria for narrative which were listed in Chapter 1, it is self-evident that narrative films contain the following features: (a) a means for emphasizing human agency or action; (b) a sequence of some sort; and (c) a sense of what is canonical, traditional or permitted as well as what is non-canonical. The fourth criterion, (d) a narrator's perspective, however, poses problems. Because of their visual nature most films, argues Chatman, "do not 'tell' their stories in any usual sense of the word" (Chatman 1990: 124). Indeed, one of the most influential contemporary analysts of film, David Bordwell, insists that film has no narrator. For him, to attribute to every film a narrator is "to indulge in an anthropomorphic fiction"; film narration, instead, is "better understood as the organization of a set of cues for the construction of a story" (1985: 62).

There is good reason for Bordwell to come to this conclusion. It follows from his argument that *sjuzet*, the way the story is organized, helps the film's spectator to *infer* the *fabula*, the 'raw materials' or action of the story (Bordwell 1985: 49–53). Furthermore, the *sjuzet* itself invariably becomes a norm or 'mode' across a body of films, rendering individual agency in the production process largely immaterial (1985: 147–334). Clearly, it makes good sense to emphasize in the analysis of narrative the commonly learned practices of reading and the way that readers bring knowledges of phenomena outside the text to the reading process. However, it must be said that Bordwell's work focuses on the period of film production dominated by narrative, from around 1917 until the 1960s (see Bordwell et al. 1985). If the history of film can be split up into two main periods of innovation this would probably consist of the years from 1895 to 1917, a period of rapid development and change which is, itself, made up of two periods of mainly 'non-narrative' film (1895–1908) and the emergence of narrative techniques (1908–17), plus the period from 1917 to the 1960s, the epoch of 'narrative' film during which there is seen to be little fundamental change or innovation (Elsaesser 1990: 408). Interestingly, the evolution of film as a 'modern' technology in the period 1895 to 1917, *before* its metamorphosis into a form of enunciating narrative, has a great deal to reveal about the role of the 'narrator' and other narrative levels.

It must be remembered that early audiences went to see machines demonstrated rather than watch films (Gunning 1990a: 58). The film historian, Barry Salt, suggests that "The only absolute demand from audiences was that films be photographed (and printed) sharply in focus and with the correct exposure" (1990: 31–2). Film was a new technology for recording and reproducing moments in time and space rather than a medium for narrative. Film was not accompanied by sound recording and motion pictures were actually made up of numerous still photographs which the modern camera now exposes at twenty-four frames per second. As the product of a modern technology, early one-shot films were often involved in recording details of modern life and other new technologies. Most famously, the Lumière brothers' 1895 demonstration, *L'arrive d'un train en gare*, featured the arrival of a train; but there were many other one-shot films devoted to departures, embarkations and arrivals of other forms of transport (see

Christie 1994: 31–6). Undoubtedly, the idea of a journey had the power to invoke both time and space; yet, it is probably not coincidental that the 'journey' was a staple of the narrative tradition very much associated with the development of the self.

Most early films in the period up to 1906 were 'actualities', recordings of real events. However, when events were *staged*, film displayed affinities with theatre and a demand grew for spectacle, constructed situations and tableaux (Brewster and Jacobs 1997: 8, 29). Moreover, the spectacle that film offered differed greatly from the solitary pleasures encouraged by print. Projection allowed films to be consumed by large numbers of people in public places, and the experience could be repeated. The rapid development of cheaper theatres in the United States, the 'nickelodeons', accelerated cinema's claim to be a mass medium and created a more visible 'interpretive community'. But narrative did not yet dominate interpretive activity; as Christie notes:

> No one went to see a *particular* film until around 1907 at the very earliest. They went to the biograph, the cinematograph, the moving pictures, the nickelodeon: it was a *place* and an *experience* long before identifiable works and their makers emerged to claim their niche in history.
>
> (Christie 1994: 8)

For at least the first eight years of its life, film was not strictly narrative-based but part of a 'cinema of attractions' (Gunning 1990a) presenting spectacles and the equivalent of magic tricks or illusions (Gunning 1990b: 102). Even though, as Gaudreault suggests, any film comprising one shot is a narrative in that it presents a series of events with at least some semblance of beginning and end, the earliest films lack the organization which is usually attributed to narrative form (Gaudreault 1990a: 71).

The crucial issue in early film is the role of the narrator. Gaudreault asserts that "There was no filmic narrator at the beginning of cinema" (1990a: 73); but, in the terms that we have discussed, there was certainly an *Implied Author* by virtue of the fact that some agency selected a particular object to be shot, from a specific position and within a certain frame. The role of this entity becomes clearer with the development of multi-shot films.

However, Gaudreault explores the roles of the *Narrator*, *Implied Author* and *Real Author(s)* of early films through the term 'monstration' (1990a). Early films were emphatically 'shown' to audiences by a 'monstrator', operating from behind the camera and/or in the movie theatre, whose role was more akin to that of a circus ringmaster than a contemplative narrator. Even in early legal cases concerned with the plagiarism of films, it was not clear what precise agencies were involved in the individuality of the artefacts in question; however, judgements were made which indicated that specific organizations of photographic frames in sequence were as much the subject of copyright as individual photographs (see Gaudreault 1990b). Multi-shot films displayed the agency involved in their production, but, still, the monstration process continued in the cinema: in addition to live music in the film theatre, motion pictures until around 1910 were often accompanied by a live 'monstration': a 'lecturer' in the film theatre who commented on the action. The lecturer's work was, thus, a little like that carried out by the voice-over in narrative films (Gaudreault 1990c: 280). Elsewhere, the film's shots could be explicated by the use of intertitles containing dialogue or commentary on the action; however, as film was sold by the yard, the over-use of intertitles could be costly.

'Monstration' from behind the camera was undeniably an act of showing. As such, it took place in the service of mimesis and imitation, and it often added the human voice, as a further showing and an oral quasi-telling by the lecturer, to a soundless representation. In the early years of the twentieth century, though, film, for a number of reasons, started to develop 'internal' means for telling, an agency which might have been called 'the poet's voice' by Aristotle and Plato, but which is more a matter of the fluid categories associated with narrative levels. From around 1903 to 1906, one of the most popular types of motion picture was the 'chase film' (Salt 1990). Quite simply, this involved one person in pursuit of, or in flight from, another, sometimes in vehicles. As Gaudreault notes, the lecturer was not needed with chase films because the action was fairly explicit (1990c: 278) and this explicitness resulted from the fact that "pursuer and pursued were always in the same shot, due to the absolute priority of spatial coherence in the representation of causal relations or sequential action" (Elsaesser and Barker 1990: 296). The artistic limitations in this kind of film were clear. Alternatively, in 'non-chase' films, the insertion of intertitles remained costly and the use of the lecturer continued to be cumbersome. Both chase and non-chase films, then, benefited from the introduction of an organizing principle into the very fabric of the motion pictures. This organizing principle was known as 'parallel editing' or 'cross-cutting'.

The film-maker D. W. Griffith (1875–1948) is most associated with the development of the parallel editing process although it is clear that it had appeared before he commenced his major innovations (see Gaudreault 1990d: 133 and Salt 1990: 39). Parallel editing involved the depiction of simultaneous or near-simultaneous actions in a sequence. In the chase film, for example, parallel editing would perhaps involve a single shot of the pursued scurrying along alone within the frame, followed by a cross-cut to a shot of his pursuer steadily gaining on him. The process could be extended to scenarios far more complex than this and, as Gunning argues, "Through parallel editing Griffith could create suspense by interrupting action and delaying information, make moral judgments, underscore characters' desires and reveal motivation" (1990c: 345). Using this and a number of other narrating devices, Griffith supplemented the mimetic aspect of film and, as Richter argues, abolished the "viewpoint from the stalls" (1986: 75). His films featured shots composed with action taking place simultaneously in the background, middleground and foreground. Where characters in scenes had often been viewed from a distance and their emotions inferred by broad, expressive, theatrical gestures, Griffith's films used close-up shots to depict emotion on the actors' faces. In sum, the act of cutting within a scene to a more detailed or different-angled shot, as well as the act of cutting to a new scene, betrayed the work of a narratorial agency in film.

Such standardization of narrative devices which was to take place over the period 1908 to 1917 was also augmented by other significant developments. Film-makers started to focus on objects other than real events, news, vaudeville and burlesque routines. They started to adapt major novels in the Western tradition, partly as a ploy to attract to the cinema a bourgeois reading public who demanded more sophisticated character psychology in their narratives (Belton 1994: 12–3). Specially prepared scripts came into use in the planning of films round about 1910 (Chanan 1996: 243); and there were developments with regard to what is called 'style' within film narrative: camera angle, distance and movement, lighting, musical accompaniment and editing techniques beyond cross-cutting. That film in the second decade of the twentieth century was experienced as a *re*-presentation or the working of *sjuzet* on *fabula* was clear; Tsivian notes that the typical Russian film spectator saw narrative form as progressing intermittently:

> For example, a critic in *The Projector*, reviewing Wladslaw Starewicz's *In the Fire of Passions and Sufferings* ... pointed out what he saw as the film's narrative paradox: 'The action is drawn out in places. But at the same time you get the feeling that important scenes have been left out – for example, there is no concert scene, and all you get is the ovation that follows'.
>
> (Tsivian 1994: 165)

The new narrative medium suffered the doubts of its early audience in a way that is analogous to that of the eighteenth-century novel. In a statement which might constitute the core of Tristram Shandy's implied critique of early novelistic narrative, Tsivian says of the Russian film audience that the "general opinion was that cinema failed to distinguish the important from the trivial" (1994: 185).

Clearly, narrative film had to struggle to establish itself before 1917. Devices that are now considered transparent and taken for granted in audio-visual production took time to comprehend. One example is the 'Kuleshov effect'. Named after a Russian film-maker, this effect consisted of "any series of shots that *in the absence of an establishing shot* cues the spectator to infer a spatial whole on the basis of seeing only portions of that space" (Bordwell and Thompson 1993: 258); it was not automatically accepted by audiences used to seeing not just two actors in close-up but also, as in theatre, the room or street in which the action took place. Similarly, in the early 1920s, the use of what is now an almost omnipresent motion picture device, 'montage', had to be explicated by its key innovator, Sergei Eisenstein (1898–1948). His films proceeded by inviting a connection between otherwise unconnected shots which were edited continuously. For example, a sequence in Eisentein's *The Battleship Potemkin* (1925) involves an image of a marble lion leaping up in protest but is composed "of three shots of three stationary marble lions at the Alupka Palace in the Crimea: a sleeping lion, an awakening lion, a rising lion" (Eisenstein 1985: 112). Although the shots of the lions refer to part of the landscape in which the action takes place, they emphatically conjure an image of strength in reference to the revolutionaries whose actions are contained in the previous and subsequent shots (cf. Lothe 2000: 70). More straightforward, perhaps, is an example from an episode of the long-running British television drama *Coronation Street* screened in 2000: during a hostage siege in the local supermarket, police marksmen are called to the scene and there is a shot of two police operatives moving towards the store with rifles poised. The identity of the police operatives and even their gender is obscured by the armed strike force uniform in which they are dressed. The next shot pans the faces of the hostages within the supermarket but starts and lingers slightly with the manager of the store. If the viewer does not make the connection in the montage it is certainly made clear later that the armed police operative seen in the earlier shot, underneath the uniform, is another regular character in the narrative: a policewoman who just happens to be the supermarket manager's girlfriend.

There can be little doubt that the single images in such sequences are 'mimetic' in their orientation; they show events. Yet, their juxtaposition is not simply a matter of showing two separate and unconnected incidents; instead, new meanings are invited. The connection made between the two characters, the identity of the police operative being initially obscured, is plainly an act of narration. As Wood puts it, invoking a linguistic metaphor, "the moment we put two shots together we have a syntax" (1999: 222); the connections between different elements can be learned with practice. Indeed, there seems to be a direct parallel to montage in the seemingly straightforward sequencing of apparently unrelated sentences in printed hard-boiled fiction (see Chapter 4). On occasion, these too will invite a meaning beyond that yielded by mimesis: that is to say, like film images, sentences in printed narrative do not simply present events and characters; they also *re*-present events and characters as 'connected', and *re*-present things which are *not* events and characters. These latter include such phenomena as thoughts, feelings, motivations and, importantly, the *very connections* between represented objects.

The other juxtaposition which film exploits concerns 'time' rather than 'space' and it, too, has parallels with printed and oral narrative. The 'temporal order' of film narrative, the sequencing of its *fabula*, might be thought of as 'ABCD'; yet a flashback can transform it to 'BACD'. A character might stop to think about something for a moment, and then, what s/he is thinking about, such as a scene from his/her childhood, is narrated before returning to the character in the present. The film *D.O.A.* (1946; remade 1988), for example, consists almost entirely of a flashback in which a man recounts the events surrounding his ingestion of fatal poison: a sequence, therefore, of CABD. Of course, *The Odyssey* implemented the flashback technique copiously over two and a half thousand years ago (see, especially, Books IX–XII); but the device has become synonymous with film.

Similarly, film will sometimes use the opposite of flashback, a 'flashforward'. Here the duration is: AB, then D, followed by C (Bordwell and Thompson 1993: 70–1). What is interesting about the flashforward in so many narrative films is that it often aligns itself with a character's psychology rather than a mere *re*-presentation of events. In *Don't Look Now* (1973), either there is a flashforward or the protagonist has a vision of three mourners, including his wife, at a funeral in Venice, the place where he is killed in the closing scene of the film. More controversially, *The Last Temptation of Christ* (1988) depicts what is either a flashforward or a hallucination of desire which Jesus experiences while on the cross: the scene depicts Jesus alive, married to Mary Magdalen and settled with a family. In these examples, the narrative device might be said to be 'close to', or even 'very much tied up with', the character's psychology or perspective. Indeed, most films require the character's understanding of events to be the foundation of the narrative because of what Bordwell and Thompson call 'temporal duration' (1993: 71): the fact that the *story* in a narrative may derive from a *plot* which ranges into the past, even into a period before the protagonist was born, as is the case with the novel, *Oliver Twist* (see Chapter 1).

Thus, the modern technology of film established its own powerful narrative devices. After 1917, especially, narrative film also made character psychology integral to its operation, to the extent that its 'subjective' mode of delineation of character, presenting the events from a position close to the protagonist, for example, often resembled that of modernist print narrative. Yet film retained aspects of its heritage, specifically the orientation to the theatrical and spectacular. In fact, as Gunning shows, the mixed influences within film irked those modernists such as the Italian 'Futurist', Filippo Marinetti, who exalted the power of technology. For them, there existed excitement at the medium's potential but also disappointment at the way in which it was still enslaved to traditional forms such as theatre and literature (see Gunning 1990a: 56). It is probably this double-edged nature of film that makes it difficult, as Bordwell argues, to identify what is 'modernism' in film (1985: 310).

However, the mixed heritage of film, as well as its narrative devices, can also be seen as the essence of its modern status. One salient feature of film narrative throughout its history has been the fact that it does not betray an omniscient, controlling consciousness. The authority and legal rights of authors had become firmly established with the rise of written narrative and especially in the wake of the Enlightenment. Yet early film narrative was clearly not simply the product of the writers of film scripts. As with theatre, there was the work of the actors to consider, the work of the producer who staged the acting or financed the production, the work of the set designer, the work of the lighting engineer and, especially, the work of the director. Indeed, most frequently in the second part of the twentieth century, attempts were made by critics to emphasize the special controlling role of the film director. In France, most notably, film critics put forward the notion of the director as an 'auteur' of film narrative, a relatively free creator of narrative meaning by dint of his/her juxtaposition of images, choice of camera angles, lighting, sound and sets (see Caughie 1981: 35–67). The extent to which this notion caught on, especially in traditional academic circles, is considerable, leading to references to films as the products or 'possessions' of their directors. The present book, it must be said, is no exception in this respect.

Against the 'auteur' argument, however, is the fact that the film director works within strict economic restraints, with specific technology, within a fairly fixed repertoire of narrative devices and in collaboration with an extensive range of personnel. Furthermore, for audiences the most important seat of creativity in a narrative might not be the director but, rather, the actor, the scriptwriter, the genre, the producer or, in some cases, such as the films made by Ealing Studios in Britain during the 1940s and 1950s, the production company. Nevertheless, these factors did not prevent experimentations with motion picture narrative, the desire to "set cinematographic technology against the vulgar naturalistic theatricality of the fiction film" (Richter 1986: 59) and attempts to establish authorship of films.

## THE CINEMA AND MODERNISM

According to Yuri Tsivian, early Russian film-makers began to adapt classic Russian novels, many of which were extremely long. To economize on length, and anticipating that the narratives would already be well known to the audience, the films often contained key scenes only. For audiences, argues Tsivian, the films felt like modernist narratives (1994: 166). Continuity was therefore sacrificed in favour of spectacle, and *re*-presentation was foregrounded as so many events were omitted. The most deliberate assault on narrative continuity and coherence in film during the first three decades of the twentieth century, however, came from Surrealism. Surrealism was a movement which embraced painting, film-making, performance and, especially, writing. It took as its central concern the manifold nature of the Freudian unconscious and, most importantly, the idea that modes of *conscious* representation are not the only ones available to humans (see Gershman 1969; Germain 1978; Rosemont 1978; Jean 1980; Alexandrian 1989; Breton 1991; Stitch 1991). Bordwell and Thompson suggest that "Surrealist cinema is overtly antinarrative, attacking causality itself" (1993: 465).

Probably the most famous Surrealist film, *Un Chien Andalou* (1927), was made by a painter, Salvador Dalí (1904–1989) and a film director, Luis Buñuel (1900–83). For seventeen minutes the film depicts a range of scenes with a limited ensemble of characters, set to music from Wagner's opera, *Tristan und Isolde*, as well as a tango. Buñuel stated on more than one occasion that the images chosen for the film were totally meaningless and their intent was to exclude "all narrative sense, all logical association" (Buñuel quoted in Etherington-Smith 1992: 115). Such statements invite *interpretations* of the spectacle and there has been no shortage of these since the film was first screened. In fact, the film's lack of conventional devices to indicate causality and, sometimes, space and time, seems to encourage speculation about meaning.

In the first scene a man (Buñuel) prepares a razor and then, instead of shaving someone, he slices open the eye of his female sitter. Just as he does so an image of a cloud cutting across the moon is revealed. The images are striking but they are more than this because of the way that the moon has traditionally been associated with madness or 'lunacy'. Moreover, the moon is a spherical object, much like the eye in the scene and the eye the spectator uses to view the film. Already, this reading of the image invokes associations because of the lack of narrative support for a stable interpretation. For example, the image clearly shows penetration, and 'penetration' is frequently the word used as a quasi-clinical synonym for sexual intercourse.

Yet the cutting of the eye might also echo the culmination of the Oedipus myth which was so important to Freud (1976b: 363–5). As shown in Sophocles' play, *King Oedipus* (429–20 BCE), the eponymous protagonist discovers that he has not only unknowingly murdered his father but that the woman he then took as a wife and who bore him two sons and two daughters, Jocasta, is his own mother. Appalled, Oedipus blinds himself in penance and self-retribution. Yet this self-punishment is curious: Oedipus destroys one spherical object in his body, his eye, when in fact the incestuous damage has been committed by another bodily sphere, the producer of sperm, the testicle. The punishment of the eye rather than the testicle is what Freud would call, in dream analysis, a 'displacement' (1976b: 314ff.). The emotion evoked by one image is *displaced* onto another, seemingly innocuous one; instead of gouging the offending object, his testicle, Oedipus *displaces* his self-aggression upwards to the eye.

This kind of 'sexual' reading of the film's image has no doubt been encouraged by the previous observation on 'penetration'. Furthermore, it is a man and a woman that are involved in the scene's transaction and a second viewing of the film will reveal that although the man wears a collarless shirt in the first shots, the close-up leading to the razor-cut shows him in a stripy tie which changes size. As is popularly assumed, Freud does make references to phallic and vaginal symbols in some of his analyses, albeit in a limited way, in the *Introductory Lectures* (1973c: 187– 99). Using such tools which make up only a minuscule part of the psychoanalytic enterprise, the tie would seem to be an obvious phallic image here. Whatever it means, the cutting of the eye contains many different interpretative possibilities and is consequently an example of the process in dreams that Freud calls "condensation" (1976b: 383–413).

The next scene, for no apparent reason, depicts a cyclist wearing frills. Clearly, the cyclist is a man, but he has taken on 'feminine' paraphernalia. This might refer to Freud's perspective on the development of human sexuality (1977b) in which culture, not just biology, has a crucial role to play. That is to say that gender and sexuality are not the result of biology alone but also of the constructed identities that lie in wait for the child within a given culture. In addition, the intertitle announces "eight years later", which seems to follow from the film's opening caption of "Once upon a time ..." So far, the film does not contravene the temporal protocols concerned with cinematic causality. However, subsequent intertitles announce "three o'clock in the morning", "in the Spring", and so forth, which produces precisely the feeling of the narrative proceeding non-sequentially in fits and starts, with a great number of events seemingly left out. In short, the subversion of film's conventional way of rendering time is almost like the disorientation experienced in a dream and, indeed, Freud had suggested that, in dreams, the unconscious exercises its own means of representation, a means in which time, sequence and logical connection associated with conscious life have no purchase (1976b: 119–23).

Such analysis of the disjointed scenes of *Un Chien Andalou* could continue, suggesting that $x$ means $y$ in a mechanistic way which Freud himself would find difficult to approve. And in fact this is Raymond Durgnat's approach in his analysis, supplemented by a countenancing of different readings of the film as a whole. The film might be read in general as the chronicle of a life beginning with the sex act, through infantile sexuality and the Oedipus complex, the rape scene in the middle of the film and the 3 a.m. bedroom scene, through to death, with frills on the beach, and ultimate decay, figures buried in sand. Alternatively, the scenes might be read in reverse with the initial seed of a lovers' liaison, in spring, followed by the idea to have a child, frills on the beach, Oedipal conflicts, infantile sexuality and the social world, culminating in a violent death by razor. But Durgnat also adds that,

> *Un Chien Andalou*, apparently so drab, short and summary, reveals itself at each viewing to be richer and more indefinable, as the sensitivity of its shades of mood become apparent: the sad, apathetic rhythms, the sinister indifference of passers-by, the tenderness of the slow-motion flashback.
>
> (Durgnat 1977: 38)

What is clear from this discussion is that although the film-makers may have striven to make the film as nonsensical and lacking in rational sense as they could, they actually failed. The film does not abolish narrative.

## JUST ANOTHER 'REALISM'?

Like *Un Chien Andalou*, Dalí's Surrealist painting had knitted together associations without regard for the rationalization that is characteristic of conscious life. Where conscious reasoning might assert that 'x' goes with 'y', 'knife' goes with 'fork', 'cat' goes with 'dog' and so on, Dalí was happy to trust to unconscious impulses when they dictated that 'cherries' goes with 'couple', 'woman' goes with 'praying mantis', 'lobster' goes with 'telephone' and 'clock' goes with 'fried eggs'. Yet at the same time as it draws together seemingly disparate associations, Dalí's painting is also suffused with expert realist draughtsmanship. A painting such as 'The ghost of Vermeer of Delft which can be used as a table' (1934) not only carries the absurd image of Vermeer viewed from the back with an outstretched leg used as a perch and a long, thin crutch, it also pays tribute to the ultra-realist style of the seventeenth century Dutch master. Landscapes and body parts, although 'otherworldy' in Dalí's paintings, are nevertheless recognizable, unlike the 'pure' abstractions or 'automatism' of painters such as Kandinsky (1866–1944). This tension in Dalí's work suggests something which bears on *Un Chien Andalou*. His paintings often seem to be reproductions of strangely juxtaposed images of dream life and, far from abolishing the act of narration, they seem to depict mimetically the twisted logic of the unconscious.

*Un Chien Andalou* and Surrealism might also provide an insight into the relation between narrative and modernist representation as a whole. The comedian Les Dawson often presented a hilarious routine in which he would play a tune on the piano and, repeatedly, at crucial points, hit a discordant note; the supreme ability to time these notes plainly demonstrated a high level of proficiency in 'conventional' piano playing. Likewise with modernism, narrative experiments were probably underpinned by a strong conventional narrative sense of how elements should combine in a story or representation, a sense which necessarily preceded the intent to subvert narrative principles. Modernist narrative, as well as attempts at anti-narrative, 'understood' the representational heritage which they sought to surpass. Indeed, Auerbach's comments on the work of Virginia Woolf suggest that what is at the heart of modernist representation is an attempt "to put the emphasis on the random occurrence, to exploit it not in the service of planned continuity of action but in itself" (Auerbach 1968: 552). Auerbach reveals in his analysis of a passage in *To the Lighthouse* that the novel is made up of sequences in which seemingly inconsequential events such as the measuring of a stocking are drawn out in all their richness.

What is emphasized in this novel, then, is not the movement towards conclusion but the *detour* for its own sake. What are expanded are those minor realistic details which seem to push the narrative to its end, but which also work in the service of a *detour* and in the service of presenting convincing details, the phenomenon that Barthes labelled "the reality effect" (see Chapter 3). In this way, modernist narrative seems intent on new modes of depiction which are more adequate to the objects that are depicted; and these objects are invariably concerned with the human self, be they inner psychological states or the emotional experiences of such phenomena in the modern world as bureaucracy. Time in modernist representation is frequently depicted not as a uniform, linear phenomenon but as dragging or fitful depending on the consciousness that is experiencing it; space is equally 'de-structured' so that a character such as Joseph K in Franz Kafka's *The Trial* (1916) can find that his home, his workplace or the courtroom, all of which are supposedly separate spaces, may be linked merely by a door. Generally, narrative is not so much absent in modernism but is put to different or more detailed purposes. *A Portrait of the Artist as a Young Man* initially seeks to reproduce the thought-patterns of infancy; Surrealism attempts to depict unconscious associations; Marcel Proust's narratives are concerned with the evocation of memories and sensations; Kafka's novels and stories depict a nightmare world with a heightened sense of domination by the alien structures of society. In short, modernist representation seeks to be more 'accurate', getting closer than ever before to what it chooses to render.

Like the print narrative of the early decades of the twentieth century, the modern technology of motion pictures undoubtedly promised the power of recording events with immense accuracy. Yet the extent to which film embodied modernism and, certainly, the extent to which it fulfilled its promise of accuracy in the way that modernist representation, with its nuanced depiction of psychological states, might have desired, remains debatable. What is clear is that while film developed the main components of its narrative apparatus by 1917, the question of whether film harboured a narrator was still unanswered.

It cannot be denied that much of the narration of motion pictures, as Bordwell argues, is embedded in the very form of film as a series of cues to the viewer. However, it does not necessarily follow that the agency of the *Implied Author* and the *Narrator* should be overlooked. The 'monstration' of early film, its explicit disposition to 'show', always entailed an *Implied Author*, the agent who set up the camera for the shot. The later development of editing was the product of a similar agent, responsible for ending a scene at a particular moment, cutting to another shot, omitting some details from a frame and leaving in others. But it does seem that these agencies, while similar, are qualitatively different, with the latter taking on a role more akin to a traditional narrator, as opposed to a character/narrator in the story, and certainly as opposed to the previous cinematic monstrator. Cinematic narrative devices are not identical to those of oral and print narrative, but they manifest the same impulse to supplement their 'showing' with a degree of 'telling'. Editing and cinematic 'style' *re*-present and, as we have observed of narrative in general, facilitate the meaningful relations which will transpire with human input.

Perhaps Noël Burch is correct when he suggests that many English and American critics see the earliest days of cinema as a lost paradise and prefiguration of modernism (1990: 225). It seems that the first eight years of cinema presented a modern technology with great promise and power, a means to make humans see differently which has apparently not been borne out by the technology's subsequent history. On the other hand, there *is* something in early cinema which seems, for some, to hint at a representative form which can subvert narrative. To be sure, the exact nature of early film is difficult to ascertain; as with other historical documents, much of early film production has been lost and film history has been left to extrapolate from what remains (see, especially, Gallagher 1986). Nevertheless, Gunning argues that the 'cinema of attractions' constantly established contact with the viewer; whether it featured comedians smirking at the camera or conjurors bowing to a presumed audience, the early film was "willing to rupture a self-enclosed fictional world for a chance to solicit the attention of the spectator" (1990a: 57). The spectacle of early cinema remained in films up to the most sophisticated digital imaging available to modern film today. But, as Gunning suggests, the 'rupturing' effect 'went underground' as a device in *some* avant-garde films. Not all avant-garde films embraced such self-consciousness: it is notable, for instance, that one encouragement to read *Un Chien Andalou* as a narrative rather than an anti-narrative is that at no stage in the film is the production process revealed. The same characters and the same actors appear throughout the film and they act out the scenes without nodding to the audience, speaking to the camera operator or moving beyond the scenery in which they act. Yet, as narrative survived beyond its re-orientation by modernism, the 'rupturing' device was to find a footing in both print and film.

# 7

## POSTMODERNISM

John Fowles' novel *The French Lieutenant's Woman* was published in 1969 but deals mainly with story events that took place in the year 1867. At one point in the narrative, the heroine, Sarah Woodruffe, returns to her room and unpacks some goods she has bought. The sequence is narrated as follows:

> Slowly and carefully she lifted out one after the other a row of wrapped objects and placed them on the green cloth. Then she put the basket on the floor, and started to unwrap her purchases.
>
> She began with a Staffordshire teapot with a pretty coloured transfer of a cottage by a stream and a pair of lovers (she looked closely at the lovers); and then a Toby jug, not one of those garish-coloured monstrosities of Victorian manufacture, but a delicate little thing in pale mauve and primrose yellow, the jolly man's features charmingly lacquered by a soft blue glaze (ceramic experts may recognize a Ralph Leigh). Those two purchases had cost Sarah ninepence in an old china shop; the Toby was cracked, and was to become re-cracked in the course of time, as I can testify, having bought it myself a year or two ago for a good deal more than the three pennies Sarah

was charged. But unlike her, I fell for the Ralph Leigh part of it;
she fell for the smile.

(Fowles 1977: 241)

What is clear about this passage is that part of the narration exists as
a very conventional third-person, past tense, realist account, telling
what Sarah did in a manner that would not be alien to a history book
and which seems fitting for a novel written just over a hundred years
after the period that it depicts. Yet another part of the narration
consists of an almost unseemly interruption of the events by the
narrator, who offers first-hand information about one of Sarah's artefacts and its present-day fate. Before analysing this passage further,
it is worth saying that the narrator's comments constitute a typical
example of the 'rupturing' effect in fiction, an effect which consists
of the narrating agency revealing itself and which is frequently
called 'postmodernist'.

In such cases, the 'straightforward' realist narrative is supplemented by a voice that sometimes comments on the narrative,
sometimes overwhelms it or even undermines it. Italo Calvino's
celebrated novel *If on a winter's night a traveller* is made up of
twelve chapters, nearly all of which are preceded and followed by
a chapter devoted to commentary on reading the main narrative,
as in the opening sentences of Chapter 1: "You are about to begin
reading Italo Calvino's new novel *If on a winter's night a traveller.*
Relax. Concentrate" (1982: 9). Similarly, Tom Stoppard's play,
*The Real Inspector Hound* (1968), features two critics watching and
commenting on the performance of a 'whodunit' drama which is
itself enacted on stage. And even an episode of the final series of
the British television comedy, *One Foot in the Grave*, broadcast in
2000, cleverly implements the device. At the opening and conclusion of the episode scenes from a humorous play are shown.
The play is concerned with a cantankerous senior citizen and his
long-suffering wife who are the victims of extraordinary coinci-
dences; the set, actors, characters and situations are typical of

those of the regular *One Foot in the Grave* narratives and they mirror almost exactly the events in the life of Victor Meldrew (Richard Wilson) which make up the middle of the episode. It transpires in the narrative that the Meldrews' new cleaner has written the play whose scenes are shown; however, when she tries to vouch for the verisimilitude of the play's narrative to a potential theatrical financier he expresses his doubt at the credibility of events using Victor Meldrew's own exasperated catchphrase: "I don't believe it".

This kind of effect has been the focus of a considerable amount of commentary. Indeed, it has been suggested that there is an entire body of narrative characterized by rupturing which is known as 'metafiction'. The designation is apt because the prefix 'meta' is used to refer to levels of narrative which lie 'after', 'behind' or 'outside' the supposedly main narrative. Patricia Waugh argues that the

> increased awareness of 'meta' levels of discourse and experience is partly a consequence of increased social and cultural self-consciousness. Beyond this, however, it also reflects a greater awareness within contemporary culture of the function of language in constructing and maintaining our sense of everyday 'reality'. The simple notion that language passively reflects a coherent, meaningful and 'objective' world is no longer tenable. Language is an independent, self-contained system which generates its own meaning. ... 'Meta' terms, therefore, are required in order to explore the relationship between this arbitrary linguistic system and the world to which it apparently refers.
>
> (Waugh 1984: 3)

In a more famous formulation, the semiotician and novelist Umberto Eco suggests that the kind of avant-garde 'destruction' or superseding of past modes of representation characteristic of, say, modernism tends to reach an impasse. Eventually, instead of 'destroying' or consigning the past to the realm of oblivion or error, there must be revisiting of the past, this time avoiding the 'mistakes' that the past has made. The revisiting is therefore *ironic*:

> I think of the postmodern attitude as that of a man who loves a very cultivated woman and knows he cannot say to her, 'I love you madly', because he knows that she knows (and that she knows that he knows) that these words have already been written by Barbara Cartland. Still, there is a solution. He can say, 'As Barbara Cartland would put it, I love you madly'. At this point, having avoided false innocence, having said clearly that it is no longer possible to speak innocently, he will nevertheless have said what he wanted to say to the woman: that he loves her, but he loves her in an age of lost innocence.
>
> (Eco 1985: 67)

What is being suggested by these theorists, then, is that there is a form of expression in narrative which retains the traditional realist devices. Modernists had rebelled against realism but sought to displace the nineteenth-century forms of narrative by challenging the authoritative voice of the narrator in favour of presenting different consciousnesses. 'Metanarratives', on the other hand, do not seek simply to open up realist fiction in order to present different consciousnesses or amplify the experience of commonplace events. Instead, they indicate the *re*-presentative nature of narrative in toto.

## 'META' LEVELS

This possibility of introducing a 'meta' level of narrative is the result of distinct capacities of narration to be found in some languages. The French linguist Émile Benveniste identified two orders of language use which bear directly on narrative and meta-narrative. One of these was *histoire*, a 'historical' utterance character-izing past events, without any intervention of the speaker. The historian using such utterances, argues Benveniste, will not use per-sonal pronouns such as *je* or *tu*; instead, everything will be imper-sonal and, importantly, the present moment of the utterance will be excluded. An alternative form of utterance is *discours*, which takes place in the present tense, assuming "a speaker and hearer, and in the speaker, the intention of influencing the hearer in some way" (Benveniste 1971: 209). The point of this separation for some narra-tive theorists is that *discours* corresponds to the kind of 'meta' level where the narrator of a novel such as *The French Lieutenant's Woman* enters the action and relates his knowledge of a ceramic pot; *histoire* consists of presenting the laying out of objects on a table by a charac-ter, for example, without mentioning that one is narrating, and pos-sibly creating a situation whereby "the events seem to narrate themselves" (Benveniste 1971: 208; see also Easthope 1983: 41–7, Silverman 1983: 43–53, Lapsley and Westlake 1988: 49–52 and Metz 1982: 91–3).

Something similar to the separation of *discours* and *histoire* is to be witnessed in film, although it should be noted that the precise fit of these capacities of language with cinematic narration has been questioned (see Bordwell 1985: 21–4). Alfred Hitchcock's *Spellbound* (1945), for example, contains at least one sequence that indicates different levels of narration. In the penultimate scene of the film, initially narrated by means of a conventional shot and countershot, Constance (Ingrid Bergman) reveals to Dr Murchison (Leo G. Carroll) that she has found out he is a mur-derer. Consequently, he pulls a gun on her and she tentatively makes to leave the room, trying to convince Dr Murchison that he will not commit a second, premeditated murder that will call into question the possibility that he committed the first while suffering mental illness. At the climactic moment the narration proceeds with a shot which clearly comes from Dr Murchison's position, showing the barrel of the gun following Constance as she crosses the room to the door. As she leaves, the gun is reversed by Dr Murchison's hand; he pulls the trigger and fires straight into the camera. Undoubtedly, this indicates that he commits suicide; but it also plays upon the untenability of *really* firing into a camera without destroying it and the fact that this is a *movie* subject to specific modes of *narration*.

It is telling, too, that most films cannot sustain the equivalent of *discours* throughout their duration. They constantly require some level of *histoire* and frequently move from one level to another as smoothly as possible. Spike Lee's *Do the Right Thing* (1989) is a skilful example of this. In one scene, Pino (John Turturro) and Mookie (Spike Lee) attempt to discuss why Pino professes to hate black people, yet his favourite celebrities in sport and show business are African Americans. The scene takes place in the pizza parlour, a recurrent location in the film, and is presented in conventional shot/countershot mode. However, as soon as the conversation ends on an aggressive and inconclusive note, there is a cut to a series of short scenes populated by one character, beginning with Mookie. In each of these, an individual of a more or less recognizable ethnicity is featured in an outdoor location; the camera zooms in on him and he delivers to the camera a tirade of specific racial invective: Mookie delivers an angry monologue of racial stereotypes of Italians, Pino does the same for African Americans, an Irish American police operative rages about Hispanics, a Korean shop-owner rails against Jews, and so on. All of these, in speaking to the camera, expose the act of narration. However, before returning to the mode of *histoire* in the pizza parlour, the sequence is completed by an intermediary scene. The local DJ (Samuel L. Jackson), who acts as a chorus in the rest of the film, delivers his own impassioned monologue in which he calls for people to cool off. At first sight, the narration looks exactly like that of the previous sequence. Yet it becomes clear that the camera does not zoom in on the DJ; rather *he* 'zooms' towards the camera in his castor-equipped chair. Nor is he looking at the camera; his eyes are covered by dark sunglasses and he is working at his console. His speech is not even addressed to the camera as in the previous scenes; as DJ, his microphone and broadcasting equipment allow him to speak to the other characters in the community depicted by the film. It is an example of *histoire* disguised as *discours*.

This smooth movement from *discours* to *histoire* in film actually reveals something significant about the written example which commenced this chapter. The passage from *The French Lieutenant's Woman* seems to begin with conventional *histoire*, only to be ruptured by *discours* as the narrator explicitly enters the scene. However, it is worth noting that the narrator's presence seems to be phased in gradually in the passage. In the second paragraph, it is narrated in brackets that Sarah "looked closely at the lovers". Who decided to narrate this and why was it put in brackets? Is it an aside or is it something significant about the love story in the rest of the novel? Then details of the Toby jug are narrated: it is not one of "those garish-coloured monstrosities of Victorian manufacture". The word "those" is an instance of the phenomenon known as *deixis* in linguistics, a term which is derived from the Greek word meaning 'to point'. Thus 'those' is a word like 'I', 'you', 'this' and 'these' which cannot be understood simply on its own within a discourse but which *points* to a solid context usually outside the discourse (see Lyons 1981: 171–242). Such a context needs to be known by both speaker and listener and, in this case, it is as if the narrator is nodding to the implied reader in order to indicate that 'we' both know that some Victorian pots are "garish-coloured monstrosities". From the interpolation "ceramics experts might recognize a Ralph Leigh", in which an explicit appeal is made to an implied reader but *not* some real readers who are not ceramic experts, it becomes obvious that the narrator has intruded and made apparent that this sequence *is* narrated.

Yet the fact that questions might already have been raised in the smooth transition from *histoire* to *discours* poses problems. If it is possible to ask 'Who decided to narrate this and why was it put in brackets?', it is just as easy to ask of the first two sentences 'Who sees fit to say that Sarah slowly and carefully lifted out one after the other a row of wrapped objects and placed them on a green cloth?' or, 'Why is it important that she put the basket on the floor and started to unwrap her purchases?' As with film or any form of *re*-presentation, there is the possibility that the beholder of the *re*-presentation will calculate that while one scene is narrated, another is left out; while one character is the focus of scrutiny, another is not; and while one view of events is offered, another view of the same incidents might have been possible. All this is to say that, although the mode of *histoire* operates to *efface* the act of narration, the outcome is not successful. If narration were completely effaced, the audience of narrative would imagine that the events they behold *really happened* as depicted. Such a response is rare and takes place only in special circumstances.

Owing to the long tradition of storytelling in Western culture, readers are well aware of the act of narration, even in modes which make futile attempts to efface it. Indeed, as the work of the Bakhtin school is at pains to point out, narration is one of many discourses which cannot possibly close itself off; it cannot be 'monologic' because it is always orientated to an 'other' (see Vološinov 1973), and because it entails a narrator and characters it is heteroglot in nature. Put another way, *histoire*, like *discours*, also assumes a speaker and hearer which readers are likely to recognize. The distinction between the two different orders, *discours* and *histoire*, then, does not, ultimately, enable a definitive understanding of how narrative is received. While not as explicit, perhaps, *histoire*, it appears, can be seen to demonstrate its narration just as much as *discours*. However, the distinction does indicate that further key questions need to be asked about the status of narrative and, especially, its use in the recording of facts.

## HISTORY

As we showed in Chapter 2, the work of Hayden White and others has been concerned with the way in which the relating of historical events cannot evade narrative form. It has become conventional to think that *histoire* is the most appropriate way of relating historical events; yet, *histoire* is very much a narrative mode. Indeed the work of White or, more briefly, the comments of David Lodge on the writing of the historian Thomas Carlyle reveal this quite clearly. *Pace* Benveniste, they show that novelistic methods have been quite common in historical discourse and have been accepted in the past (see White 1973 and Lodge 1992: 201–5). Ultimately, however, the fact that narrative is woven into history but is associated with poetic exposition entails the blurring of the common-sense distinction of 'fiction' and 'nonfiction'. If there are two broad categories of writing designated by the terms 'non-fiction' and 'fiction', one might assume that they are fundamentally different. Fiction could be said to deal with imagined events while non-fiction takes as its raw material facts about the real world. Yet even if this is correct, such a definition does not take into account the shared factors such as narrative tropes in their respective articulations of their raw material.

In America, especially, in the two decades leading up to the 1980s, postmodernist writers challenged notions concerned with the status of the non-fictional. Novels by Truman Capote, E. L. Doctorow, Norman Mailer and William Styron among others dealt with documentary subjects in innovative ways. Treating real events or real people within imaginary situations or imaginary people in historical situations, these works served to problematize the distinction of fiction and non-fiction. Summarizing the reflections of one of the exponents of such work, Tom Wolfe, David Lodge identifies four techniques of the 'non-fiction novel':

(1) telling the story through scenes rather than summary; (2) preferring dialogue to reported speech; (3) presenting the

events from the point of view of a participant rather than from some impersonal perspective; (4) incorporating the kind of details about people's appearance, clothes, possessions, body language etc., which act as indices of class, character, status and social milieu in the realistic novel.

(Lodge 1992: 204)

Using the same techniques, less valorized texts such as Irving Stone's books or Alex Haley's *Roots* (1976) also demonstrated the narrowness of the line between biography and novel, "the extent to which the discourse of the historian and that of the imaginative writer overlap" (White 1987: 121).

Nevertheless, it is worth adding that the similarity of signs in fiction and signs in non-fiction is not simply based on a general understanding of their work in depicting. Even those signs in historical accounts which eschew the excessive use of Lodge's and Wolfe's four techniques nevertheless will tend to do something more in the act of *re*-presentation: it is likely that they will demonstrate a propensity to narrativize, to incorporate a trajectory in their sequence of signs. Consider the following two passages taken almost at random from separate non-fictional works:

It is a paradox that no important people or forces in France of 1789 wanted revolution. Revolutions may begin, as wars often begin, not because people positively want them. They happen because people want other things that, in a certain set of circumstances, implicate them in revolution or war.

(Thomson 1966: 24)

The governance of a modern society is an enormous task. In Great Britain, for example, half of the nation's national income flows through the hands of the government, and some 30 per cent of the labour force are employed in the state sector. Government is therefore 'big business'.

(Byrne 1981: 17)

What both of these texts manifest is an orientation to narrative. Both contain over-arching statements about the way that things *are* in the world that they describe. However, and more importantly, the statements are about motivation, offering a driving narrative force behind what they are presumably going to discuss: the role of people's desires in revolution and the role of business in national governance.

While these examples seem to concentrate on verifiable fact, there are some non-fictional discourses which take matters a step further. John Lukacs' avowedly narrative history of events in eighty days of 1940, *The Duel* (1990), does not shrink from a narrative thrust and goes so far as to state the motivating factors in the minds of Hitler and Churchill at the time. In postmodern 'non-fiction novels' or 'faction' narratives, such depiction of protagonists' motivations is even more conspicuous. The acknowledgements signed by Truman Capote at the beginning of *In Cold Blood* (1966) testify that the work is based throughout on official documents or interviews pertaining to the real-life case that it relates (Capote 1966: 9); thus, like Lukacs' *The Duel*, speculations on characters' thoughts in Capote's account are likely to be the result of scrutiny of such artefacts as diary entries or transcripts. *In Cold Blood* does begin with a recounting of knowable facts, as might be expected; and it does go on to give details of verbatim dialogue which, at least sometimes, might have been derived from the historical record; but, crucially, it also presents the *thoughts and feelings* of the protagonists. More telling still are those sequences when the narration not only presents thoughts but shifts to a mode of free indirect discourse or *skaz*:

A thousand people! Perry was impressed. He wondered how much the funeral had cost. Money was greatly on his mind, though not as relentlessly as it had been earlier in the day – a day he had begun 'without the price of a cat's miaow'. The situation had improved since then; thanks to Dick, he and Dick

> now possessed a 'pretty fair stake' – enough to get them to
> Mexico.
>     Dick! Smooth. Smart. Yes, you had to hand it to him. Christ
> it was incredible how he could 'con a guy'.
>
> (Capote 1966: 194)

The presence of such sequences in the account of events entailed
that, for many, *In Cold Blood* was an affront. As Sauerberg (1991:
20ff.) shows, critics felt that Capote had not been loyal to the
objective standards of historical truth, a particularly fraught matter in this case because the narrative dealt with multiple murder
and the families of the victims were still alive. Capote was
thought to be guilty of adding literary embellishments which
were felt inappropriate to a work of non-fiction and, indeed, *In
Cold Blood* was transferred to the catalogue of *fiction* in the 1980s
by its British publisher.

That such 'literary' flourishes could upset the fragile distinction between fiction and non-fiction in narrative is probably
unsurprising. As Bruner points out "The fact that the historian's
'empirical' account and the novelist's imaginary story *share* the
narrative form ... has challenged thoughtful students of imaginative literature and of history since Aristotle" (1990: 45).
Speculation on protagonists' psychologies seems to follow natu-
rally from the use of narrative devices; narrative, from its oral origins, has been inextricably tied to the actions of characters.
Psychology therefore adds to the 'motivation' of the character and
the narrative. Yet the assault on the dividing line of fiction and
non-fiction which took place in the latter decades of the twentieth century, and of which such psychological speculation is a part,
appears especially concerted because it came as part of a larger
context in which narrative is implicated: postmodernism.

## THE DECLINE OF THE 'GRAND NARRATIVE'

Narrative is absolutely crucial to an understanding of postmodernism. Yet, like modernism, postmodernism is a slippery concept which evades definition. Additionally, definitions are hampered by the fact that postmodernism co-exists with a phenomenon called 'modernity' or, sometimes, 'postmodernity', the latter of which is important for understanding 'postmodernist' narrative and narrative as a whole, especially in its relation to history. For the purposes of focus, it should be mentioned that, in some quarters, a critical consensus seems to be forming on what postmodernism and (post)modernity are. In (post)modernity, there exists a new set of material conditions arising from a decline in mass production in favour of flexible specialization; a sovereignty of information and service industries over the traditional products of manufacture; an emphasis on consumption rather than production; the dissolution of traditional, class-based politics into politics centred on 'identities'; and the development of communication technologies which have served to shrink distances between people across the globe and have made representations much more accessible (for an account of these changes, see Harvey 1988 and Bertens 1995). In fact, this last feature of postmodernity has been so important for narrative and, reciprocally, has made narrative so important for postmodernity, that it requires some detailed comment later in this chapter. *Postmodernism*, on the other hand, is generally thought to consist of the styles of representation and the characteristics of critical thinking which result from, or co-exist with, the material conditions of postmodernity (Hutcheon 1989: 23–42); indeed, Fredric Jameson (1991) has dubbed postmodernism 'the cultural logic of late capitalism'.

The 'rupturing' effect which we have observed, or what Hutcheon suggests is "the simultaneous inscribing and subverting of the conventions of narrative" (1989: 49), can undoubtedly be analysed as part of a postmodernist cultural 'logic'. Yet it might also be observed that this and other narrative devices in the postmodern armoury are by no means to be considered new innovations. Eighteenth-century narrative and indeed early film are renowned for utilizing all manner of rupturing devices and copiously employing *discours*. Sterne's *The Life and Opinions of Tristram Shandy*, which was discussed in Chapter 3, is one of the most well-known examples of an early novel which uses, but at the same time dramatizes the conventional problems of, mimetic representation in narrative. *Tristram Shandy* can be seen as a response to a 'crisis' in representation as the novel form of narrative sought to stake out its territory; the recurrence of rupturing devices in postmodernism might similarly lead to the conclusion that narrative in the late twentieth century underwent a similar crisis. There are, however, significant differences between the moment of the early novel and the postmodern 'condition'.

Famously, for Jean-François Lyotard, the issue which to a great extent defines the postmodern condition is knowledge. Narrative form is central here because, as we have seen, the origins of narrative are to be found in the need of ancient oral cultures for a means to store knowledge. Lyotard recapitulates this point for postmodernity, asserting that "narration is the quintessential form of customary knowledge" (1984: 19). For him, narrative is not only the means for storage but, additionally, it has come to pervade almost every aspect of human knowledge. He identifies four aspects of narrative in society which indicate its knowledge function (1984: 20–1). First, the actions of a hero in a narrative are important: the hero's recurrent failure or success in narratives indicates the legitimacy or otherwise of certain goals, outcomes or institutions within that society. Second, narrative lends itself to a great variety of 'language games'; not only does narrative include statements which describe its 'content', it also contains statements which suggest what is to be done about these described contents. Plato had drawn out the didactic orientation of mimesis and we have seen how this inclination continued to exist through the development of the novel. Lyotard suggests that didacticism is woven into the fabric of narrative by way of such devices as questions posed and then answered, or evaluations offered or implied by the actions and statements of protagonists, for example.

Like Bruner, Lyotard insists on a third aspect of narrative, the rules of the "pragmatics of transmission". That is to say that narratives imply a speaker or narrator, a protagonist and a listener. Indeed, Lyotard's comments on this issue seem to have important implications for human subjects and their relation to knowledge. As Readings suggests, the pragmatics of transmission can mean that there is no subject position outside of narrative (1991: 67). Lyotard explains this with an anthropological example: he refers to the way in which storytellers from the South American Indian tribe, the Cashinahua, rely on a formula for commencing and concluding a tale. In fact, the formula to which Lyotard refers is precisely the kind discussed at length by Lord and which is evident in *The Odyssey*; a formula in which the storyteller might identify him/herself and the listener of the story, adding, crucially, that this is the story as it has been told many times before. Although, as we have seen, Lord is keen to credit the oral storyteller with at least some measure of creative authorship, Lyotard's point is that *narrative* assigns roles to its 'pragmatic' participants. Narrative has a tendency to formulate knowledge such that "it determines in a single stroke what one must say in order to be heard, what one must listen to in order to speak, and what role one must play ... to be the object of a narrative" (Lyotard 1984: 21). For Lyotard, the fact that humans, especially in their relation to knowledge, *inhabit* narrative means that they are also compelled to occupy those roles offered to them which are a necessary part of the narrative form.

Fourth, narrative is bound up with human perceptions of time. Narrative form clearly involves a foreshortening of the world, a *re*-presentation in which, at its simplest, there is a beginning, *detours* in the middle and an end. Enshrined also in narrative, from its formulaic oral origins, is a repeatable pattern manifest in either simple phrases such as "wine-dark sea" or in more complicated configurations of rhythm at the level of sentences, paragraphs or entire episodes. For Lyotard, this entails that narratives pass on knowledge without the receivers of the knowledge necessarily being aware of it in the customary sense. It is as if the message is in the rhythm itself, as in the way one can remember nursery rhymes taught to one as an infant or proverbs with their formulaic knowledge which make up the currency of everyday life. Where memory might be thought to exist by way of an ability to recount the strict linear sequence of events in time, Lyotard suggests that, instead, the rhythms of narrative provide a new temporalization. "A stitch in time, saves nine" is a little narrative of the virtues of quick action and the benefits of prevention over cure. However, it is likely that it is remembered not simply because of the wisdom contained therein but because of the easily recalled rhythm and rhyme. Furthermore, the knowledge it encapsulates may have been specific to a 'primal' moment in time when the analogy between sewing and immediate preventative action was made; but this relation to time is exceeded by the fact that the proverb relates most pressingly to the here and now. Like Ricoeur, then, Lyotard sees in narrative the ability to render time in the services of *memory* and *expectation*.

In general, for Lyotard, narrative has been crucial for human existence because it has been the pre-eminent form of representation, allowing the world to be apprehended in a specific form by humans, recording the details of a culture, but also *legitimating* its own arrangement or *re*-presentation of that culture. Narratives, he writes, "define what has the right to be said and done in the culture in question, and since they are themselves part of that culture, they are legitimated by the fact that they do what they do" (Lyotard 1984: 23). Narrative has not had sovereignty over all representation, however. In its oral form it is generally thought to have been less beneficial in recording the more abstract knowledge which is characteristic of science and, as we have seen, written forms took on the latter task. Nevertheless, Lyotard argues that scientific knowledge, especially in the last few centuries, has sought to legitimate itself not by validating its own internal procedures but by appealing to a narrative outside itself, a 'grand narrative'. Among these he lists narratives driven by "the dialectics of Spirit, the hermeneutics of meaning, the emancipation of the rational or working subject, or the creation of wealth" (1984: xxiii); but, in general, he sees two grand narratives at work in the legitimation of science. One is associated with the Enlightenment and is concerned with human emancipation from bondage and oppression; the other is the philosophical narrative associated with the development of a more self-conscious human being or an evolved 'Spirit'. In short, scientific knowledge has justified itself by referring to, and placing itself within, a narrative of progression to the greater human good.

In Lyotard's own narrative of the development of scientific knowledge, a range of factors contribute to a changed situation in the second part of the twentieth century. The reliance of 'modern' science on 'grand narratives' or 'metanarratives', as he sometimes calls them, and which we should not confuse with our earlier use of the term to describe features of postmodern fiction, gave way to a postmodern condition. "Simplifying in the extreme", he writes, "I define *postmodern* as incredulity toward metanarratives" (1984: xxiv). Developments took place in the last fifty years of the twentieth century which forced Lyotard to report that "The narrative function is losing its functors, its great hero, its great dangers, its great voyages, its great goal" (1984: xxiv). "The grand narrative has lost its credibility", he adds "regardless of what mode of unification it uses, regardless of whether it is a speculative narrative or a narrative of emancipation" (37). Somewhat notoriously, Lyotard is vague about the material causes of the decline of grand narratives and this has enabled a plethora of commentators on postmodernity to augment his somewhat sketchy comments, identifying features in society such as the demand for specialized production resulting from postwar economic policies which encouraged citizens to enjoy goods and services; and the emphasis on consumption, self-determination and identity politics (see, for example, Kaplan 1988, Connor 1989 and Giddens 1991).

What is clear is that the devices witnessed in postmodern narrative fiction appeared at a time when there was a broader questioning of the functions of narrative, not just in narrative fiction but in the much wider field of knowledge. Thus the questions presupposed in the implementations of such devices made postmodernist narrative fiction different in quality from previous manifestations of the 'rupturing' effect. In the practice of history, especially, there were debates over the ability of narrative to provide a guarantee of the veracity of that which it *re*-presented. These debates took place during the same period in which the notion that narrative was a self-perpetuating phenomenon advertising its own truth was undermined in fiction. Simultaneous with both, scientific knowledge was called into question for the way in which it relied on a 'grand narrative' which no longer spoke to the localized, 'little' narratives of personal pleasures, identity and circumstances. Famously, Kuhn (1970) argued that science, rather than being concerned with absolute truth, was more a matter of a paradigm which might change from one epoch to another. Such a paradigm or conceptual framework would be accompanied by set practices which dictated the procedure and findings of scientists. Succeeding all of these, the idea was abroad in the 1990s that narrative was in its final throes largely as a result of the 'triumph' of liberalism and capitalism witnessed in the fall of Communist regimes, and that the grander narratives of human emancipation which such regimes promised would be superseded by highly individual narratives sustained by the market (see Fukuyama 1992). The extent to which postmodernity is a long-range phenomenon and the extent to which the fall of Communism represents an 'end' of large historical narratives is highly questionable (see, especially, Eagleton 1996). Moreover, as Klaus Bruhn Jensen, echoing Marshall McLuhan, puts it "Postmodernism is itself a grand narrative, announcing the death of another grand narrative in its rearview mirror" (1995: 11). However, the fate of contemporary narrative has been greatly affected by a general phenomenon which is identified as part of the postmodern mosaic.

## NEW TECHNOLOGIES

Writers on postmodernism hold that, in the late twentieth century, grand narratives ceased to be 'grand' any longer and that history was no longer sustainable by traditional historical discourse. At the same time, commentators such as Jean Baudrillard see the same period as dominated by the constant action of signs referring to themselves in an all-encompassing realm of 'simulation', where signs take on value not because they refer to real, material things in the world but because they refer only to each other (Baudrillard 1981, 1983, 1988, 1995). What is clear is that technologies which reproduced signs and, in particular, narrative signs, developed rapidly in the twentieth century and made diverse narratives more familiar, more frequent and brought them within easy reach. Some of these technologies were certainly not designed simply to be the bearers of narratives and continued to perform functions which did not necessarily require narrative organization. However, the extent to which narrative suffused new technologies was notable.

Radio is a good case in point. It is a technology which results from the ability to transmit messages in the form of electromagnetic waves through the air, its most famous early application being that of the Marconi company which transmitted Morse code across the Atlantic in 1901. This system of communication had obvious military uses but the main manifestation of radio came through domestic wireless sets. By the 1930s, following a boom in radio transmissions in the 1920s, practically every home in the advanced industrial West had a radio set (Cardwell 1994: 397). In the United States commercial radio stations brought music, the voice of news, documentary features and a great deal of fictional narrative into the home; in Europe, similar kinds of radio transmissions were dominated by public institutions. What characterized radio as a medium was that its messages were transmitted from a central location, yet they arrived in masses of specific places: sometimes in factories but, more often than not, in individual homes. From the outset, then, it was not unusual for listeners to be engaged in something else in addition to listening to the radio.

As an 'invisible' or 'sightless' medium, sounds on radio needed to be more nuanced than in other media. One of these customary sounds, music, has always been a staple of the medium; but the spoken word and *how* it was spoken are crucial. It is frequently observed that the domestic location of the wireless set encouraged an informal tone of speech on radio, the employment of conversational patterns and the maintenance of closeness, warmth and a sense of connection with the audience (see, for example, Shingler and Wieringa 1998: 35–6). This was to have repercussions, too, as radio transmitted narratives. Radio developed its own version of a narrative format which had previously been associated with the novel: the serial. This consisted of equal-length episodes which would be broadcast at regular intervals, perhaps weekly or daily. Such serials as *The Shadow*, broadcast by CBS in the United States, or *Fu Manchu*, broadcast by the BBC in Britain, gained a strong following in the 1930s. Yet such narrative serials differed from their novelistic counterparts. Radio sought to encourage the listener's creation of images in a fashion thought to be similar to that of the same action performed by printed words on a page. But, as with oral narrative, the images could not be checked, re-checked and memorized by flicking back a few pages.

Radio, especially in serial drama, therefore had to resort to a formula: repetition, a small ensemble of characters, an emphasis on the conversational patterns of scene as opposed to more abstract summary and a limiting of sub-plots (cf. Shingler and Wieringa 1998: 72–87). On the other hand, radio serials had the advantage of being able to elaborate their scenes without the restrictions of time, space and money; that is to say, the medium had no need of elaborate sets and costumes, and the actors' dialogue was used, where necessary, to conjure an image of distant times and places. Because the medium was so new, dramatic narrative on radio, like that on film, initially relied on pre-existing models; as John Drakakis notes "early practice measured itself against that of the traditional live theatre" (1981: 111). Nevertheless, one of the most famous radio broadcasts in the history of the medium exploited to the utmost the lack of visible scene settings. Orson Welles' single-episode adaptation of H. G. Wells' *War of the Worlds* (broadcast in 1938) presented the narrative of an extra-terrestrial invasion through a series of simulated news broadcasts, a narrative device which was so powerful that it actually caused some panic among listeners (see Cantril et al. 1940).

The reliance of radio wholly upon sound meant that narrative could maintain an important presence in the domestic environment. Yet its dominion was exceeded by the visual technology of television. The possibility of transmitting moving images and sound was first realized by way of broadcasting antennae which sent radio waves through the air to a receiver. From the 1950s onwards experiments with transmission through cable continued and, in the 1990s, more precise sound and images for television were to be produced digitally. These developments in enhancing the medium reveal the importance of its visual nature; as Corner and Harvey put it

tele-vision (literally 'seeing at a distance') seemed even more miraculously to bridge the gap between world and home, opening out a corner of the home onto a range of changing

> vistas, recorded and live, in a way which initially had all the allure of magic. Like radio, it too was a 'sociable' medium, often addressing the viewer as a member of a known community, sometimes perhaps as a friend. However, it was the 'sights' that television offered – variously mundane, extraordinary, intimate, grand, informative and thrilling – which gave it its distinctive identity and force as a cultural technology.
>
> (Corner and Harvey 1996: xi)

Unlike cinema, where one was required to buy a ticket for a publicly received spectacle in a darkened theatre where one would witness a large image for a delimited duration of time, television messages were transmitted to the home, were displayed on a small screen and were largely continuous (see Ellis 1992: 111–2). The domestic availability of television was very much part of its sense of contemporaneity, its 'nowness' (Fiske 1987: 145; Ellis 1992: 145), especially as so many of its transmissions were concerned with 'live' events.

As television sets became affordable domestic commodities in the 1950s and 1960s, television was marketed as a commodity which enabled a communal experience to take place in the relative isolation of the home. Television brought another world into the domestic sphere, but broadcasters wished to provide narratives which were as familiar and unthreatening as possible. Programmers developed the 'family situation comedy' in which humorous events in the unchanging lives and environments of an American family could be played out weekly in episodic form (Spigel 1992: 142–6). Sacrificing some aspects of the world in the act of providing unity, harmony and continuous action, it is precisely this form of narrative *re*-presentation which is satirized in the film *Pleasantville* mentioned in Chapter 1.

The domestic bearing of television also entailed that its narratives were, in general, less heroic in the grand sense. Like radio, but unlike film, writing and oral modes, the immediacy and domesticity of television lent itself to informality. Raymond Williams argues that postwar British and American television drama is characterized by "the 'exploring eye' of the camera, the feel for everyday ordinary life, the newly respected rhythms of the speech of work and the streets and of authentic privacy" (1974: 57). Numerous analysts of television go further than this, suggesting that television narratives in the second part of the twentieth century consistently fulfilled a 'bardic function' (Fiske and Hartley 1978: 85–100); that is to say, like the oral poets who sustained cultures by disseminating their own stories to them, television became a central institution of society, circulating and reinforcing commonly held views, acting as the foremost producer of 'consensus narrative' (Thorburn 1988: 56–62).

The extent to which this 'bardic' function is real depends on one's view of the extent to which television narratives are involved in expressing and reinforcing consensual values. Researchers have found, for instance, that, as a domestic appliance, television is treated in quite a cavalier fashion by its users, and by no means commands undivided attention to the narratives it disseminates (see, for example, Morley 1986). What is certain, however, is that television has been responsible for the diffusion of a *huge amount* of narratives as well as a diversification in their form. Writing well before the mushrooming of academic discourse regarding postmodernism, Raymond Williams argued that

> In societies like Britain or the United States more drama is watched in a week or weekend, by the majority of viewers, than would have been watched in a year or in some cases a lifetime in any previous historical period. It is not uncommon for the majority of viewers to see, regularly, as much as two or three hours of drama, of various kinds, every day ... It is clearly one of the unique characteristics of advanced industrial societies that drama as an experience is an intrinsic part of everyday life.
>
> (Williams 1974: 59)

Despite the use of the term 'drama', Williams is clearly referring to fictional narrative here. If plain 'narrative' is substituted for 'drama', however, the phenomenon Williams identifies becomes even more pronounced. Where cinema is dominated by fictional narrative despite the occasional production of prize-winning documentaries, television is characterized by its ample presentation of both fiction and non-fiction. "Any model of televisual narration", writes Ellis, "would have to give pride of place to this division of TV products" (1992: 145). Furthermore, non-fiction on television is overwhelmingly presented within a narrative format. As Kozloff adds, "the only television formats that consistently eschew narrative are those that are highly structured according to their own alternate rules: game shows, exercise shows, news conferences, talk shows, musical performances, sports contests" (1992: 69). Indeed, it is not difficult to argue that even these formats usually contain at least an element of narrativity.

In spite of this emphasis on the diversity and number of television narratives it is nevertheless worth mentioning a couple of recurrent features. Like radio, which had extended the form from the novel, television presents serial narratives. Some of these last the length of a season, such as adaptations of classic novels; others, such as the British drama *Coronation Street*, which notched up forty years at the top of the television ratings in December 2000, are more long-running. The first type of serial comes to some kind of conclusion, but the second kind delays a definitive ending: "Its characteristic mode is not one of closure or totalising vision; rather it offers a continuous refiguration of events" (Ellis 1992: 147). This latter point is noteworthy not only in itself but also because it is illustrative of a great deal of television output, including non-fictional genres such as news and current affairs.

The other narrative form in which television specializes, especially in fiction, is the series. Usually this will revolve around one or more characters in a basic situation which does not fundamentally change from week to week. The USS Enterprise is on a "five-year mission" in *Star Trek*, itself a fact worth iterating because, like many television series, the underlying narrative drive is the traditional theme of 'the journey'. However, as with other series, the situation and range of regular characters in each episode of *Star Trek* is basically the same. Rather than coming to a conclusion, a single adventure with a beginning, *detours* and a denouement is presented each week in the series, with the characters' 'seriality' guaranteeing that neither death or a total life change will prevent the steady repetition of their escapades. There *have* been a few notable exceptions to this pattern: the final episode of the long-running US comedy *M\*A\*S\*H\**, set in a mobile hospital during the Korean War, narrated the return of the protagonists to their homes and the end of a war that had actually lasted for less time than the series ran on television; similarly, the concluding episode of the British series, *The Prisoner*, saw the protagonist, No. 6, escape from the Village where he had been imprisoned by the government for the entire series and reveal at least some of the mystery behind his torment. Yet the series and serial formats as described in general terms here have been integral to television narrative and have been so also because they are excellent means of conforming to a certain length. The half-hour comedy series on a commercial channel, for example, contributes to a schedule by consisting of two 12.5 minute parts, preceded, followed and split by an advertising break.

In consonance with the institution of the serial and series, the characteristic of television which has been found most notable is its continuity or, in the formulation of Williams, its "flow". For him, this is the chief experience and the "defining characteristic of broadcasting, simultaneously as a technology and as a cultural form" (1974: 86). The idea of the television 'programme' was derived from the experience of an individual concert or theatrical performance; yet a collection of programmes actually becomes a 'flow' because it is not just one narrative but a sequence of different kinds of narratives or narrative plus non-narrative programming. Television, rather than yielding to the exigencies of narrative alone, is, above all, dictated by a schedule "modeled on the modern working week – day time, prime time, late night or weekend" (Mellencamp 1990: 240). Indeed, as Williams points out (1974: 91–3) in a prediction that has come to pass, an individual narrative on television might be broken up by commercial breaks and even trailers for other programmes. This kind of description of television flow emphasizes the extent to which the medium does not command the kind of attention to narrative that a delimited event such as cinema does. Moreover, the increasing use of remote control handsets has enabled television viewers, with a minimum of effort, to 'zap' or change channel from the flow of one schedule to the flow of another, and, possibly, to 'graze', enjoying a narrative or part of one before going on to another or part of one.

These aspects of television which distinguish it from cinema or theatre, might be seen to assault the 'integrity' of narratives by making them susceptible to 'undisciplined' reading. In the last two decades of the twentieth century, however, homes adopted further technologies which had the potential to restore 'traditional' modes of reading. The availability and rapid uptake of home video cassette recorders (VCRs) in the 1980s meant that 'flow' could be interrupted. The schedules of television which collude with the temporalization of work might be circumvented by recording a programme broadcast during the day in order that it might be viewed during an evening, a phenomenon known as 'timeshifting' (Cubitt 1991). Also, a programme on one channel might be recorded with a VCR in order to allow the viewer to watch a programme on a different channel at the same time. Programmes might also be singled out for recording not only in order that they could be watched later but also, if they are shown on a commercial channel, so that advertising breaks could be edited out or elided by way of fast-forwarding. The particularly keen viewer, like the reader of a book, might even also *rewind* certain sequences in a narrative to check details or re-experience their narration.

Following the proliferation of VCRs in the home, satellite and cable television companies attempted to appeal to television viewers' preference for specific kinds of narratives and modes of viewing. In the final years of the twentieth century companies began to offer particular 'themed' channels; these included non-narrative programming such as sports events, as well as narrative programming: films, documentaries, classic drama and other narrative forms. In the early years of the twenty-first century, some companies have taken advantage of digital technologies and offer a range of mixed programming, the difference from regular channels being that the viewer may select the exact *times* that s/he wishes to watch individual programmes; other companies promise to arrange compilations of programmes on the basis of narrative and non-narrative genres favoured by the paying viewer.

Ultimately, the foolproof means of maintaining audience investment sought by the economic interests involved in producing programming for radio, terrestrial, cable, satellite and digital television was not to be found. As with the audience for oral narrative whose collective mind could be elsewhere, or the reader of written narrative who skips some pages and reads the denouement, or the radio listener who is more concerned with chopping vegetables, or the television viewer who keeps nipping out to make a cup of tea, narratives among specialized programming could be ignored or given only partial attention, or even recorded with the viewer fast-forwarding through sequences s/he did not care to see. Nevertheless, many narratives continued to be produced, in television and elsewhere, which retained the traditional virtues of a beginning, *detours* and conclusive endings.

The way that film, television and radio embodied narrative had profound effects on twentieth-century consciousness. Each medium contributed to the proliferation of narratives and each made narratives so much more accessible than they had been in previous epochs. 'Flow' in television and, to a lesser extent, in radio meant that audience members could 'tune in to' and 'tune out of' narrative in their own homes and almost at will. This did not necessarily mean that individuals lost the ability to find narrative captivating; but it did mean that narrative no longer assumed a commanding public role. This was compounded by the fact that these new technologies also problematized the role of 'authorship' and 'authority' in narrative. Despite the attempt of film theorists to posit an 'auteur' of movies, film narrative continued to be produced largely as a result of its form rather than, or even in spite of, its auteurs. For this reason, the analyses of Bordwell and other 'formalists' is most important. Similarly, radio's distinctive voice and that of the companies responsible for broadcasting it were arguably as important as individual, named narratives. Yet perhaps the most serious undermining of the concept of the author came from television. Its 'bardic' bearing, based on formats rather than individual producing consciousnesses, and the fact that so many bodies such as television companies, channels, actors, directors, camera operatives and so forth are involved in the production and broadcasting of its narratives means that a traditional notion of 'authorship' in the medium is untenable.

Specifically, television programming and the technologies which supplemented it had had three important consequences for the development of narrative. First, the widespread uptake of television in the West, to the extent that the television set not only took up one space in the domestic environment by the end of the twentieth century but also took up others in kitchens and children's bedrooms, for example, meant that opportunities to witness narratives proliferated on an unprecedented basis. Second, those myriad narratives were not only fictional; they were also non-fictional, such as those presented by the flagship of programming, news and current affairs. The narrative nature of the bulk of non-fictions became more familiar than it had ever been, and on a much greater scale than could be achieved by the work of historiographers or non-fiction novelists. Third, the shape of narratives in programming was dictated by the episodic requirements of scheduling and flow, which favoured open-ended serial and episodic series formats.

In the light of these developments, it is hardly surprising, then, that producers of narratives might be "oppressed by the fear that whatever they might have to say has been said before, and condemned to self-consciousness by the climate of modern culture" (Lodge 1992: 207). This emblem of postmodernism haunts *The French Lieutenant's Woman*: it is a novel whose narration is cautious of definitively pronouncing on history because of the knowledge that history partakes of what is more commonly known as a 'fictional device'; it self-consciously refers to the processes of narration and authorship; and it is wary of producing a conclusive ending. Instead, it provides *two* endings, one of which presents an unfavourable outcome for at least one of the protagonists, and one which narrates a favourable outcome for at least one of them. The narration of *The French Lieutenant's Woman* acknowledges that the novelist has traditionally stood next to God and may still do so (Fowles 1977: 85); but "There is only one good definition of God: the freedom that allows other freedoms to exist" (86). As such, the narrator does not possess a freedom born of omniscience and control of her/his characters; rather freedom is constituted to the extent that characters possess a degree of autonomy from the narrator born of their social situations.

In a fashion similar to that of fictional postmodern narratives, the freedom promised in the pursuit of knowledge since the Enlightenment has been found to have been sustained by a belief in the possibility of omniscience. Rather than proceeding unquestioned towards a point in which the human good was equated with ultimate awareness, knowledge was found to be validated, underpinned and given impetus by narratives of its own progression. Moreover, these 'grand narratives' were little different in form from the narratives consumed in large numbers in domestic settings by citizens of the West in the twentieth century.

It is interesting, then, that the undecidability which characterizes postmodern fiction anticipates the fate of narrative as it has been embodied by a further technology developed in the last decades of the twentieth century: a technology that, like radio and television, has contributed to the demise of traditional narrative authority and to new formulations of identity; a technology which has also operated in an environment in which there is increasing awareness of the characteristics of genres and an enhanced sense of the capacity for participation in narrative.

# 8

---

# IN THE END: THE BEGINNING

Following the advent of modernism, the concept of time that had been prevalent in realist narrative underwent a challenge. Realism offered what seemed a linear exposition of time, appearing to present discrete moments along a straight line of temporality but actually effacing the process of lingering or digressing in scenes, or, at the very least, making the transition from summary to scene as smooth as possible. The expansion of the 'reality effect' in scenes, narrating minor details and impressions at length that was characteristic of modernism, explicitly contravened the concept of linear time as an onward procession of equally proportioned moments. Similarly, so-called 'postmodernist' narratives often demonstrated a wariness of the formulation of history as a steadily unfolding series of events. Frequently, they coupled this with a display of awareness of the thoroughly constructed nature of narrative and the impossibility of producing true closure of time and space through the device of a conclusive ending. In the final years of the twentieth century, however, these ideas had become so commonplace that they were almost 'naturalized'; indeed, they contributed to the basic assumptions of many narratives produced by technologies which superseded and incorporated film, radio and television.

## NARRATIVE IN CYBERSPACE

In the film *Sliding Doors* (1998) Gwyneth Paltrow plays the role of a woman who lives in a London curiously uncluttered by litter, foul air and crime, who *does* and *does not* have a happy relationship with an ideal partner (John Hannah). The crux of the narrative is the moment when she is running for an underground train: in one scenario she catches the train and the pattern of events which ensues results in her happy relationship; in an alternative scenario presented by the narrative, she misses the train and the relationship does not take place. Such a notion of alternative scenarios is actually derived from the findings of some branches of quantum physics which posit a 'multiverse' or parallel, rather than singular, universe(s) (see Deutsch 1997: 32–54, 321–43). This idea that there may be not just one world where time unfolds in a linear fashion, but actually an infinite number of universes existing in tandem has become a favourite of science-fiction narratives. Another recurrent theme of science-fiction narratives, especially in the last quarter of the twentieth century, consists of the possibility that humans can be inserted into the 'physical world' of a story. In the TV series *Star Trek: The Next Generation* crew members avail themselves of the 'holodeck', a device that allows individuals temporarily to take on narrative roles such as that of Sherlock Holmes, along with an entry to the appropriate environment in which the character's actions are played out.

Both of these possibilities provide the starting point for Janet Murray's (1997) analysis of the fate of narrative after the advent of computer technology. The computer is a data-processing device whose early prototype was the 'analytic engine' devised by Charles Babbage in Britain in the 1830s. Variants of such devices were developed throughout the following century and applied to a range of military and other purposes. The *digital computer* which has become available as a business necessity and a domestic commodity since the 1980s is characterized by the tiny amount of physical space required for storing information. There are a number of implications for narrative arising from these facts. First, like television, the computer's status as a domestic appliance means that narratives and other information a computer is capable of storing or retrieving can be made available with ease. Second, the minuscule size of the physical equipment required for computing, such as a 'laptop' machine which is the size of a large-format book, coupled with the massive amount of tasks it can perform and the data it can store require a new conceptualization of space. The metaphor which has most often been used for this purpose is 'cyberspace', taken from a novel by William Gibson entitled *Neuromancer* and first published in 1984.

A third implication for narrative requires a little more explication. In the final decade of the twentieth century especially, the proliferation of computer links between individuals and organizations generated a network for transferring data known as the 'Internet'. This network is largely made up of a massive information retrieval service called the 'World Wide Web' which gives computers access to a huge number of documents connected to each other by means of a form of writing which is called 'hypertext'. Such a 'hypertext' allows words to be highlighted in 'hypertext markup language' (html) within web documents, thus indicating that specific issues to do with that topic in the text can be accessed separately by an instant transfer to another place in cyberspace. A hypertext on the topic of narrative, for example, may contain underlined words such as <u>identity</u>, <u>representation</u>, <u>time</u>, <u>space</u>, <u>signs</u> and <u>technologies</u>, indicating that other pages may be accessed which address these topics more closely.

What this means for narratives produced on Web pages should be clear: hypertext not only allows alternative endings to a narrative in a manner related to the strategy of *The French Lieutenant's Woman*, it also allows alternatives *within* the body of a narrative, "exploring what in print culture would be described as 'digressions' as long and complex as the 'main' text" (Snyder 1998:

127). The kind of reading that hypertext encourages is not new, however. The term was actually coined in the 1960s, but an old sacred text such as the Talmud, surrounded by the commentaries of religious scholars, incorporates the hypertext principle, as do many literary works characterized by an immense depth of allusion, from the *The Divine Comedy* to *The Waste Land* (Murray 1997: 91, 56). The differences between the general hypertext principle applied to written narratives and computer-generated narratives are, however, significant. Contemporary readers of such works as *The Divine Comedy* apprehended the depth of allusion by means of their affiliation to traditions whose history required an immense amount of commitment to learn and understand. Readers of computer-generated narratives, on the other hand, as they use hypertext to access pages instantly, are less likely to be committed in the same way, and perhaps know less about the genesis, heritage and traditions of specific narratives. Nevertheless, following the ascendancy of the television serial with its continuity, multiple storylines and wealth of possibilities, hypertext seems a particularly apposite development in narrative technology. Murray analyses such hypertext serial dramas as *The Spot*, in which, for example, in-depth information compiled for a specific character, can be accessed at the click of a computer mouse (1997: 86).

Given the nature of the metaphor of cyberspace as it has been applied to computer technology, it is hardly surprising that the traditional 'journey' story, a recurrent feature of narrative in other media, is prevalent on the Web (Murray 1997: 137). From *The Odyssey* onwards, journeys have unfolded as narratives, offering a series of episodes but also creating a sense of space. Likewise, because of the way that computer technology and its use encourages episodes and a conception of unfolding space, Murray also predicts that the major form of storytelling in the future will be the serial drama (1997: 254). For her, the computer is an "incunabula" (28), a technology whose major uses have not yet developed; rather like printing and the movie camera in their early days, the computer has still to find its forte in narrative. When seen as "a truly revolutionary invention humankind is just on the verge of putting to use as a spellbinding storyteller" (2), the computer offers narrative a number of possibilities.

First, Murray insists that the computer is not to be considered the enemy of writing or the book (1997: 8). For many commentators on the end of the twentieth century, the image dominates current human communication (see, for example, Denzin 1991, Collins 1992 and McRobbie 1994); yet a great many of the narratives that Murray considers are *written* ones using the benefits of hypertext. However, second, visual narratives will converge with written ones. Already, the technologies of television and the computer are starting to merge, with the Internet and email being available on the same screen as broadcasting. Along with the development of digital manipulation of images, this will have consequences for the act of *re*-presentation. For example, Murray points out that viewers of films on the Internet or on a converged TV/computer may want to follow characters out of frame and see their actions from different angles (1997: 258), in much the same way that viewers can choose a specific camera for spectating televised sports events. While digital imaging will make this possible, it should be said that the possibilities will not be infinite: as a *re*-presentation there will be some features shown and not others. Nevertheless, these developments are an indication of one crucial factor in the development of narrative: the power of the reader.

## READING NARRATIVE

The technological embodiments of narrative in the late twentieth century have forced a re-evaluation of the role of readership in narrative. Hypertext in written computer narratives makes explicit the degree of choice involved in the ways in which readers construct narratives, delineating the reader as 'agency' (cf. Murray 1997: 51, 153). This has encouraged the production of narratives by the growing number of people who have access to the relevant technology. Similarly, where print was once a medium of authority, enacted by experts on behalf of a chosen few whose work a publisher might choose to finance, the many people who possess laser printers and computers can now produce their own novels in formats not too different from those that grace libraries and bookshops. Owners of camcorders, webcams, digital cameras and the relevant software can produce their own visual narratives and distribute them to a wide range of Internet users. It is even possible to reconfigure existing written narratives with the use of a scanner, or visual narratives with the use of editing software, to produce new narratives which combine existing material with home-produced narrative input.

Yet it should be recognized that the *active* nature of narrative readership did not begin with the interactivity of computers. Immediately before the advent of home computers, the VCR was "itself a kind of production device" (Cubitt 1991: 4) in the way that it allowed users to interfere with the flow of television programming, playing back and re-running sequences. Before this the development of the tape recorder and especially the cassette/radio allowed listeners to engage in timeshifting with regard to aural narratives. One might even suggest that the element of choice involved in television viewing on different channels is a kind of reader activity. What is at issue here is not that readers can now be active; instead, a fairly established feature of the reception of narrative has become crystallized in postmodernity, and this is a result of a combination of the proliferation of narratives and the availability of technology for their reproduction. Choice, albeit merely the choice to consume a diversity of, or parts of, narrative, is greater than it has ever been.

As Iser pointed out in relation to print narrative, texts are shot through with 'indeterminacy' which requires a great deal of reader activity in order for a text to be read. The very difference between the narrative levels of *Implied Reader* and *Real Reader* suggests a quotient of *active* engagement embedded in each entity. Furthermore, the gap-filling activity demanded by the existence of indeterminacy is also evident in visual narratives such as films. As the reading of narratives proliferated in the twentieth century so too, then, did the level of readerly activity. The consequences of this are that, first, the sheer *number* of narratives and the reader activity required for their consumption detracted from the authority of the purveyors of narratives. Where, in previous epochs, most narratives were produced by individuals with access to technology, and represented their interests to the extent of carrying an individual stamp or mark of authorship, the twentieth century saw the growth in demand for narratives which, as we shall see below, often played down or made irrelevant individual authorship. Moreover, authorship was to become demystified further when certain kinds of narratives were more widely produced as technology became more accessible. Second, the specific personal or group investments integral to the act of reading constituted an 'exercising' of identity which expanded along with the consumption of narratives.

The most visible result of these factors has been the erosion of the dividing line between 'high' and 'popular' culture in the twentieth century. It is true that, for some commentators, the collapse of the high/low distinction in culture derives from a critique of the elitism of the theory of mass culture propounded by academics on both the political right and left, from a playful incorporation of popular narratives into high art since the 1960s and from a breaking of the repressive constraints of 'educated good taste' (Huyssen 1986; Collins 1989; Ross 1989). More important than all of these, however, is the role of narrative, particularly its embodiment in new technologies in the period. The reason for this is also tied to one of the 'old' technologies. As Murray reiterates (1997: 188–9, 277), the 'bardic' or 'folkloric' oral tradition of narrative identified by Parry and Lord is not so much concerned with the 'authorship' and 'authority' of narratives, but with the formula that allows them to be transmitted. As has been demonstrated, 'authorship' of oral narrative is almost impossible to establish; yet the kind of *authority* upon which an elite concept of 'high' art can be based requires a thoroughgoing delimitation and identification of authorship. Written narrative, along with the Enlightenment notion of the individual, provided the basis for the concept of 'high' art, and the authority of written narrative was consolidated by the rise of the novel in the eighteenth century, the establishment of the powerful narratorial voice in realism during the nineteenth century, and the anti-democratic strain of modernism in the early twentieth century. However, the new technologies of narrative that we have discussed were less susceptible to 'authorship' claims.

As we have seen, the attempt of film theorists to posit an 'auteur' of movies did not stop films being produced largely as a result of their *form*, making formalist analysis most important. Similarly, radio's distinctive voice and that of the companies responsible for broadcasting it were arguably as important as individual, named narratives. Television's supposed 'bardic' bearing and the plethora of personnel involved in production also challenge notions of authorial control. Narratives generated with the help of computers further problematize the concept of authorship and even seem to encourage interactivity and a participation. And as television and computer technology converge, the same phenomena will probably be enhanced.

As the work of Jenkins (1992), Lewis (1992) and others attempts to demonstrate, late twentieth-century narrative cemented the rise of a 'participatory culture' in which ardent consumers of narratives such as 'fans' not only used narrative for the purposes of formulating aspects of their own identities but also changed the nature of the narratives with which they interacted. This latter could consist of reading and re-reading narratives, producing one's own narratives or taking aspects of existing narratives and developing them. An example of these are the 'alternative' *Star Trek* narratives written and circulated by fans of the television series. The other way of changing the nature of narratives might result from feedback to the producers of narratives, such as the petitioning of television companies to run further series of TV programmes or the extension of narratives into other fora such as the kind of fan conventions satirized in the early stages of the film *GalaxyQuest* (2000). Clearly, the newly recognized power of the reader is one further indication of the demise of narrative authority. The narrative of Stephen King's novel *Misery* (1985), for example, in which an injured writer is held captive by a fan and forced to rewrite a narrative, presents a disturbing picture of the assault on authorial autonomy. Yet it is clear that the possibility of participating in the production and circulation of narrative has never been greater than in the early years of the twenty-first century.

## DIVERSITY AND GENRES

There can be little doubt that human consciousness is now suffused with narrative. In the West, narrative is the focus of a number of lucrative industries, and narratives proliferate as never before. Consider the breadth and diversity of some of the most popular contemporary narrative production. Among younger consumers of stories in the early years of the twenty-first century, the 'Harry Potter' novels of J. K. Rowling sell in the millions. More curious than the enthusiasm for print fiction in this example, however, is the novels' subject matter. Secondary characters have names such as 'Hermione' and 'Neville', and in each narrative the trials and tribulations of life are reconfigured precisely in a fashion that would have pleased Matthew Arnold: as an inter-house game in a British public school. In the field of the 'adult' novel, the nineteenth century retains its influence in that realism continues to prosper, whether it is elevated by nomination of realist novels for such accolades as the Booker prize or whether it resists valorization because it is part of a genre. Meanwhile, a novel such as Mark Z. Danielewski's *House of Leaves* (2000) plays upon its very postmodernism. It purports to be the production of Johnny Truant, who, through a friend, has come into possession of a manuscript written by someone called Zampanò which is actually a quasi-academic commentary on a documentary film, as well as various out-takes, made by someone called Navidson about a house whose dimensions begin to transgress conventional understandings of time and space. Among the tricks that the narrative incorporates are different fonts for different narrators; the mixture of real and fictional references in the copious footnotes to Zampanò's commentary; the reproduction of Zampanò's erratic writing habits, such as paragraphs pasted onto the page at an angle, back to front or crossed out; a slightly raised and faded lettering whenever the word 'house' appears in the text and a note on the book's copyright page explaining that other editions of the book which, presumably, do not exist, print the word 'house' in blue or have Braille supplements.

The representation of *House of Leaves* as a palimpsest and the attendant 'rupturing' effects are not as unsettling as they may have been in the early years of the last part of the twentieth century. This is not to say that 'rupturing' effects have become completely sterile in postmodernist narrative; a master of the palimpsest, Scottish writer, Alasdair Gray, uses them to great humorous effect. Some way into his story, 'Logopandocy', which, from the outset, purports to be an 'apocryphal diurnal' written in 1645, a physical gap appears in the narrative which the implied author has annotated with the words "here a great part of the manuscript has been eaten by mice" (Gray 1984: 177); four pages later there is a further gap with a different annotation: "More excisions by the tooth of the editorial rodent" (181).

In film, a movie such as *The Limey* (1999) disconcertingly flashes forwards and backwards, revealing presumed flashbacks as flashforwards in the manner of a high modernist narrative. In *The Matrix* (1998) a terrifying vision of parallel universes is offered where, for some time, it is not really possible to discern which world is which and which world is desirable, true and good. On the other hand, *The Straight Story* (1999), made by David Lynch, "a bona fide postmodernist filmmaker" (Collins 1992: 341), is a model of simplicity and realism, comprising a conception of linear time, a beginning, a middle and an end. On television, two of the most commercially successful narratives in the last years of the twentieth century and the first years of the twenty-first century have been cartoon series, *The Simpsons* and *South Park*. The first features common characters who relate the stories of their everyday lives, especially those of the main character, significantly named Homer. The second features unrealistic, poorly drawn characters who are nevertheless recognizable and who are involved in a combination of schoolday drudgery and fantastic adventures including trips to distant planets, ravaging by gigantic Barbra Streisand creatures and the discovery of parallel universes. The contrast with one of the equally popular narratives produced for American television, *Friends*, in which a group of extremely well-heeled young white people share an apartment, could not be greater. In contemporary Britain one of the most popular television narratives, *The Royle Family*, consists of episodes in which the members of an extended working-class family speak to each other, frequently in a stilted fashion, in one or two rooms, usually slumped in front of the television, and without any disruption of the actual time in which the action takes place. Its narrative is the very model of Aristotelian mimesis, although it must be mentioned that, in at least two respects, it fails in its acts of showing. First, *The Royle Family* is not fully Aristotelian; rather, in consonance with the television series format, it does not bring any action to a completion. Second, it is undoubtedly a *re*-presentation in that there are many features of everyday working-class life in Britain, such as racist discourse, which simply do not appear in its narrative.

In the world of new narrative technologies, the bleak vision of Stephen King's *Misery* has not prevented him from trusting to participatory culture in order to extend one aspect of the circulation of narrative. Circumventing the usual routes to publication and dissemination of narrative, King placed the first two instalments of his new novel *The Plant* (2000) on his Web page, promising to write and publish further instalments on the page on the condition that 75 per cent of those who download the instalments pay him one dollar (see www.stephenking.com). In a more participatory vein, Web sites have also enabled 'unknown' producers of narratives to find an audience; camcorders have allowed the broadcast of personal narratives such as 'video diaries'; and desktop publishing has continued the tactile traditions of the book.

Amidst the diversity of narrative over the last hundred years readers might have been in danger of floundering as a result of their inability to choose what narrative is appropriate for them and what offers the potential of enjoyment. It is significant, then, that the twentieth century saw the renewal of the term 'genre' in connection with narrative. On radio, in film, in print, television and cyberspace genres flourished. Many of them also had deep roots: tragedy, comedy and epic obviously emanate from Ancient Greece. Yet the more ossified popular genres of the twentieth century had their own long heritages: the development of science fiction can be traced to utopian narratives of the seventeenth century and, more specifically, to such critiques of technological hubris as Mary Shelley's *Frankenstein* (1818); the thriller's inception is usually associated with the work of Edgar Allan Poe in the 1840s, particularly his stories of deduction or 'ratiocination'; the modern romance genre has roots in the form from which it is distinct, the medieval romance, but became established in the patterns of narratives produced by novelists such as Jane Austen and Charlotte Brontë in the nineteenth century. Other genres easily recognizable today had slightly different roots: the stage and film musical derived from traditions of theatre, reaching its pinnacle in the Hollywood film; soap opera, on the other hand, was a genre defined by its enunciation, being a long-running serial drama on American radio financed by the sponsorship of soap companies and eventually evolving into a form on television exemplified by such serials as *Peyton Place*, *Dallas* and *Dynasty*.

In a sense, the importance of popular genres in current narrative is an index of the demise of authorship and the return of certain of the premises of oral narrative in which formula and repetition are more important than the identification of an individual producer. Nevertheless, it is important to be clear that genre and formula in narrative are not the same thing. Although Lord is at pains to point out that the oral poet will introduce innovations, the formula of the narrative will remain basically the same. Yet the fact that an audience can enjoy the same formula over and over again suggests that, although it might be demonstrably identical on each occasion, the pleasures that the audience derives from it are subject to change. Identical experience of the repetition of a formula has little mileage in terms of enjoyment; changing experience of a formula, on the other hand, even when the changes are small or subtle, offers a greater potential for pleasure. In the latter case, such change may involve a different performance by the oral storyteller or slightly different content to the narrative; equally, though, it will involve changed investments by the reader, sometimes prompted by the variation in performance or contents.

While formula is demonstrable, then, its reception is less easy to define. Genre, in contrast to formula, is concerned precisely with the issue of how audiences receive narrative conventions (Cobley 2000: 15–33). Every consumer of narratives has a rough idea of what 'genre' means: a shorthand textual classification, determining whether a particular fiction is expected to conform to previous experiences of texts on the part of the consumer. As such, then, genre is properly an 'idea' or an 'expectation' harboured by readers. However, academic commentary has repeatedly assumed that genre designates an entity which is objective and concrete like a formula. Stemming from the analyses of Aristotle, it has been thought that factors internal to narrative such as structure, plot, character and setting have constituted genre. Twentieth-century critics such as Vladimir Propp (1968) and Northrop Frye (1957) have attempted to define genre by reducing a narrative's elements to a limited number of 'functions' or 'archetypes'. Whilst a genre text *may* be shown to possess the internal textual organization that genre theorists have discerned, displaying key elements such as a hero, problem-solving, and so on, the manner in which these features are read is more problematic.

These facts about genre reveal a significant amount about narrative in general. Clearly, all texts, even non-narrative ones, carry a multiplicity of meaning or polysemy; yet, when a text operates within a generic system the potentially wide range of interpretations is, to use Rick Altman's phrase (1987: 4), "short-circuited". As Altman is keen to point out, there is a great deal outside the text which determines a genre, such that "genres look different to different audiences" (1999: 207). For Altman, a cultural commodity such as a genre is 'made' through the action of readers who harbour expectations about it. Such expectations are not just created by publicity surrounding a narrative; nor are they, unproblematically, the products of existing belief. Instead, they are the products "also of knowledge, emotions and pleasure" (Jost 1998: 106). Generic meaning is derived partly from competence in reading other narratives in the genre but also from a more diffuse set of knowledges, attitudes, values and experiences brought to the reading of a specific narrative, all of which are in a complex interplay.

Undoubtedly, short-circuiting is necessary for generic narrative to function. Unless the range of expectations about a narrative formula is limited, the narrative will be multiplicitous and diffi-cult to pin down. It therefore follows that the phenomena of selection and expectations being harnessed are easy to swallow in relation to generic texts. After all, genre has so frequently been associated with a demonstrably reductive formula which might be found within narratives. Yet it might equally be the case that narrative in general has been seen as a short-circuiting device and that, in fact, the principle has been enshrined by analysts of nar-rative. Let us consider this in some concluding comments.

## CLOSURE, VERISIMILITUDE AND THE NARRATIVE SIGN

By way of conclusion, and in the manner of the intrusive narrator, I would like to request the reader's indulgence of a personal story. As a youth in the early days of home video, I watched a recording of the 1970s paranoid thriller *Capricorn One* (1978). The film's narrative is concerned with a future manned space flight to Mars which is aborted at the last minute because of technical difficul-ties caused by private contractors failing to maintain standards of safety. The fact that the journey does not take place is concealed from the public and the astronauts are blackmailed into enacting the Mars landing in a film studio in order that public faith in the space programme might continue. As the astronauts realize that the public will be told that they have been fictionally killed on re-entry into the earth's atmosphere, they decide to escape the clutches of their captors and flee into the nearby desert. Two of the astronauts are caught and presumably executed, but a maver-ick journalist (Elliott Gould) rescues one of them (James Brolin) and brings him back to the astronaut's home town, ironically just in time to attend his own funeral and to greet the media that are assembled there. This is the final scene of the film. However, the point of this summary is that whilst I was watching the film, my mother was also in the room, her attention divided between the narrative and the task of ironing clothes. At the film's conclusion she expressed disappointment and stated that she would have been keen to view the inevitable ensuing court case, the media coverage and the ultimate fate of the conspirators.

Two issues seem to be raised by my mother's reading. One is to do with the concept of closure and the other is to do with verisimilitude. Let us consider the issue of closure first. The reading of *Capricorn One*, above, harbours specific ideas about when the narrative should end or close; that is to say, it is concerned with what is represented and what is left out. Nearly all analysis of narrative has been devoted to the way that narrative forecloses reality and this is true of the present analysis. From the outset we have emphasized the way in which narrative is a *re*-presentation of the world, selecting and articulating some things while leaving others out. At the beginning, we discussed representation in terms of the *re*-presenting of sequence, time and space, and the separation of the processes of *re*-presentation into plot, story and narrative. Repeatedly, we have discussed analyses of narrative which attempt to demonstrate how it closes or short-circuits the world in specific ways. Narrative has been used to store information about identities and as a foundation for cultures; but, in doing this, it has been selective, leaving some details out of the formulation of a culture in favour of others. Narrative has also been transfigured as it has become embodied in different technologies or forms of enunciation. The differences between oral narrative, written narrative, print narrative, cinematic narrative, radio narrative, television narrative and narrative in cyberspace are plain to see, even though they are united by the way in which they *re*-present rather than *present*.

We have seen that the mixed mode of mimesis and the poet or narrator's voice has been responsible for a didactic, instructive and authoritative thrust in narrative. Once again, this has been a matter of one view of the world represented in favour of another. The dominant mode of the nineteenth century, realism, has even been seen by analysts of 'classic realist texts' to set up a hierarchy in which the omniscient narratorial voice overwhelms or under-mines those of characters. Early modernist narratives, by contrast, attempted to pit narrative levels against each other and make mani-fest the selectivity involved in narrative. Yet such selectivity remained, as it did in modernist narrative which, in fact, increased the focus on selected moments and consciousnesses. Even postmod-ernism's attempt to draw attention to the nature of *re*-presentation could be construed as an admission of failure on the part of narrative to present the world.

Arguments about the way that narrative has foreclosed the world have been sustained since the 1960s by a discipline which provides crucial technical tools for narrative analysis. 'Narratology' draws attention to the building blocks of narrative, exploring the various combinations that can appear in narrative texts and the devices that readers come to learn and accept. Among these are many of the concepts we have witnessed in this book: narrative levels from *Real Author* to *Real Reader*; free indirect discourse; omniscient narration; intrusive narration; unreliable narration; flashbacks and flashforwards (cf. Genette 1982, 1988; Rimmon-Kenan 1983; Chatman 1990). Indeed, narratology can also be seen as a continuation of work by analysts who have been men-tioned earlier such as Vladimir Propp, A. J. Greimas, Claude Lévi-Strauss and Northrop Frye. Furthermore, the work of these 'proto-narratologists' and narratology itself have been largely responsible for the formation of genre study in the twentieth cen-tury, identifying the formulas and devices which were thought to make up a genre, without paying due attention to the processes of short-circuiting and reception.

Undoubtedly, the kind of close textual analysis exemplified by genre study, myth analysis and narratology is useful and, indeed, indispensable. However, narratology has recently been criticized for its limited purview. Fludernik (1996: 330) suggests that nar-ratology has been insufficiently "holistic", but Gibson hits right at the heart of the matter when he discusses the way in which narratology is the culmination of a 'geometric' tendency in the Anglo-American analysis of narrative (1996: 5–6). For him, narratology reveals "a drive to universalise and essentialise the structural phenomena supposedly uncovered" in narratives, a tendency he traces back through the work of the French critic Gerard Genette to the American critic Wayne Booth, and all the way to the eighteenth-century English novelist Henry Fielding (Gibson 1996: 5). Gibson clearly believes that narratological analysis leaves out something that is absolutely fundamental to narrative. As we have also seen, in the first chapter of this book, Ricoeur feels the same about narratology or, what he somewhat misguidedly calls, the 'semiotics of narrative'. Ricoeur's main point concerns the way that narratology tends to 'dechronologize' narrative and reduce it to a series of dominating 'paradigmatic' functions, leaving sequence to the mercy of the common-sense linear interpretation of time. However, it is worth revisiting his criticism of narratology in the light of what we have said about the tendency in narrative analysis to emphasize the foreclosing, *re*-presentative nature of narrative; especially important is Ricoeur's implicit criticism of the *text-centredness* of some narrative analysis and the conception of the *sign* which underpins it.

Before proceeding to this, however, we should explore the other, related, issue which arises from the above reading of *Capricorn One*. We have already said that the reading is concerned with the matter of when it is apposite for the narrative to close and, therefore, it is concerned with what is represented and what is left out. Yet, this observation also implies a more general concern of narrative that we have discussed on a number of occasions, its verisimilitude. In Chapter 3, we noted the way in which Pamela's extended recounting of the events of her wedding day in Richardson's novel strains credibility because the profusion of events would not have allowed her time to narrate them at such length and simultaneously in her diary entries. Similarly, Tristram Shandy's extended narration of his life in Sterne's novel constitutes a concerted assault on verisimilitude because of the way in which he narrates so much that he is prevented from getting on with the story. In the century after these novels were published, realism forged an effective compromise between the mimetic showing of detail in a scene and the manipulation of time, space and character in a summary. Yet, despite the implementation of a certain kind of verisimilitude, it is important to be clear that realism and verisimilitude are two different things. Moreover, the distinction is important not just because it is a technical issue in the history of narrative but because it sheds light on the very nature of the narrative sign.

Once more, the consideration of generic narratives can assist in the understanding of narrative as a whole. Todorov (1977) identifies two sets of criteria by which a work or set of statements is said to have verisimilitude: the 'rules of the genre' and 'public opinion' or *doxa*. When somebody bursts into song during a musical, this is not, according to the rules of that particular genre, an indecorous act at odds with the statements in the text; instead, the song is part of a specific regime of verisimilitude and falls within a range of expectations on the part of the audience that such acts, while extremely infrequent in real life, are legitimate within the bounds of the genre. Similarly, 'public opinion' is not identical to the real world; it plainly consists of a set of *expectations and understandings* of the world by readers rather than the world considered as a referent, and it is therefore itself a regime of verisimilitude. As Todorov explains (1977: 87), it is hence more accurate to consider verisimilitude as a principle of textual coherence rather than as an area in which there exists some relation between the fictional and the real world.

Verisimilitude is therefore based upon a *public opinion* about what is credible, which itself will be subject to change, revision and learning anew of its principles; plus a learned sense of what happens in different kinds of narratives or, as Bruner put it and as we discussed in Chapter 1, a sense of what is canonical and what is not. What has made realism such a durable mode of narrative is the way that its mixture of mimesis and the narrator's voice, or scene and summary, has aligned itself with verisimilitude. Fundamental to expectations about realism is the maintenance of a general level of 'credibility' which matches as closely as possible that which is held by the *doxa*. As Bruner suggests, the act of 'telling a story' cannot simply be understood by interrogating the logical principles of sense and reference contained in the act; instead "we interpret stories by their verisimilitude, their 'truth likeness' or, more accurately, their 'life likeness'" (1990: 61).

A durable narrative mode such as realism thus attempts to achieve harmony between the consistency of representation in the narrative, the mixed mode of mimesis and narrator's voice, and what is believed to be credible politically, socially and topically at a given moment by public opinion. Clearly, one result of this is that it is easy to make the mistake of believing that realism is more 'realistic' than other modes of narrative. However, this should not offer licence to narrative analysis to proceed in the opposite direction, overstressing the closure in narrative and the failure to present the world adequately. Although we have suggested that much narrative analysis does this, there are also ways of analysing narrative which draw attention to its purposes, its richness and to its potential breadth of allusion to the world.

One important argument about narrative in this book which has been especially important in discussing realism has been that of Bakhtin regarding heteroglossia. For him, the discourse of the novel form of narrative cannot avoid being *dialogical*. The signs in a novel will always be related to other signs, thus preventing the kind of closure which a narratorial voice might attempt to achieve. That is to say, even for characters the signs that pass between them are 'concrete', the site of struggle, because they can be hurtful, helpful, vindictive, true and many other things. The insuperable relation of signs to other signs also implies a richness within the supposedly closed world of realist narrative.

Approaching the question of realism's richness from a different angle, it is probable that many expected Roland Barthes' book *S/Z* to expose the entire system of realism and sound its death knell. After all, Barthes took a short story by the arch-realist, Balzac, and showed how it could be broken down into discrete units and analysed with reference to just five codes. It seemed that the exercise was like those of Propp on the Russian folktale or Lévi-Strauss on myth. However, what *S/Z* revealed was that the Balzac short story was incredibly rich and full of signs which, far from being reduced by the codes, actually competed with each other.

A similar surprise was in store for viewers of David Lynch's film *The Straight Story* at the end of the last century. As we have mentioned, Lynch has been considered, paradoxically, a postmodernist auteur; that is to say, a controlling authorial presence in an age when authors of narratives disappeared from view or lost their authority. *The Straight Story*, however, bears all the hallmarks of the most traditional realism. The narrative concerns an old man, Alvin Straight (Richard Farnsworth), who hears that his brother (Harry Dean Stanton) has just suffered a stroke. The brothers have not spoken to each other for many years, for reasons of animosity that they have both now largely forgotten. They are also separated by over 300 miles and both are poor. Alvin determines that he wants to see his brother and sets out on the only transport he can afford: a converted lawnmower. Far from making the narrative comical, the lawnmower trip converts it into an epic odyssey; the journey that Alvin makes becomes, in the established tradition of Western narrative, a voyage to the self. As Alvin makes his way to his destination there are various *detours* in which he is befriended by an ordinary family who fear for his welfare and where he meets similar senior citizens in a bar and discusses experiences in the Second World War. The film is cut and lit in a conventional way, mimetic scenes are allowed to play themselves out and long-distance aerial shots of the mid-western

American countryside are used to summarize the size of the land-scape and the duration of Alvin's odyssey.

*The Straight Story* is based on a true series of events and it is a happy coincidence that the protagonist of those events was called Alvin Straight in real life. Few narratives could be as *straightfor-ward* as this one. Simultaneously, of course, the word 'straight' has multiple connotations. Indeed, the film demonstrates the same point as *Middlemarch* demonstrates for David Lodge: not that it becomes closed as a result of attempting to represent the world in as close and comprehensive a fashion as possible, using mimetic modes in a controlled, authorial way; but that it "sur-vives, to be read and re-read, without ever finally being closed or exhausted" (Lodge 1981: 236). Despite its realism, *The Straight Story*, along with other realist texts, does not simply make refer-ence to reality. It does *re*-present the world, to be sure, but its use of specific mimetic devices to do so does not mean that the sum of those devices is the sum of narrative; put another way, "people do not deal with the world event by event or with text sentence by sentence" (Bruner 1990: 64). What is important in the act of narrative is frequently something else: the representation of the world for a purpose. Bruner offers 'praying' as an analogy with narrative in that an utterance such as "Give us this day our daily bread" is not to be considered a request but rather an act of rever-ence or trust (64). As we have stressed from the outset, narrative has made reference to the world; yet its origins lie not in refer-ence but the larger purpose of allowing humans to affirm and re-affirm identities.

The narrative sign, therefore, carries a great deal of baggage. However, as we saw earlier, narratology was underpinned by a notion of the sign derived from the work of the Swiss linguist Ferdinand de Saussure (1983) who, despite his prediction of a general science of signs, semiology, did not anticipate this bag-gage. In his conception, users of signs operated within an abstract system of signs, *la langue*, in which a sign's 'value' could only be determined by virtue of its difference to all the other signs. Such a closed formal system, when used as the basis for a discussion of narrative, was bound to generate a form of analysis which emphasized a tendency towards closure and its difficulty in making full reference to the world. It would tend to focus on the way that signs combine with each other rather than the motivation behind the making and linking of signs. Furthermore, the Saussurean sign was a linguistic one only; it had to be strained to become in any way applicable to cinematic or televisual narratives. The discussions in this book of the purposes of narrative, its metamorphoses, the causal connections within it and behind it, and its changing embodiments in oral, written, visual, aural and mixed technologies, as well as its dialogical nature, should indicate that there is a need to analyse narrative on the basis of a different, more general, concept of the sign. Such a concept of the sign will allow the observation that narratives refer to specific objects; that they allow, encourage and cannot preclude reference well beyond those objects; and that they serve the purpose of creating a new world. Such a concept is offered by the sign theory of Charles Sanders Peirce.

## THE FUTURE OF THE NARRATIVE SIGN

In terms of technical proficiency in the production of narratives, one of the worst things one can do is to introduce a new character right at the closing stages of the story. When the character is a thinker with a repertoire as huge as that of Peirce, the error is compounded. In this instance, the late introduction of a figure should be forgivable: despite the unavoidable tendency to narrativize, this book is not supposed to be a narrative. Furthermore, the understanding of narrative which Peirce's sign theory allows and on which I will comment briefly here should be implicit in all that has been argued already in this book.

Peirce's sign is different from most other conceptualizations of signs in that it is triadic (1955). He envisages a 'sign' or 'representamen' which is the entity that acts as a sign of something else. That something else which the 'representamen' signifies he calls an "object". An 'object' can be *dynamic* and exist in the real world, but it can also be *immediate*; that is, an object as it is represented in a sign. Where Saussure's linguistic sign envisages sound patterns and concepts, this first aspect of Peirce's sign that we have discussed immediately makes it more suitable for understanding narrative. A 'representamen' can be related to an object in the real world, but it can also be caught up in the act of *re*-presenting what is not in the real world; as Peirce states,

> The Objects – for a sign may have any number of them – may each be a single known existing thing or thing believed formerly to have existed or expected to exist, or a collection of such things, or a known quality or relation or fact, which single Object may be a collection, or whole of parts, or it may have some other mode of being, such as some act permitted whose being does not prevent its negation from being equally permitted, or something of a general nature desired, required, or invariably found under certain general circumstances.
>
> (Peirce 1955: 101)

Thus, Peirce's sign theory at once demonstrates that it can accommodate the referential *and* the fictional function of narrative; the Peircean sign can stand for objects believed formerly to have existed such as London in the 1880s, or things expected to have existed such as 221b Baker Street.

However, the third part of Peirce's sign triad is more illuminating still. The relation between 'representamen' and 'object' is subject to a third entity, what Peirce calls the 'interpretant'. This is not to be confused with an 'interpreter' of a sign. If I point with my finger (representamen) at an item in a room (object) and a person in the room turns to look at it, a triad is completed. The person's action of turning to look is the 'interpretant' connected to the 'representamen' and the 'object', and encapsulates two things: first, it is the *result* or 'significate effect' of the pointing to the item; second, it is a *mediator* in that it brings the pointing finger and the item together in a relation which can be called a 'sign'. In the Saussurean sign there is no sense of causality: the relation between sound pattern and mental concept is construed as 'arbitrary' and the 'value' of signs is a result of their difference from other signs. By contrast, the Peircean sign consists of an in-built propensity for causality: how something such as a pointing finger becomes a sign happens with reference to an 'idea' that Peirce calls a "ground" (1955: 99). The making of a sign is therefore the result of a cause, be it a convention or even some notion of resemblance between 'representamen' and 'object'.

From the outset, we have stressed that narrative is bound up with causality. Plot, in particular, binds together story events; for Ricoeur it is the chain of causality in emplotment which ensures that narrative is the human relation to time. Even non-fiction narratives which are usually expected to be devoid of plot demonstrate a motivation which makes the events they relate cohere. The mediating role of the interpretant, then, is important in the way that it allows for connections between the 'representamen' and 'object' to be construed as a sign, thus creating a new world with principles different from those of the real one and based on sign-specific relations.

Furthermore, there is a larger causality behind narrative beside the internal one which connects story events within it. As we have seen, narrative is not simply a matter of reference to the world. It is a *re*-presentation of the world whose original purpose was the recording and storing of knowledge about identity. The signs in a narrative are not the same as those in the world: they are transformations of the world, invariably into stories of human action. Narrative signs are *re*-presentations even though, ultimately, they may refer to *dynamic* objects. They are specific to a narrative, operating as narrative signs rather than some kind of other sign; this is because the interpretant can mediate a connection between a 'representamen' and an *immediate* 'object'; that is, the object as it is represented by the sign. Thus, fundamentally 'unrealistic' narratives supposed to be lacking referentiality, such as musicals or fantastic science fiction, can have verisimilitude or credibility because of the consistency of each 'representamen' within them standing for an *immediate*, rather than a *dynamic*, 'object'.

Peirce also shows that a sign can operate on different bases than just an arbitrary connection between a sound pattern and mental concept. Something can become a sign because it possesses a quality, because it exists or because it constitutes a general law; it can signify an object by resemblance, by being affected by the object, or by a law or convention; it can be a sign of possibility, a sign of existence, or a sign of laws and conventions. In fact, Peirce recognized ten basic classes of signs and towards the end of his life claimed to have identified 59,049 different classes of signs (Peirce 1966: 407). The point of this for our purposes is that signs are variable enough to allow them to be embodied in different narrative forms and media. The narrative signs to be found in cinema, for example, are characterized by the following: they evince a quality through such devices as camera angle or lighting; they give the impression that they *exist* as, say, actors or scenery; even as projected onto a flat screen, the signs resemble the colour, shape, sound and other facts of their objects; they appear on screen as signs because they were present, affecting the purview of camera; they embody general laws such as the connection between a hero and 'goodness'. As this example demonstrates, a proper understanding of narrative therefore requires an appreciation of the general potential of the sign.

Above all, what the Peircean theory of the sign offers the analysis of narrative is a means to understand its capacity for metamorphosis, its dialogic openness and its dynamism. We have already emphasized the chains of causality which occur throughout narrative. However, the example in this chapter from a reading of the film *Capricorn One* demonstrates the dynamic nature of this chain: not only can narrative set up relations between signs in such a way as to effect a movement from a start point to an end point, characterized by *detours* in between, it also has the potential to extend that chain *beyond* the endpoint. Undoubtedly, narratives do come to some sort of an end by their very definition, and this has prompted narrative analysts to pay so much attention to issues of closure. However, readers and spectators of narrative with the relevant technology such as books or video recorders can dwell for some time on passages of narrative, re-reading or replaying them, or simply musing on them at length to take them *beyond* the flow to an end point. In the *Capricorn One* example, on the other hand, the reader actually envisaged what went on *after* the formal ending, and desired its narration.

The chief reason that narrative can 'move beyond itself' in this way is to be found in two important features of the Peircean understanding of the sign. First, as we saw in the example of the pointing finger, a sign, in order to *be* a sign, must be a sign *for someone*. In a sense, my pointing finger can be a sign for me, but unless it is recognized by another who looks in the direction of the pointing, it is useless to the point of not being a sign. Thus, the sign is dialogic: it must always open out and be subject to an 'other' in order to exist. The signs in narrative are open to the many ways that they will be used by different readers, including those readers who will dwell upon them at some length.

The second feature relevant here is related to the first. The connection between my pointing finger and the item to which I point is effected by another who provides the interpretant in the act of turning his/her head and looking in the right direction. If the item I point to is a cloud of billowing smoke in the corner of the room, not only will the other person have provided the mediation to make my pointing a *sign*, s/he will also be likely to embark on his/her own process of making signs: 'Fire!', 'Let's get out of the room', 'We should sound the alarm', 'Round everyone up!', 'Don't use the lifts!', 'Take the back staircase!', 'We can reach safety outside' (cf. Merrell 2001). Indeed, it is easy to see that there is almost a little narrative here. This is because an 'interpretant' always has the capacity to become a 'representamen'; a 'representamen' will have a connection to an 'object' effected by an 'interpretant' which can also be a 'representamen', and a 'representamen' will have a connection to an 'object' ... and so forth. The only reason that this does not go on forever is that the practical necessities of everyday life often interfere with the process.

Thus, it is true to say that it is in the very nature of narrative to have an ending, in the same way as it is true that humans have other things to do besides adding to the chain of new interpretants. However, the potential for openness is nevertheless omnipresent in the dialogicality of signs and the impulse to proliferate interpretants. Narrative undoubtedly *re*-presents features of the world, leaving some out in favour of others. It *re*-presents time, space and sequence; it facilitates the remembrance and exploration of identity; it imbues its representations with causality; it envisages an end; and it does all of these according to the specificities of the technologies in which it is embedded. Yet in spite of what might be understood as narrative's limiting action, it harbours astounding complexity and offers us the opportunity to partake of the unlimited potential of signs.

# Glossary

**Auteur theory** Theory within the study of the cinema which holds that, in spite of the dominance of the forms of cinematic narrative and the power of the industries that finance those forms, a creative individual can produce artistic cinematic works which transcend these restrictions. Individual actors or screenwriters might be seen as auteurs in their own right but, usually, auteur status has been associated with the work of the director.

**Bardic function** Function attributed to oral poets who sustained cultures by disseminating their own narratives to them. The function has also been attributed to television as it became a central institution of society in the late twentieth century and was believed to circulate and reinforce commonly held views.

**Classic realist text** Associated especially with the nineteenth-century novel, a narrative in which there exists a strict hierarchy of subordinate discourse (characters' discourse rendered in **mimesis**) and dominant discourse (the **voice** of the **narrator**). The narrator's voice in classic realism, because it is so strongly associated with the task of providing **summary** and detail in narrative, appears to be almost 'objective' and hence more reliable than that of the character. Indeed, the narrator's discourse, couched in prose rather than within inverted commas, seems to efface its status as a voice and appears to become mere 'commentary'.

**Cyberspace** Term coined by William Gibson in his 1984 novel *Neuromancer* to indicate the ways in which the notion of 'space' can be conceptualized within a computer's activities. The 'cyber' aspect of the term is derived from 'cybernetics', which, in the mid-twentieth century, was a science concerned with machines such as robots, and computers. However, 'cyber' is actually derived from the Greek word for navigation.

The word 'cyberspace' now invokes the minuscule size of computer equipment allied with its almost unimaginably huge capacity to carry out tasks, including the creation of new worlds through narrative.

*Detours*   *see* **Hermeneutic code**

**Dialogue**   For Bakhtin, dialogue is the defining feature of the signs passed between humans, and dialogue entails that there is always a *relationship* between sign users no matter how much a sign user may think that s/he is not in dialogue with an *other*. In narrative fiction, the **heteroglossia** which makes up languages, and which is the result of dialogue between individuals in specific situations, is refigured; the many different social situations which determine the existence of specific languages are recreated in narrative through the speech of characters, but this is itself always placed in a relation of dialogue with the voice of the narrator.

**Discours**   Order of language identified by the French linguist, Émile Benveniste. *Discours*, unlike *histoire*, takes place in the present tense, assuming a speaker and hearer who might be referred to as *I* and *you*. *Discours* corresponds to the kind of intervention in **metafiction** whereby a **rupturing effect** by a narrator who speaks directly to an **implied reader** interrupts any existing *histoire*. *Discours* can be found in audio-visual narratives as well as written ones.

**Early modernism**   Period of narrative production roughly situated in the late nineteenth century and early twentieth century which precedes **modernism**. Where modernist narrative eschews the concept of linear time and expands the **reality effect**, early modernist narrative tends to challenge realist modes by focusing on the theme of a 'reasonable' self and an 'unreasonable' other as it plays itself out in relation to characters, and by experiments with **narrative levels**.

**Editing**   *see* **Parallel editing**

**Epic**   Large-scale narrative, often associated with the theme of national or cultural identity whose main archetypes in Europe have been the narratives of Homer, *The Iliad* and *The Odyssey*. Although originally rendered in verse, epic, unlike drama, mixes **mimesis** and the 'poet's' **voice** to relate stories of (usually mythical) heroism. Epics strongly influenced the development of the novel, and some early novels such as Fielding's *Tom Jones* have been evaluated as epics in their own right. Some large film and television productions which range over vast territories and which are concerned with major themes of heroism have also been called 'epics'.

**Fabula**   Term introduced by the Russian Formalist critics to refer to the chronological sequence of events which make up the raw materials of a **story**; the term designates the 'prior events' that are to be narrated, whether they are fictional or real.

**Flow**   The way in which a collection of programmes consists of not just one narrative but a sequence of different kinds of narratives or narrative plus non-narrative programming. Television programming, dictated by a schedule modelled on the modern working week, is concerned more with channel loyalty and the viewer choosing to consume a selection of programmes than strict attention to individual narratives as is the case with, say, cinema. (The psychologist, Mihalyi Csikszentmihalyi also uses the term 'flow' in an unrelated sense to refer to humans' capacity to sense an immense satisfaction, commitment, rejuvenation and even joy in certain occupations and pastimes; the capacity was frequently found to be spurred by an early engagement with narrative as a tool for making meaning of the world.)

**Free indirect discourse**   Anglophone term which refers to an extension of the mixed mode of **mimesis** and the poet's or narrator's voice. In free indirect discourse, the voice of the character becomes embedded in the voice of the narrator; thus, the character's habit of speech is present, but direct imitation and quotation marks are not. Bakhtin calls this **skaz** or an orientation towards someone else's speech.

*Genre*   Generally thought to be a 'type' of text, although the question of what is a 'type' has hidden difficulties. Originally, in ancient Greek criticism, the main genres existed in drama, tragedy and comedy, and were contrasted to the non-dramatic genre of **epic**. From this time, the verifiable features of some kinds of texts led to the belief that genres were objective categories associated with the formulas to be found in narratives. It has become clear with the proliferation of popular genres and their constant overlaps that the term 'genre' more suitably refers to a set of expectations harboured by readers about given narratives and their **verisimilitude**.

**Grand narratives**    Term used by Lyotard to refer to philosophical narratives which 'validate' scientific knowledge and which are seen to be in decline in the period of **postmodernism**. He argues that scientific knowledge, especially in the last few centuries, has sought to legitimate itself not by validating its own internal procedures but by appealing to a narrative outside itself, a 'grand narrative'. In general, he sees two grand narratives at work in the legitimation of science: one associated with the Enlightenment and concerned with the emancipation of humans from bondage and oppression; the other a philosophical narrative associated with the development of a more self-conscious human being or an evolved 'Spirit'. Both contain a narrative of progression to the greater human good. Confusingly, Lyotard sometimes refers to grand narratives as 'metanarratives', a term best reserved for the discussion of the **rupturing effect** in postmodern narrative fiction, but which is nevertheless present in his definition of the 'postmodern' as "incredulity toward metanarratives".

**Hard-boiled narrative**    Form of narrative derived from the prose style of Ernest Hemingway and others, but whose development is mainly associated with American pulp detective fiction of the 1920s and 1930s. Hard-boiled narrative is mainly defined by its prose, which involves a 'tough', 'no-nonsense' depiction of objects and people, eschewing complex verbs, excessive use of adjectives, subordinate clauses and other 'flowery' effects. Frequently, hard-boiled sentences which purport to be bald statements of fact can, through their juxtaposition, produce complex new meanings.

**Hermeneutic code**    Code in narrative identified by Roland Barthes in *S/Z* (1974); the code has a dual function in relation to the establishment of narrative 'space' and 'time' because it (a) pushes the narrative forward towards disclosure; and (b) simultaneously retards a narrative's progress. The code is manifested in narrative events by **story** features such as 'equivocation', 'snares' and 'false replies'. Brooks (1982) refers to such events as *detours*.

**Heteroglossia**  Literally, different languages. For Bakhtin, language is not to be considered a unitary phenomenon; rather, it is 'heteroglot'. It is divided up into languages which represent interests within dialogical relations such as the specific language uses which facilitate exchanges between humans within particular social groups, within professional groups and within particular genres. 'Literary' language itself is part of this heteroglossia and, furthermore, is itself subdivided into specific heteroglot language uses such as those of characters in **dialogue** according to their social, professional or generic positions. The **novel**, more than any other form of poetic discourse, is manifestly heteroglossic because of its ability to present numerous characters and situations, its ability to report or reproduce speech and, especially, its ability to parody different language uses by embedding them within the general narratorial, 'authorial' or 'poet's' voice.

*Histoire*  Order of language, especially found in writing, identified by the French linguist, Émile Benveniste. *Histoire* is a 'historical' utterance, invariably characterizing past events and is frequently used by historians. In *histoire* there is no intervention of the 'speaker' or 'enunciator' into what is written; a historian using *histoire* will not use personal pronouns such as *I* or *you*, and everything to do with the present moment of the utterance will be excluded. *Histoire* attempts to be impersonal and, even, objective. *See also* **Discours**.

**Hybridity**  Term used to describe the way in which cultures can never be considered as 'holistic' or 'organic'. Rather, cultures are hybrid; in a culture's attempt to construct narratives about itself it is forced to 'edit out' features of 'other', 'alien' cultures which might appear in such narratives. Narrative's re-presentation may facilitate such a process of constructing a 'pure' culture by electing *not* to narrate a given culture's constant incorporation of, and dialogue with, aspects of putatively 'other' cultures.

**Hypertext** Written script to be found in computers and, especially, on Internet Web sites, which is presented in 'hypertext markup language' (html). Hypertext allows specific parts of text to be highlighted, such that clicking on those parts with a computer mouse effects an instant transfer to another place in **cyberspace**. At this place, a further, separate page will be presented, itself written in hypertext.

**Identity** The perception and feeling of belonging to a particular group as a result of commonalities of experience, status and physical existence. Such commonalities can revolve around social class, gender, sexuality, age, occupation, ethnicity, nationality, and so on. Identity can also derive from the experiences of much more local phenomena such as individual or familial circumstances. Since the existence of early oral cultures, narrative has been a traditional, yet often informal, means of maintaining and recalling identity by embodying facts or events in stories of human action.

**Implied Author** The organizing principle of the text, the guiding star responsible for the presentation of the text's materials in a specific way. The Implied Author is that entity among **narrative levels** responsible for ordering scenes, facilitating the narration of certain objects and events and the non-narration of others, structuring the **plot** and so forth. *See also* **Real Author, Narrator, Narratee, Implied Reader** and **Real Reader**.

**Implied Reader** A specific *reading* which is a detailed response to the various ordering processes of the **Implied Author**. As such, the Implied Reader is an anthropomorphization: it is a reading of a narrative which does not diverge from the cues for reading and interpretation given in the arrangement of such narrative features as the **plot** or sequencing of events. *See also* **Real Author, Narrator, Narratee** and **Real Reader**.

**Interpretant** Third element in the relation between **representamen** and **object** which not only *effects* the relationship between representamen and object but is also the *result of* it. The interpretant is not to be confused with an 'interpreter' of a **sign**. If I point with my finger (representamen) at an item in a room (object) and a person in the room turns to look at it, a triad is completed. The person's action of turning to look is the 'interpretant' connected to the 'representamen' and the 'object'. On the one hand, it is the *result* of the pointing to the item; but, at the same time, it is a *mediator* in that it brings the pointing finger and the item together in a relation which can be called a 'sign'. Additionally, in creating this whole new sign by the action of bringing a representamen into relation with an object, the interpretant as new sign has the capacity to come into relation with a further object in a relation *mediated by* the result of a new interpretant. This process has the potential to continue indefinitely if allowed.

**Intrusive narrator**   A narrator who directly addresses the **Implied Reader** or **Narratee** using such phrases as "dear reader". Like his/her forebears in oral narrative, the intrusive narrator often begins a narrative with a formula such as "Let me tell you the tale of …".

**Metafiction**   Written fiction which is characterized by varieties of the **rupturing effect**. It is usually associated with **postmodernism** because it involves one narrative mode being 'ruptured', 'undermined' or 'invalidated' by another, as when a narrative mode such as *discours* may throw into question a passage of *histoire*.

**Mimesis**   In Plato's work mimesis is considered a reflection of an 'eternal model' of the world in language, in the thought of the philosopher, and in material things; it is seen as mimicry of a visual, behavioural or impersonatory kind; and it is discussed as the making of poetic, musical and choreographic images. Since Plato mimesis has been frequently considered merely as a dramatic *imitation* of events and characters. In opposition to the *reporting* of events and characters which 'tells' what occurs in narrative and is more readily prone to the charge of didacticism, mimesis in this formulation simply 'shows' to readers or spectators what goes on in a narrative. The latter perspective is largely derived from the sketchy comments of Aristotle in his *Poetics*.

**Modernism**   Phase of artistic and scientific endeavour, especially in the first half of the twentieth century, which consisted, in part, of a backlash against previous trains of thought, especially those of the nineteenth century. One important part of modernist thought is the way in which its apprehension of **identity** as complex, constructed and lacking unity, constituted a major leap forward in knowledge. In narrative, this was manifest in artistic devices which indicated a new faith in the ability to explore human identity. Where nineteenth-century **realism** offered considerable organization of the contents of narrative, especially through a linear exposition of time in which discrete moments along a straight line of temporality were represented, modernism sought to expand the **reality effect**. Consequently, many modernist narratives are characterized by their narration at great length of minor details and impressions, explicitly contravening the concept of linear time as an onward procession of equally proportioned moments.

**Monstration**   Term used to discuss the act in which early films were emphatically 'shown' to audiences. The 'monstrator' of film, operating from behind the camera as the photographer of scenes and/or as the impresario in the movie theatre, occupied a role more akin to that of a circus ringmaster than a contemplative **Narrator**. In addition to live music in the film theatre, motion pictures until around 1910 were often accompanied by a live monstration: a 'lecturer' in the film theatre who commented on the action (the modern version of this variant of monstration has been subsumed by the device of the voice-over in narrative films). Another monstration device used by early film was the intertitle: the film's shots could be explicated by the use of intertitles containing dialogue or commentary on the action. *See also* **Mimesis**.

**Narratee**   Theoretically, the narratee is the ideal entity to whom the text is narrated, an entity that will accept largely uncritically all that the text has to offer and the way that it is offered. In order for a narratee to exist, s/he must be embodied by someone to whom the narrative is told. The main **Narrator** of *Heart of Darkness* is, interestingly, also one of the narratees of Marlow's narrative. In narratives without an embodied narratee, it is usually not possible to separate this entity from the **implied reader**. *See also* **Real Author, Implied Author, Narrator** and **Real Reader**.

**Narrative**   A movement from a start point to an end point, with digressions, which involves the showing or the telling of **story** events. Narrative is a *re*-presentation of events and, chiefly, *re*-presents space and time.

**Narrative levels** *see* **Real Author, Implied Author, Narrator, Narratee, Implied Reader, Real Reader**

**Narratology** Discipline which draws attention to the building blocks of narrative, exploring the various combinations that can appear in narrative texts and the devices that readers come to learn and accept, such as **narrative levels**. Although narratological studies proliferated after the 1960s, narratology can also be seen as a continuation of work by analysts involved in **structuralism and the structural study of narrative and myth**, such as Vladimir Propp, A. J. Greimas, Claude Lévi-Strauss and Northrop Frye. Much of this work is 'text-centred' and takes the passivity of the reader for granted. It is possibly for this reason that Ricoeur, somewhat erroneously, refers to narratological work as the 'semiotics of narrative'.

**Narrator** Narrative voice which tells the **story** in the first or third person, for example, sometimes as a character in the story and, on occasion, even through **omniscient narration**. *See also* **Real Author, Implied Author, Narratee, Implied Reader** and **Real Reader**.

**Naturalism** Intellectual movement within the **novel** form derived from the work of the French scholar Hyppolite Taine, and exemplified by the novels and critical writing of Emile Zola. Taine's 'positivist' psychology, history, philosophy and literary theory sought to stress the constant play of heredity and environment in the life of humans. Naturalism, in the work of Zola and others, embodies the dominance over individual **voices** of social and natural forces which seemingly render the narratorial voice redundant. In the United States in the late nineteenth century the movement metamorphosed in specific ways to become 'American naturalism'.

**Non-fiction novel** A **genre** which developed in the 1960s and 1970s, especially in the United States and among writers such as Truman

Capote, E. L. Doctorow, Norman Mailer and William Styron. Such novels took real, true, documentary subjects and explicitly represented them by way of devices associated with narrative fiction such as verbatim dialogue, the points of view of a participant/character in the action and detailed description of peoples' clothes, possessions and so forth.

**Novel** Extended narrative form which developed mainly in the eighteenth and nineteenth centuries but which has its antecedents in the epic, the romance and even the 'ancient novel' of the first century. Novels, which have been predominantly rendered in written prose, contain the mixed mode of **mimesis** and the 'poet's' **voice**, thus facilitating their own specific **heteroglossia**. They have also been concerned with the psychology of individuals and especially the way in which psychology is implicated in the social relations which exist in complex situations. Since the nineteenth century, the concerns of the novel have been most strongly associated with those of **realism**. However, as narratives, novels have also been subject to their own form: for example, in the nineteenth century, when novels were customarily serialized in periodical publications, there was a demand for novel narratives to be episodic. The influence of the novel on later technologies of narrative such as film, radio, television and the computer has been considerable.

**Object** The thing that a **sign** or **representamen** refers to. For Peirce, an object is anything that is represented in a sign. An object can be 'immediate', that is an object as it is represented to the human being as a sign; or it can be 'dynamic', the thing that causes the representation in a sign but does not necessarily appear in the representation.

**Omniscient narration** Narration which is all-knowing and god-like. In the act of *re*-presentation, omniscient narration selects some areas of knowledge for narration and deselects others, but is always in possession of the complete knowledge of characters, time and space of a narrative. In print narrative, omniscient narration is fairly straightforward; in cinematic narration it is more difficult to discern as the limited view offered by the cinematic frame always necessitates **editing** in order to exceed its limits and throws into question the extent to which the camera can 'see' and 'know' all.

**Parallel editing**   Process in film where actions filmed separately, at different times, can be spliced together in a finished movie in order to facilitate the depiction of simultaneous or near-simultaneous actions in a sequence. In *The Blue Lamp* (1950), for example, the climactic car chase through West London is interspersed with shots of the police control room in Paddington where desk-bound police operatives are engaged in the parallel action of tracking the pursuit of the villain and sending radio messages about his current location. The origins of parallel editing of this kind are frequently associated with the work of the American film-maker D. W. Griffith. Sometimes, parallel editing is called 'cross-cutting'.

**Plot**   The chain of causation which dictates that **story** events are somehow linked and that they are therefore to be depicted in relation to each other. The 'plot' or, in Ricoeur's terms, derived from Aristotle, *muthos* or emplotment, drives the story events.

**Postmodernism**   Term used to describe a period of artistic and scientific crisis in the latter half of the twentieth century. Postmodernism co-exists with a phenomenon called 'modernity' or, sometimes, 'postmodernity'. In (post)modernity, there exists a new set of material conditions arising from a decline in mass production in favour of flexible specialization; a sovereignty of information and service industries over the traditional products of manufacture; an emphasis on consumption rather than production; the dissolution of traditional, class-based politics into politics centred on 'identities'; and the development of communication technologies which have served to shrink distances between people across the globe and have made representations much more accessible. Sometimes postmodernism is conflated with postmodernity but, more frequently, is thought to consist of the styles of representation and the characteristics of critical thinking which result from, or co-exist with, the material conditions of postmodernity. Narrative is integral to postmodernism because of a perceived crisis of representation. On the one hand, this was manifested in the **rupturing effect** witnessed in many individual postmodern narratives. On the other, the status of knowledge was thought to need rethinking as a result of the general fate of narrative in the world, evidenced particularly by the decline of **grand narratives**.

**Real Author**   An empirical entity in **narrative levels**: the human being – or human beings in an organization – responsible for the production of a narrative. *See also* **Implied Author, Narrator, Narratee, Implied Reader** and **Real Reader**.

**Real Reader**   An empirical entity in **narrative levels**: the human being(s) who actively read a narrative. Often, real readers are human beings who share specific sociological characteristics which contribute to their common meaning-making. *See also* **Real Author, Implied Author, Narrator, Narratee** and **Implied Reader**.

**Realism**   Term used to describe the relation between a certain kind of representation, especially in the nineteenth-century novel, and the world depicted. 'Realism' connotes a mode of depiction which is putatively truer to the common-sense realities of life than other modes of depiction such as those pejoratively called 'romantic', 'idealized' or 'sentimental'. Although eighteenth-century novelists attempted 'realistic' depiction in their narratives, it was in the nineteenth century that the novel came to embody realism, primarily through focusing on the depiction of complex historical and personal relations, using large and densely populated landscapes minutely detailed by means of **reality effects**. Nineteenth-century realism also emphasized psychologies of individuals and the crises of everyday existence. As with the **epic**, realism in the novel relied on a combination of **mimesis** and **narrators' voices**, tempering potentially interminable mimetic **scenes** with the **summary** of the **Narrator**, and attempting to avoid disconcerting jumps and disturbing juxtapositions. Time in realism was invariably presented as consisting of discrete moments along a straight line and any extended lingering on events took place in the service of the narrator's exposition or summary rather than as a result of characters' subjective impressions as is often the case in **modernism**. *See also* **Classic realist text**.

**Reality effect**   Those parts of narrative identified by Roland Barthes (1992) in which **verisimilitude** is maintained through the description of details such as the interior of rooms, the physical appearances of minor characters, the weather, background sounds and so on. For **structuralism and the structural study of narrative and myth** the reality effect represents a dilemma because the details with which it is concerned are superfluous by comparison to the main functions or articulations of the narrative. These latter are often concerned with **plot**, whereas details in the reality effect are more frequently a matter of "exactitude of reference, superior to all other functions" (Barthes 1992: 138). Occasionally, reality effect details will, themselves, have important functions: they may be crucial indices of class, status, demeanour, psychology and so on; in detective fiction they may also constitute significant clues in the plot. In **modernism**, the reality effect in narrative is greatly expanded for its own sake.

**Representamen**  An entity that refers to or stands in for something but is not actually that something. A representamen stands in for an object from which it is different. For example, a human finger has its own independent existence but may become a representamen in the act of pointing. In this act, it will be brought into relation with an **object** (that to which it points), which will be something other than itself.

**Romance**  Narrative form that developed in the twelfth and thirteenth centuries, originally, as the terms suggests, 'in the Romance language', but later in English through such works as *Sir Gawain and the Green Knight* (late fourteenth century) and Malory's *La Morte d'Arthur* (1470). Romances were originally tales of heroism and chivalry rendered in verse. Prose romances in English continued into the Elizabethan age and contributed to the development of the novel form. In the twentieth century, romantic fiction derived from the models of nineteenth-century novelists such as Jane Austen crystallized into a popular **genre** frequently featuring chivalrous heroes; this, too, was called 'romance'.

**Rupturing effect**  Term used by Gunning to describe the way in which early film constantly established contact with a presumed audience, as performers interrupted their performance to address directly the camera and, by association, the cinematic spectator. In the process, performers provided a reminder that what viewers were watching was a film, constructed from a particular vantage point. In general, this action is sometimes called 'breaking frame'. The effect is analogous to the 'alienating' or 'estrangement' effect used in theatre, particularly drama influenced by Brecht (1964). It is also analogous to *discours* as manifest in written fiction, from the parodies of early **realism** in the eighteenth century to, especially, **postmodernism** in the late twentieth century.

**Scene**   The *showing* of events, places, times and people at some length. Like drama, it is frequently the case that events depicted in a scene will contain speech which can be imitated in written narrative through the use of quotation marks. *See also* **Mimesis**.

**Serial**   Narratives which range over a number of discrete episodes, all of which are of identical or similar length and delivered at regular intervals. The serial form was immensely popular in the nineteenth century as novels were commissioned for periodical publications. It was then adopted by broadcast radio in the late 1920s and early 1930s. In the 1950s the format proved eminently suitable for television programmers. Some television series last the length of a season, while others, particularly in the genre of 'soap opera', may run for decades while delaying a definitive ending. The serial format has also become established in computer-generated narrative as part of the general culture of updating Internet Web sites.

**Series**   Narrative form which developed within written fiction but which, arguably, has its roots in oral culture with selected tales of individuals such as Sinbad or tales of groups such as the heroes of Troy. Unlike the **serial** format, the series does not foreground development and progression towards an end. Typically, it will involve consecutive adventures in the life and career of an individual. In the late nineteenth century, series developed around characters such as Sherlock Holmes or Nick Carter, whose successive exploits would be related in regular instalments in periodicals. Some early comics of the period also relied on series characters. The series format later found its firmest footing within television, where some series, especially those within the 'situation comedy' genre, were able to run for decades.

**Sign**   Any entity that stands for something else and does so for an interpreter. In human terms, a sign is 'dialogical' because in order to be a sign it needs to be interpreted by someone as such. Furthermore, interpreters may transform and augment signs. Narrative signs stand for the world by means of a relation of *re*-presentation: that is, *re*-presentation of relations of space, time and sequence. Thus, narrative signs can refer to specific fictional or real **objects**; they can prompt reference well beyond those objects; and they can serve the purpose of creating new worlds. *See also* **Dialogue.**

*Sjuzet* Term introduced by the Russian Formalist critics to refer to the way in which the chronological raw materials of a **story** are *organized*. The story events which are to be *re*-presented by a narrative may have taken place, for example, within a particular chronological sequence; *sjuzet* can act to 'rearrange' this sequence or ensure that the narration of some events is more extensive than others. *See also* **Summary** and **Scene.**

*Skaz* *see* **Free indirect discourse**

**Story** All the events which are to be depicted in a narrative and which are connected by means of a **plot.**

**Structuralism and the structural study of narrative and myth** Understandings of narrative in which the overall 'structure' of a narrative is thought to bear the fundamental meaning. Once this structure is identified it can be considered to be like a 'grammar'; that is, it will be discovered to be capable of 'generating' new narratives. Alternatively, the 'structure' of narrative can be considered a vessel into which new contents might be poured; the sentences or the contents themselves are not nearly as important as that which gives them shape. Claude Lévi-Strauss identifies the structure of myths within a set of basic oppositions and relations. Yet, as with the work of related narrative theorists such as Claude Bremond, A. J. Greimas, Vladimir Propp and Northrop Frye, it is difficult to demonstrate that such structures are objective entities.

**Summary** A form of prose in a narrative, such as a **novel**, which *tells* about events or people without imitating them. It sums up events, places, times and people rather than giving a full account of them.

Summary allows a novel to move to a later point in time, passing over quickly what happens in between narrated events; alternatively, summary allows movement from one place to another, more distant one, within the same time frame. *See also Sjuzet.*

**Surrealism** Modernist movement which embraced painting, film-making, performance and, especially, writing. Surrealism took as its central concern the manifold nature of the Freudian unconscious and, most importantly, the idea that modes of *conscious* representation are not the only ones available to humans. Some surrealist films seek to banish narrative from their representations while others, such as *Un Chien Andalou* (1927), in an oblique way, affirm it.

**Timeshifting** Process of television viewing facilitated by domestic use of video cassette recorders (VCRs) which interrupts flow. VCRs enable viewers to deviate from the schedule of programmes offered by broadcasters by recording television programmes and watching them at a different time. Also, a programme on one channel might be recorded with a VCR in order to allow the viewer to watch a programme on a different channel at the same time. The particularly keen viewer, like the reader of a book, might even timeshift *within* a narrative, rewinding certain sequences in a recorded programme to check details or re-experience their narration.

**Transmission model of narrative** Understanding of narrative production which, in its simplest manifestation, involves an author sending a message which is then unproblematically decoded and understood by a reader. The model is implicitly extended in approaches to narrative which rely on biography or valorize the individual 'genius' of authors.

**Verisimilitude** A logical and meaningful connection between described objects as opposed to a completely detailed analogue of them. In opposition to a strict sense of what is 'realistic', verisimilitude consists of a range of readers' expectations about what is legitimate, believable and consonant with common wisdom, and therefore acceptable for representation in narrative. Verisimilitude can involve totally unrealistic, but acceptable, acts such as bursting into song during a musical; it is therefore a principle of textual coherence rather than an area in which there exists an unproblematic relation between the fictional and the real world.

**Voice**   For Plato, epic poets such as Homer used two modes of narrative *re*-presentation: one which consisted of an imitation of the voice of characters, and another which is not imitative and which he called the 'poet's own voice'. The latter clearly conflates the role of an 'author' and a **Narrator**. Bakhtin suggests that the distinction between characters' voices and those of authors/narrators, when necessarily employed in representing **heteroglossia** in novels, is a 'double-voiced discourse'. That is, the voice of a character is represented by a narrator even when the character's speech is a direct imitation in quotation marks. It is as if the voice of the narrator and the voice of the character are always in conversation or **dialogue**. The voice of the character is therefore always tied to that of the narrator's intentions; equally, though, the voice of the narrator is always embroiled in the social circumstances that give rise to heteroglossia.

# BIBLIOGRAPHY

Achebe, C. (1998) 'An image of Africa: racism in Conrad's *Heart of Darkness*' in
   A. M. Roberts (ed.) *Joseph Conrad* Harlow: Longman.

Adorno, T., Benjamin, W., Bloch, E., Brecht, B. and Lukacs, G. (1980) *Aesthetics and
   Politics* London: Verso.

Åhnebrink, L. (1950) *The Beginnings of Naturalism in American Fiction: A Study of
   the Works of Hamlin Garland, Stephen Crane, and Frank Norris with Special
   Reference to Some European Influences* Cambridge, MA: Harvard University
   Press.

Alexandrian, S. (1989) *Surrealist Art* London: Thames and Hudson.

Altman, R. (1987) *The American Film Musical*. Bloomington: Indiana University
   Press.

—— (1999) *Film/Genre* London: British Film Institute.

Ammons, E. (1995) 'Expanding the canon' in D. Pizer (ed.) *The Cambridge
   Companion to American Realism and Naturalism: Howells to London*
   Cambridge: Cambridge University Press.

Anderson, B. (1991) *Imagined Communities* rev. edn, London: Verso.

Anderson, M. (1998) 'Folklore, folklife and other bootstrapping traditions' in
   R. Kevelson (ed.) *Hi-Fives: A Trip to Semiotics* New York: Peter Lang.

Appignanesi, L. and Forrester, J. (1992) *Freud's Women* London: Weidenfeld and
   Nicholson.

Aristotle (1996) *Poetics* trans. and intro. M. Heath, Harmondsworth: Penguin.

Arnold, M. (1980) *Culture and Anarchy* in L. Trilling (ed.) *The Portable Matthew
   Arnold* Harmondsworth: Penguin.

Atkins, J. (1964) *The Art of Ernest Hemingway: His Work and Personality* London:
   Spring Books.

Auerbach, E. (1968) *Mimesis: The Representation of Reality in Western Literature*
   Princeton: Princeton University Press.

—— (1984) *Scenes from the Drama of European Literature* Manchester:
   Manchester University Press.

Austen, J. (1985) *Persuasion* Harmondsworth: Penguin.

Baines, J. (1971) *Joseph Conrad: A Critical Biography* Harmondsworth: Penguin.

Bakhtin, M. M. (1981) *The Dialogic Imagination: Four Essays* Austin: University of
   Texas Press.

—— (1984) *Problems of Dostoevsky's Poetics* ed. and trans. Caryl Emerson,
   London and Minneapolis: University of Minnesota Press.

Balzac, H. de (1992) 'Balzac on his role as secretary to society', reprinted from the
   preface to the *The Human Comedy*, reprinted in L. Furst (ed.) *Realism*
   Harlow: Longman.

Barron, J. and Nokes, D. (1993) 'Market, morality and sentiment: the eighteenth-century novel' in A. M. Roberts (ed.) *The Novel: From its Origins to the Present Day* London: Bloomsbury.

Barthes, R. (1974) *S/Z* trans. R. Howard, New York: Hill and Wang.

—— (1992) 'The reality effect' in L. Furst (ed.) *Realism* Harlow: Longman.

Baudrillard, J. (1981) *For a Critique of the Political Economy of the Sign* trans. C. Levin, St Louis: Telos.

—— (1983) *Simulations* New York: Semiotext(e).

—— (1988) *The Ecstasy of Communication* trans. B. Schutze and C. Schutze, New York: Semiotext(e).

—— (1995) *Simulacra and Simulation* trans. S. F. Glaser, Ann Arbor: University of Michigan Press.

Beattie, O. and Csikszentmihalyi, M. (1981) 'On the socialization influence of books' *Child Psychology and Human Development* 11 (1): 3–18.

Bell, M. (1990) 'How primordial is narrative?' in C. Nash (ed.) *Narrative in Culture* London: Routledge.

Bell, M. D. (1993) *The Problem of American Realism: Studies in the Cultural History of a Literary Idea* Chicago and London: University of Chicago Press.

Belton, J. (1994) *American Cinema/American Culture* New York: McGraw-Hill.

Bennett, T. (1990) *Outside Literature* London: Routledge.

Benveniste, É (1971) *Problems in General Linguistics* trans. M. E. Meek, Coral Gables: University of Miami Press.

Berger, A. A. (1997) *Narratives in Popular Culture, Media and Everyday Life* Thousand Oaks and London: Sage.

Bernal, M. (1987) *Black Athena: The Afro-Asiatic Roots of Classical Civilization*, vol. 1, London: Free Association Books.

Bertens, H. (1995) *The Idea of the Postmodern: A History* London: Routledge.

Berthoff, W. (1981) *The Ferment of Realism: American Literature, 1884–1919* Cambridge: Cambridge University Press.

Bettelheim, B. (1976) *The Uses of Enchantment: The Meaning and Importance of Fairy Tales* Harmondsworth: Penguin.

Bhabha, H. K. (1990a) 'DissemiNation: time, narrative and the margins of the modern nation' in H. K. Bhabha (ed.) *Nation and Narration* London: Routledge.

—— (1990b) 'The third space: interview with Jonathan Rutherford' in J. Rutherford (ed.) *Identity: Community, Culture, Difference* London: Lawrence and Wishart.

Bishop, J. P. (1959) 'Homage to Hemingway' in M. Cowley (ed.) *After the Genteel Tradition: American Writers Since 1910* Gloucester, MA: Peter Smith.

Booth, W. C. (1961) *The Rhetoric of Fiction* Chicago: University of Chicago Press.

Bordwell, D. (1985) *Narration in the Fiction Film* London: Methuen.

Bordwell, D. and Thompson, K. (1993) *Film Art: An Introduction* 4th edn, New York: McGraw-Hill.

Bordwell, D., Staiger, J. and Thompson, K. (1985) *The Classical Hollywood Cinema: Film Style and Mode of Production to 1960* London: Routledge.

Borus, D. H. (1989) *Writing Realism: Howells, James and Norris in the Mass Market* Chapel Hill and London: University of North Carolina Press.

Bradbury, M. and McFarlane, J. (1976) 'The name and nature of modernism' in M. Bradbury and J. McFarlane (eds) *Modernism* Harmondsworth: Penguin.

Branigan, E. (1992) *Narrative Comprehension and Film* London: Routledge.

Brantlinger, P. (1985) '*Heart of Darkness*: anti-imperialism, racism or impressionism' *Criticism* 27: 363–85.

Brecht, B. (1964) *Brecht on Theatre* ed. and trans. J. Willett, London: Methuen.

Breton, A. (1991) *What is Surrealism?* London: Pluto.

Brewster, B. and Jacobs, L. (1997) *Theatre to Cinema: Stage Pictorialism and the Early Feature Film* Oxford: Oxford University Press.

Brink, A. P. (1998) *The Novel: Language and Narrative from Cervantes to Calvino* London: Macmillan.

Brooks, P. (1982) 'Freud's master plot' in S. Felman (ed.) *Literature and Psychoanalysis The Question of Reading: Otherwise* Baltimore and London: Yale University Press.

—— (1984) *Reading for the Plot: Design and Intention in Narrative* Cambridge, MA: Harvard University Press.

Bruner, J. (1990) *Acts of Meaning* Cambridge, MA and London: Harvard University Press.

Budd, L. J. (1995) 'The American background' in D. Pizer (ed.) *The Cambridge Companion to American Realism and Naturalism: Howells to London* Cambridge: Cambridge University Press.

Burch, N. (1990) 'A primitive mode of representation?' in T. Elsaesser with A. Barker (ed.) *Early Cinema: Space, Frame, Narrative* London: British Film Institute.

Butler, C. S. (1994) *Early Modernism: Literature, Music and Painting in Europe, 1900–1916* Oxford: Clarendon Press.

Byrne, T. (1981) *Local Government in Britain: Everybody's Guide to How It All Works* Harmondsworth: Penguin.

Calvino, I. (1982) *If on a winter's night a traveller* London: Picador.

Campbell, J. (1975) *The Hero with a Thousand Faces* London: Abacus.

Cantril, H., Gaudet, H. and Herzog, H. (1940) *The Invasion from Mars*, Princeton: Princeton University Press.

Capote, T. (1966) *In Cold Blood: A True Account of a Multiple Murder and Its Consequences* Harmondsworth: Penguin.

Cardwell, D. (1994) *The Fontana History of Technology* London: Fontana.

Carr, D. (1991) 'Discussion: Ricoeur on narrative' in D. Wood (ed.) *On Paul Ricoeur: Narrative and Interpretation* London: Routledge.

Caughie, J. (ed.) (1981) *Theories of Authorship* London: Routledge and Kegan Paul in association with the British Film Institute.

Chanan, M. (1996) *The Dream that Kicks: The Prehistory and Early Years of Cinema in Britain* London: Routledge.

Chandler, R. (1944) 'The simple art of murder' *Atlantic Monthly* December: 62–8.

—— (1948) *The Big Sleep* Harmondsworth: Penguin (originally 1939).

—— (1984) 'Letter to Frederick Lewis Allen, May 7, 1948' in D. Gardiner and K. Sorley Walker (eds.) *Raymond Chandler Speaking* London: Allison and Busby.

Chatman, S. (1978) *Story and Discourse: Narrative Structure in Fiction and Film* Ithaca and London: Cornell University Press.

—— (1990) *Coming to Terms: The Rhetoric of Narrative in Fiction and Film* Ithaca and London: Cornell University Press.

Chaucer, G. (1966) *The General Prologue to the Canterbury Tales* ed. J. Winny, Cambridge: Cambridge University Press.

Christie, I. (1994) *The Last Machine: Early Cinema and the Birth of the Modern World* London: British Film Institute.

Clark, R. W. (1982) *Freud: The Man and the Cause* London: Granada.

Cobley, P. (2000) *The American Thriller: Generic Innovation and Social Change in the 1970s* London: Palgrave.

Cohn, D. (1966) 'Narrated monologue: definition of a fictional style' *Comparative Literature* 18 (2) Spring: 97–112.

Collins, J. (1989) *Uncommon Cultures: Popular Culture and Post-modernism* London: Routledge.

—— (1992) 'Television and postmodernism' in R. C. Allen (ed.) *Channels of Discourse Reassembled: Television and Contemporary Criticism* London: Routledge.

Connor, S. (1989) *Postmodernist Culture: An Introduction to Theories of the Contemporary* Oxford: Blackwell.

Conrad, J. (1973) *Heart of Darkness* Harmondsworth: Penguin (originally 1902).

Corner, J. and Harvey, S. (1996) 'Introduction' in *Television Times: A Reader* London: Arnold.

Cornford, F. (ed. and trans.) (1945) *The Republic of Plato* Oxford: Oxford University Press.

Coupe, L. (1997) *Myth* London: Routledge.

Cowley, M. (1959) 'Foreword: the revolt against gentility' in M. Cowley (ed.) *After the Genteel Tradition: American Writers Since 1910* Gloucester, MA: Peter Smith.

Crews, F. (1975) 'Conrad's uneasiness – and ours' in *Out of My System* New York: Oxford University Press.

Crystal, D. (1998) *Language Play* Harmondsworth: Penguin.

Csikszentmihalyi, M. (1992) *Flow – The Psychology of Evolution* London: Rider.

—— (1994) *The Evolving Self: A Psychology for the Third Millennium* New York: HarperCollins.

—— (1996) *Creativity: Flow and the Psychology of Discovery and Invention* New York: HarperCollins.

Cubitt, S. (1991) *Timeshift: On Video Culture* London: Routledge.

Davies, P. (1996) 'What happened before the Big Bang?' in J. Brockman and K. Matson (eds) *How Things Are: A Science Tool-kit for the Mind* London: Phoenix.

Davis, L. J. (1983) *Factual Fictions: Origins of the English Novel* New York: Columbia University Press.

Denzin, N. K. (1991) *Images of Postmodern Society: Social Theory and Contemporary Cinema* London: Sage.

Deutsch, D. (1997) *The Fabric of Reality* Harmondsworth: Penguin.

Dewberry, E. (1996) 'Hemingway's journalism and the realist dilemma' in S. Donaldson (ed.) *The Cambridge Companion to Ernest Hemingway* Cambridge: Cambridge University Press.

Dinwiddy, J. R. (1979) 'Luddism and politics in the Northern counties' *Social History* 4: 33–63.

—— (1986) *From Luddism to the First Reform Bill* Oxford: Basil Blackwell.

Donaldson, S. (1978) *By Force of Will: The Life and Art of Ernest Hemingway* Harmondsworth: Penguin.

Doody, M. A. (1998) *The True Story of the Novel* London: Fontana.

Drakakis, J. (1981) 'The essence that's not seen: radio adaptations of stage plays' in P. Lewis (ed.) *Radio Drama* London and New York: Longman.

Durant, W. (1935) *The Story of Civilization Part 1 Our Oriental Heritage* New York: Simon and Schuster.

Durgnat, R. (1977) *Luis Buñuel* Berkeley: University of California Press.

Eagleton, T. (1976) *Criticism and Ideology* London: Verso.

—— (1996) *The Illusions of Postmodernism* Oxford: Blackwell.

Easthope, A. (1983) *Poetry as Discourse* London: Methuen.

Eco, U. (1985) *Reflections on* The Name of the Rose, trans. W. Weaver, London: Secker and Warburg.

Eisenstein, E. (1979) *The Printing Press as an Agent of Change: Communications and Cultural Transformations in Early-Modern Europe* 2 vols, New York: Cambridge University Press.

Eisenstein, S. (1985) 'The cinematographic principle and the ideogram' in G. Mast and M. Cohen (eds) *Film Theory and Criticism: Introductory Readings* 3rd edn, Oxford: Oxford University Press.

Eliot, G. (1965) *Middlemarch* ed. W. J. Harvey, Harmondsworth: Penguin.

Ellis, J. (1992) *Visible Fictions: Film, Television, Video* 2nd edn, London: Routledge.

Elsaesser, T. (1990) 'Afterword' in T. Elsaesser with A. Barker (ed.) *Early Cinema: Space, Frame, Narrative* London: British Film Institute.

Elsaesser, T. and Barker, A. (1990) 'Introduction to Part III' in T. Elsaesser with A. Barker (ed.) *Early Cinema: Space, Frame, Narrative* London: British Film Institute.

Ermarth, E. D. (1998) *Realism and Consensus in the English Novel* 2nd edn, Edinburgh: Edinburgh University Press.

Etherington-Smith, M. (1992) *Dalí* London: Sinclair-Stevenson.

Evans, R. O. (1956) 'Conrad's underworld' *Modern Fiction Studies* 2: 56–62.

Feder, L. (1955) 'Marlow's descent into Hell' *Nineteenth Century Fiction* 9: 280–92.

Finley, M. I. (1979) *The World of Odysseus* Harmondsworth: Pelican.

Fish, S. E. (1980) *Is there a Text in this Class? The Authority of Interpretive Communities* Cambridge, MA: Harvard University Press.

—— (1981) 'Why no one's afraid of Wolfgang Iser' *Diacritics* 11 (March): 2–13; repr. in P. Cobley (ed.) *The Communication Theory Reader* London: Routledge, 1996.

Fiske, J. (1987) *Television Culture* London: Routledge.

Fiske, J. and Hartley, J. (1978) *Reading Television* London: Methuen.

Fitzgerald, F. (1996) 'Apocalypse Now' in M. C. Carnes (ed.) *Past Imperfect: History According to the Movies* London: Cassell.

Fleischmann, A. (1967) *Conrad's Politics: Community and Anarchy in the Fiction of Joseph Conrad* Baltimore and London: Johns Hopkins University Press.

Fludernik, M. (1996) *Towards a 'Natural' Narratology* London: Routledge.

Forster, E. M. (1962) *Aspects of the Novel* Harmondsworth: Penguin.

Fothergill, A. (1989) *Heart of Darkness* Milton Keynes: Open University Press.

Foucault, M. (1971) *Madness and Civilization: A History of Insanity in the Age of Reason* London: Tavistock.

—— (1986) 'What is an author?' in P. Rabinow (ed.) *The Foucault Reader* Harmondsworth: Penguin.

Fowles, J. (1977) *The French Lieutenant's Woman* London: Panther.

Freeman, M. (1998) 'Mythical time, historical time, and the narrative fabric of the self' *Narrative Inquiry* 8 (1): 27–50.

Freud, S. (1962) 'The question of lay analysis' in *Two Short Accounts of Psychoanalysis* Harmondsworth: Penguin.

—— (1973a) 'Femininity' in *New Introductory Lectures in Psychoanalysis* Pelican Freud Library 2, Harmondsworth: Penguin.

—— (1973b) 'Fixation to traumas – the unconscious' in *Introductory Lectures in Psychoanalysis* Pelican Freud Library 1, Harmondsworth: Penguin.

—— (1973c) 'Symbolism in dreams' in *Introductory Lectures in Psychoanalysis* Pelican Freud Library 1, Harmondsworth: Penguin.

—— (1976a) *The Psychopathology of Everyday Life* Pelican Freud Library 5, Harmondsworth: Penguin.

—— (1976b) *The Interpretation of Dreams* Pelican Freud Library 4, Harmondsworth: Penguin (originally 1899).

—— (1977a) 'Female sexuality' in *On Sexuality* Pelican Freud Library 7, Harmondsworth: Penguin.

—— (1977b) 'Three essays on the theory of sexuality' in *On Sexuality* Pelican Freud Library 7, Harmondsworth: Penguin.

—— (1984a) 'Repression' in *On Metapsychology* Pelican Freud Library 11, Harmondsworth: Penguin.

—— (1984b) 'Negation' in *On Metapsychology* Pelican Freud Library 11, Harmondsworth: Penguin.

Friedman, N. (1955) 'Point of view in fiction: the development of a critical concept' *PMLA* 70: 1160–84.

Frye, N. (1957) *The Anatomy of Criticism* Princeton: Princeton University Press.

Fukuyama, F. (1992) *The End of History and the Last Man* Harmondsworth: Penguin.

Furst, L. (ed.) (1992) *Realism* Harlow: Longman.

Gallagher, T. (1986) 'Shoot-out at the genre corral: patterns in the evolution of the Western' in B. K. Grant (ed.) *Film Genre Reader* Austin: University of Texas Press.

Gaudreault, A. (1990a) 'Film, narrative, narration: the cinema of the Lumière both-ers' in T. Elsaesser with A. Barker (ed.) *Early Cinema: Space, Frame, Narrative* London: British Film Institute.

—— (1990b) 'The infringement of copyright laws and its effects' in T. Elsaesser with A. Barker (ed.) *Early Cinema: Space, Frame, Narrative* London: British Film Institute.

—— (1990c) 'Showing and telling: image and word in early cinema' in T. Elsaesser with A. Barker (ed.) *Early Cinema: Space, Frame, Narrative* London: British Film Institute.

—— (1990d) 'Detours in narrative: the development of cross-cutting' in T. Elsaesser with A. Barker (ed.) *Early Cinema: Space, Frame, Narrative* London: British Film Institute.

Gay, P. (1989) *Freud: A Life for Our Time* London: Macmillan.

Gee, J. (1991) 'A linguistic approach to narrative' *Journal of Narrative and Life History* 1: 15–39.

Genette, G. (1982) *Narrative Discourse* Oxford: Basil Blackwell.

—— (1988) *Narrative Discourse Revisited* Ithaca and London: Cornell University Press.

Germain, E. B. (1978) 'Introduction' in *Surrealist Poetry in English* Harmondsworth: Penguin.

Gershman, H. S. (1969) *The Surrealist Revolution in France* Ann Arbor: University of Michigan.

Gibson, A. (1980) 'Authors, speakers, readers and mock readers' in J. P. Tompkins (ed.) *Reader-Response Criticism: From Formalism to Post-structuralism* Baltimore and London: Johns Hopkins University Press.

—— (1996) *Towards a Postmodern Theory of Narrative* Edinburgh: Edinburgh University Press.

Giddens, A. (1991) *Modernity and Self-identity: Self and Society in the Late Modern Age* Cambridge: Polity Press.

Gombrich, E. (1956) *The Story of Art* London: Phaidon.

Goody, J. and Watt, I. (1968) 'The consequences of literacy' in J. Goody (ed.) *Literacy in Traditional Societies* Cambridge: Cambridge University Press.

Gould, S. J. (1977) *Ontogeny and Phylogeny* Cambridge, MA and London: Belknap Press.

Gray, A. (1984) *Unlikely Stories, Mostly* Harmondsworth: Penguin.

Greenblatt, S. (1991) *Marvelous Possessions: The Wonder of the New World* Chicago and London: University of Chicago Press.

Gribbin, J. (1999) *The Birth of Time: How We Measured the Age of the Universe* London: Phoenix.

Griffin, J. (1980) *Homer* Oxford: Oxford University Press.

Guerard, A. (1966) *Conrad the Novelist* Cambridge, MA: Harvard University Press.

Gunning, T. (1990a) 'The cinema of attractions: early film, its spectator and the avant-garde' in T. Elsaesser with A. Barker (ed.) *Early Cinema: Space, Frame, Narrative* London: British Film Institute.

—— (1990b) ' "Primitive" cinema: a frame-up or the trick's on us?' in T. Elsaesser with A. Barker (ed.) *Early Cinema: Space, Frame, Narrative* London: British Film Institute.

—— (1990c) 'Weaving a narrative: style and economic background in Griffith's Biograph films' in T. Elsaesser with A. Barker (ed.) *Early Cinema: Space, Frame, Narrative* London: British Film Institute.

Hainsworth, J. B. (1992) 'The criticism of an oral Homer' in C. Emlyn-Jones, L. Hardwick and J. Purkis (eds) *Homer: Readings and Images* London: Duckworth.

Hall, S. (1997) 'The work of representation' in *Representation: Cultural Representations and Signifying Practices* London: Sage.

Halliwell, S. (1998) *Aristotle's Poetics* London: Duckworth.

Harré, R. (1990) 'Some narrative conventions of scientific discourse' in C. Nash (ed.) *Narrative in Culture* London: Routledge.

Hartley, J. (1982) *Understanding News* London: Methuen.

Harvey, D. (1988) *The Condition of Postmodernity* Oxford: Blackwell.

Havelock, E. A. (1963) *Preface to Plato* Cambridge, MA: Belknap Press.

—— (1976) *The Origins of Western Literacy* Toronto: Ontario Institute of Education.

—— (1986) *The Muse Learns to Write: Reflection on Orality and Literacy from Antiquity to the Present* New Haven and London: Yale University Press.

Hawking, S. (1988) *A Brief History of Time: From the Big Bang to Black Holes* New York: Bantam.

Hawthorn, J. (1997) *Studying the Novel* 3rd edn, London: Arnold.

Hemingway, E. (1955) 'The Killers' in *Men Without Women* Harmondsworth: Penguin.

Hirschkop, K. (1999) *Mikhail Bakhtin: An Aesthetic for Democracy* Oxford: Oxford University Press.

Holub, R. C. (1984) *Reception Theory: A Critical Introduction* London: Methuen.

Hunter, J. P. (1990) *Before Novels: The Cultural Contexts of Eighteenth-century Fiction* New York and London: Norton.

Hutcheon, L. (1989) *The Politics of Postmodernism* London: Routledge.

Huyssen, A. (1986) *After the Great Divide: Modernism, Mass Culture and Postmodernism* London: Macmillan.

Hymes, D. (1996) *Ethnography, Linguistics, Narrative Inequality: Towards an Understanding of Voice* London: Taylor and Francis.

Iser, W. (1974) *The Implied Reader: Patterns of Communication in Prose Fiction from Bunyan to Beckett* Baltimore and London: Johns Hopkins University Press.

—— (1981) 'Talk like whales' *Diacritics* 11 (September): 82–7; repr. in P. Cobley (ed.) *The Communication Theory Reader* London: Routledge, 1996.

—— (1989) *Prospecting: From Reader Response to Literary Anthropology* Baltimore and London: Johns Hopkins University Press.

James, M. R. (1992a) 'Preface' in *Collected Ghost Stories* Ware: Wordsworth.

—— (1992b) 'The Mezzotint' in *Collected Ghost Stories* Ware: Wordsworth.

Jameson, F. (1991) *Postmodernism or, the Cultural Logic of Late Capitalism* London: Verso.

Jaynes, J. (1990) *The Origins of Consciousness in the Breakdown of the Bicameral Mind* Harmondsworth: Penguin.

Jean, M. (ed.) (1980) *The Autobiography of Surrealism* Harmondsworth: Penguin.

Jenkins, H. (1992) *Textual Poachers: Television and Participatory Culture* London: Routledge.

Jensen, K. B. (1995) *The Social Semiotics of Mass Communication.* London and New Delhi: Sage.

Jones, E. (1964) *The Life and Work of Sigmund Freud* Harmondsworth: Penguin.

Josipovici, G. (1979) *The World and the Book* 2nd edn, London: Macmillan.

Jost, F. (1998) 'The promise of genres' *Reseaux* 6 (1): 99–121.

Joyce, J. (1964) *A Portrait of the Artist as a Young Man* London: Heinemann.

Kaplan, E. A. (ed.) (1988) *Postmodernism and Its Discontents: Theories, Practices* London: Verso.

Karl, F. R. (1989) 'Introduction to the *Danse Macabre*: Conrad's *Heart of Darkness*' in R. C. Murfin (ed.) *Heart of Darkness: A Case Study in Contemporary Criticism* New York: St Martin's Press.

Keen, S. (1998) *Victorian Renovations of the Novel: Narrative Annexes and the Boundaries of Representation* Cambridge: Cambridge University Press.

King, S. (1991) 'A preface in two parts' in *The Stand: The Complete and Uncut Edition* London: New English Library.

—— (1992) *Gerald's Game* London: Hodder and Stoughton.

Knight, L. (1986) *Talking to a Stranger: A Consumer's Guide to Therapy* London: Fontana.

Kovel, J. (1990) *The Complete Guide to Therapy* Harmondsworth: Penguin.

Kozloff, S. (1992) 'Narrative theory and television' in R. C. Allen (ed.) *Channels of Discourse Reassembled: Television and Contemporary Criticism* London: Routledge.

Kress, G. R. (1999a) 'A creative spell' *Guardian Education* 16 November: 8.

—— (1999b) *Early Spelling* London: Routledge.

Kuhn, T. S. (1970) *The Structure of Scientific Revolutions* Chicago and London: University of Chicago Press.

Kunelius, R. (1994) 'Order and interpretation: a narrative perspective on journalism' *European Journal of Communication* 9: 249–70.

Lacy, D. (1996) *From Grunts to Gigabytes: Communications and Society* Urbana and Chicago: University of Illinois Press.

Lapsley, R. and Westlake, M. (1988) *Film Theory: An Introduction* Manchester: Manchester University Press.

Lattimore, R. (ed. and trans.) (1967) *The Odyssey of Homer* New York: Harper and Row.

Lawson, J. and Silver, H. (1973) *A Social History of Education in England* London: Methuen.

Leavis, F. R. (1962) *The Great Tradition: George Eliot, Henry James, Joseph Conrad* Harmondsworth: Penguin.

Lehan, R. (1995) 'The European background' in D. Pizer (ed.) *The Cambridge Companion to American Realism and Naturalism: Howells to London* Cambridge: Cambridge University Press.

Levine, G. (1997) 'The narrative of scientific epistemology' *Narrative* 5 (3): 227–51.

Lévi-Strauss, C. (1977) *Structural Anthropology 1* Harmondsworth: Penguin.

Lewis, C. S. (1960) *A Preface to Paradise Lost* Oxford: Oxford University Press.

—— (1998) *Studies in Medieval and Renaissance Literature* Cambridge: Cambridge University Press.

Lewis, L. A. (ed.) (1992) *The Adoring Audience* London: Routledge.

Lodge, D. (1981) '*Middlemarch* and the idea of the classic realist text' in A. Kettle (ed.) *The Nineteenth Century Novel: Critical Essays and Documents* 2nd edn, London: Heinemann.

—— (1992) *The Art of Fiction* Harmondsworth: Penguin.

—— (1997) *The Practice of Writing* Harmondsworth: Penguin.

Loomba, A. (1998) *Colonialism/Postcolonialism* London: Routledge.

Lord, A. (2000) *The Singer of Tales* 2nd edn, ed. S. Mitchell and G. Nagy, Cambridge, MA and London: Harvard University Press.

Lothe, J. (2000) *Narrative in Fiction and Film: An Introduction* Oxford: Oxford University Press.

Lotman, J. M. (1977) 'The structure of the narrative text' in D. P. Lucid (ed.) *Soviet Semiotics: An Anthology* Baltimore and London: Johns Hopkins University Press.

Lovell, T. (1983) *Pictures of Reality: Aesthetics, Politics, Pleasure* London: British Film Institute.

—— (1987) *Consuming Fiction* London: Verso.

Lubbock, P. (1926) *The Craft of Fiction* London: Jonathan Cape.

Lukacs, G. (1969) *The Historical Novel* Harmondsworth: Penguin.

Lukacs, J. (1990) *The Duel: Hitler vs. Churchill: 10 May–11 July 1940* London: Phoenix Press.

Lynn, K. S. (1989) *Hemingway* London: Cardinal.

Lyons, J. (1981) *Language, Meaning and Context* London: Fontana.

Lyotard, J.-F. (1984) *The Postmodern Condition: A Report on Knowledge* trans. G. Bennington and B. Massumi, Manchester: Manchester University Press.

MacCabe, C. (1974) 'Realism and the cinema: notes on some Brechtian theses' *Screen* 15: 7–27.

—— (1977) 'Theory and film: principles of realism and pleasure' *Screen* 17: 46–61.

—— (1978) *James Joyce and the Revolution of the Word* London: Macmillan.

Macherey, P. (1978) *A Theory of Literary Production* London: Routledge and Kegan Paul.

Marcus, S. (1997) 'The logical and semiotic status of the canonic formula of myth' *Semiotica* 116 (2/4): 115–88.

Masson, J. M. (1986) *A Dark Science: Women, Sexuality and Psychiatry in the Nineteenth Century* New York: Farrar, Straus and Giroux.

McClary, S. (1998) 'The impromptu that trod on a loaf: or how music tells stories' *Narrative* 5 (1): 20–35.

McKeon, M. (1987) *The Origins of the English Novel 1600–1740* Baltimore and London: Johns Hopkins University Press.

McLuhan, M. (1962) *The Gutenberg Galaxy: The Making of Typographic Man* Toronto: University of Toronto Press.

McLynn, F. (1993) *Hearts of Darkness: The European Exploration of Africa* London: Pimlico.

McNair, B. (1996) *News and Journalism in the UK* 2nd edn, London: Routledge.

McRobbie, A. (1994) *Postmodernism and Popular Culture* London: Routledge.

Mellencamp, P. (1990) 'TV time and catastrophe or *Beyond the Pleasure Principle* of television' in *Logics of Television* London and Bloomington: British Film Institute and Indiana University Press.

Merrell, F. (2001) 'Charles Sanders Peirce's concept of the sign' in P. Cobley (ed.) *The Routledge Companion to Semiotics and Linguistics* London: Routledge.

Metz, C. (1982) *Psychoanalysis and Cinema: The Imaginary Signifier* trans. C. Britton, A. Williams, B. Brewster and A. Guzzetti, London: Macmillan.

Meyers, J. (1987) *Hemingway: A Biography* London: Paladin.

Miller, R. (1989) 'Killing time before Armageddon' (profile of Mickey Spillane) *Sunday Times Magazine* 17 December: 34–6, 39.

Mitchell, J. (1973) *Psychoanalysis and Feminism* Harmondsworth: Penguin.

Morley, D. (1986) *Family Television: Cultural Power and Domestic Leisure* London: Routledge.

Murfin, R. C. (1989) 'Introduction' in *Heart of Darkness: A Case Study in Contemporary Criticism* New York: St Martin's Press.

Murray, J. H. (1997) *Hamlet on the Holodeck: The Future of Narrative in Cyberspace* Cambridge, MA: MIT Press.

Nebel, F. (1965) 'Winter Kill' in R. Goulart (ed.) *The Hardboiled Dicks: An Anthology of Detective Fiction from the Pulp Magazines* New York: Pocket Books.

Nicholls, P. (1995) *Modernisms: A Literary Guide* London: Macmillan.

Norris, F. (1903) *The Responsibilities of the Novelist and Other Literary Essays* New York: Doubleday, Page and Company.

Ogdon, B. (1992) 'Hard-boiled ideology' *Critical Quarterly* 34 (1): 71–87.

Ong, W. J. (1982) *Orality and Literacy: The Technologizing of the Word* London: Methuen.

Pakenham, T. (1994) *The Scramble for Africa* London: Abacus.

Parkes, M. B. (1992) *Pause and Effect: An Introduction to the History of Punctuation in the West* Aldershot: Scolar Press.

Pearsall, D. A. (1970) '*The Canterbury Tales*' in W. F. Bolton (ed.) *The Middle Ages* London: Sphere.

Peirce, C. S. (1955) 'Logic as semiotic: the theory of signs' in J. Buchler (ed.) *Philosophical Writings of Peirce* New York: Dover.

—— (1966) 'Letters to Lady Welby' in P. P. Wiener (ed.) *Charles S. Peirce: Selected Writings* New York: Dover.

Petrilli, S. and Ponzio, A. (1998) *Signs of Research on Signs* special issue of *Semiotische Berichte* 22 (3/4).

*Picasso and Photography* (1999) Gallery Guide, Barbican Art Gallery, London.

Pinker, S. (1994) *The Language Instinct* Harmondsworth: Penguin.

Pizer, D. (1995) 'Introduction' in *The Cambridge Companion to American Realism and Naturalism: Howells to London* Cambridge: Cambridge University Press.

Porter, R. (1990) *English Society in the Eighteenth Century* 2nd edn, Harmondsworth: Penguin.

Prickett, S. (1996) *The Origins of Narrative: The Romantic Appropriation of the Bible* Cambridge: Cambridge University Press.

Propp, V. (1968) *Morphology of the Folktale* Austin: University of Texas Press (original Russian version: 1928; first English trans. 1958).

Rabelais, F. (1955) *Gargantua and Pantagruel* Harmondsworth: Penguin.

Radway, J. A. (1984) *Reading the Romance: Women, Patriarchy and Popular Culture* Chapel Hill and London: University of North Carolina Press.

Raleigh, W. (2000) *The Discovery of Guiana* (*The Discovery of the Large, Rich, and Beautiful Empire of Guiana; with a Relation of the Great and Golden City of Manoa, which the Spaniards call El Dorado, and the Provinces of Emeria, Aromaia, Amapaia, and other Countries, with their Rivers, Adjoining. Performed in the Year 1595 by Sir Walter Raleigh, Knight, Captain of Her Majesty's Guard, Lord Warden of the Stannaries, and her Highness' Lieutenant-General of the County of Cornwall*) Microsoft eBook.

Ransford, O. (1978) *Livingstone: The Dark Interior* London: Hamish Hamilton.

Ray, W. (1990) *Story and History: Narrative Authority and Social Identity in the Eighteenth-Century French and English Novel* Oxford: Basil Blackwell.

Read, D. (1958) '*Peterloo': The Massacre and Its Background* Manchester: Manchester University Press.

Readings, B. (1991) *Introducing Lyotard: Art and Politics* London: Routledge.

Rée, J. (2000) *I See a Voice: A Philosophical History* London: Flamingo.

Reilly, J. (1993) *Shadowtime: History and Representation in Hardy, Conrad and George Eliot* London: Routledge.

Reynolds, M (1986) *Young Hemingway* Oxford: Basil Blackwell.

Richardson, S. (1980) *Pamela* Harmondsworth: Penguin.

—— (1985) *Clarissa, or the History of a Young Lady* ed. A. Ross, Harmondsworth: Penguin (originally 1747–8).

Richter, H. (1986) *The Struggle for the Film* Aldershot: Wildwood House.

Ricoeur, P. (1981) 'Narrative time' in W. J. T. Mitchell (ed.) *On Narrative* Chicago and London: University of Chicago Press.

—— (1984–6) *Time and Narrative* 3 vols, Baltimore and London: Johns Hopkins University Press.

—— (1991) 'Discussion: Ricoeur on narrative' in D. Wood (ed.) *On Paul Ricoeur: Narrative and Interpretation* London: Routledge.

Rimmon-Kenan, S. (1983) *Narrative Fiction: Contemporary Poetics* London: Methuen.

Roberts, A. M. (1993) 'Theories of the novel' in A. M. Roberts (ed.) *The Novel: From Its Origins to the Present Day* London: Bloomsbury.

—— (1998) 'Introduction' in *Joseph Conrad* Harlow: Longman.

Ronen, R. (1997) 'Description, narrative and representation' *Narrative* 5 (3): 279–86.

Rosemont, F. (1978) *André Breton and First Principles of Surrealism* London: Pluto.

Rosmarin, A. (1989) 'Darkening the reader: reader-response criticism and *Heart of Darkness*' in R. C. Murfin (ed.) *Heart of Darkness: A Case Study in Contemporary Criticism* New York: St Martin's Press.

Ross, A. (1989) *No Respect: Intellectuals and Popular Culture* London: Routledge.

Said, E. (1994) *Culture and Imperialism* London: Vintage.

Salkie, R. (2001) 'The Chomskyan revolutions' in P. Cobley (ed.) *The Routledge Companion to Semiotics and Linguistics* London: Routledge.

Salt, B. (1990) 'Film form 1900–1906' in T. Elsaesser with A. Barker (ed.) *Early Cinema: Space, Frame, Narrative* London: British Film Institute.

Sauerberg, L. O. (1991) *Fact into Fiction: Documentary Realism in the Contemporary Novel* London: Macmillan.

Saunders, D. (1992) *Authorship and Copyright* London: Routledge.

Saussure, F. de (1983) *Course in General Linguistics* trans. R. Harris, London: Duckworth.

Schafer, R. (1983) *The Analytic Attitude* New York: Basic Books.

Scholes, R. and Kellogg, R. (1966) *The Nature of Narrative* Oxford: Oxford University Press.

Scott, J. A. (1984) '*The Divine Comedy*' in B. Ford (ed.) *Medieval Literature, Part Two: The European Inheritance* Harmondsworth: Penguin.

Sebeok, T. A. (2001) 'IASS' in P. Cobley (ed.) *The Routledge Companion to Semiotics and Linguistics* London: Routledge.

Seltzer, M. (1986) 'The naturalist machine' in R. B. Yeazell (ed.) *Sex, Politics and Science in the Nineteenth-century Novel* Baltimore and London: Johns Hopkins University Press.

Sherratt, E. R. (1992) '"Reading the texts": archaeology and the Homeric question' in C. Emlyn-Jones, L. Hardwick and J. Purkis (eds) *Homer: Readings and Images* London: Duckworth.

Shingler, M. and Wieringa, C. (1998) *On Air: Methods and Meanings of Radio* London: Arnold.

Shklovsky, V. (1965) 'Sterne's *Tristram Shandy*: Stylistic Commentary' in L. T. Lemon and M. J. Reis (eds) *Russian Formalist Criticism: Four Essays* Lincoln and London: University of Nebraska Press.

Shotter, J. and Gergen, K. J. (eds) (1989) *Texts of Identity* London: Sage.

Showalter, E. (1978) *A Literature of their Own: British Women Novelists from Brontë to Lessing* London: Virago.

Silverman, K. (1983) *The Subject of Semiotics* Oxford: Oxford University Press.

Smith, A. D. (1991) *National Identity* Harmondsworth: Penguin.

Snead, J. (1990) 'European pedigrees/African contagions: nationality, narrative, and communality in Tutuola, Achebe and Reed' in H. K. Bhabha (ed.) *Nation and Narration* London: Routledge.

Snow, C. P. (1978) *The Realists: Portraits of Eight Novelists* London: Macmillan.

Snyder, I. (1998) 'Beyond the hype: reassessing hypertext' in *Page to Screen: Taking Literacy in the Electronic Era* London: Routledge.

Spence, D. (1987) 'Narrative recursion' in S. Rimmon-Kenan (ed.) *Discourse in Psychoanalysis and Literature* London: Methuen.

Spigel, L. (1992) *Make Room for TV: Television and the Family Ideal in Postwar America* Chicago and London: University of Chicago Press.

Stevens, B. (1995) 'On Ricoeur's analysis of time and narration' in L. E. Hahn (ed.) *The Philosophy of Paul Ricoeur* Chicago and La Salle: Open Court.

Stitch, L. (ed.) (1991) *Anxious Visions, Surrealist Art* New York: Abbeville Press.

Stone, L. (1969) 'Literacy and education in England, 1640–1900' *Past and Present* 42: 69–139.

Sutton-Smith, B. (1997) *The Ambiguity of Play* Cambridge, MA and London: Harvard University Press.

Swingewood, A. (1986) *Sociological Poetics and Aesthetic Theory* London: Macmillan.

Thompson, E. P. (1968) *The Making of the English Working Class* Harmondsworth: Penguin.

Thomson, D. (1966) *Europe Since Napoleon* Harmondsworth: Penguin.

Thorburn, D. (1988) 'Television as an aesthetic medium' in J. W. Carey (ed.) *Media, Myths and Narratives* Newbury Park and London: Sage.

Todorov, T. (1977) *The Poetics of Prose* Ithaca: Cornell University Press.

Toker, L. (1993) *Eloquent Reticence: Withholding Information in Fictional Narrative* Kentucky: University Press of Kentucky.

Travers, M. (1998) *An Introduction to Modern European Literature: From Romanticism to Postmodernism* London: Macmillan.

Tsivian, Y. (1994) *Early Cinema in Russia and Its Cultural Reception* trans. A. Bodger, London: Routledge.

Vološinov, V. N. (1973) *Marxism and the Philosophy of Language* trans. L. Matejka and I. R. Titunik, New York: Seminar Press.

Walcutt, C. C. (1956) *American Literary Naturalism, A Divided Stream* Minneapolis: University of Minnesota Press.

Walder, D. (ed.) (1995) *The Realist Novel* London: Routledge.

Watt, I. (1963) *The Rise of the Novel: Studies in Defoe, Richardson and Fielding* Harmondsworth: Penguin.

Watts, C. (1983) ' "A bloody racist": about Achebe's view of Conrad' *Yearbook of English Studies* 13: 196–209.

Waugh, P. (1984) *Metafiction* London: Methuen.

White, A. (1981) *The Uses of Obscurity: The Fiction of Early Modernism* London: Routledge and Kegan Paul.

White, H. (1973) *Metahistory: The Historical Imagination in Nineteenth-century Europe* Baltimore and London: Johns Hopkins University Press.

—— (1981) 'The value of narrativity in the representation of reality' in W. J. T. Mitchell (ed.) *On Narrative* Chicago and London: University of Chicago Press.

—— (1987) *Tropics of Discourse: Essays in Cultural Criticism* Baltimore and London: Johns Hopkins University Press.

Williams, G. (1985) 'Newsbooks and popular narrative during the middle of the seventeenth century' in J. Hawthorn (ed.) *Narrative: From Malory to Motion Pictures* London: Edward Arnold.

Williams, R. (1965) *The Long Revolution* Harmondsworth: Penguin.

—— (1970) *The English Novel: From Dickens to Lawrence* London: Chatto and Windus.

—— (1974) *Television: Technology and Cultural Form* London: Fontana.

Wood, M. (1999) 'Modernism and film' in M. Levenson (ed.) *The Cambridge Companion to Modernism* Cambridge: Cambridge University Press.

Young, P. (1966) *Ernest Hemingway: A Reconsideration* University Park and London: Pennsylvania State University Press.

Ziff, L. (1987) 'The social basis of Hemingway's style' in L. W. Wagner (ed.) *Ernest Hemingway: Six Decades of Criticism* East Lansing: Michigan State University Press.

# INDEX

Kuhn, T. 188
Kuleshov effect 159

*L'arrive d'un train en gare* 154–5
*Last Temptation of Christ, The* 161
Leavis, F. R. 135–6, 138
Lee, S.: *Do the Right Thing* 175
Leonard, E. 86
Leopold II 123–5, 127
Léry, J. de 129
Lévi-Strauss, C. 20, 25, 33–7, 38, 217,
Lewis, C. S. 69
Lewis, L. 208
Lewis, W. 149
*Limey, The* 211
literacy 24, 26–7, 32–4, 51–3, 56–61, 70,
    77–80, 86, 117–18, 187, 205, 208,
    216, 223
Livingstone, D. 123–5
Lodge, D. 45, 63–4, 104, 108, 116,
    179–80, 222
Loomba, A. 133
Lord, A. 45–6, 47, 52–3, 56, 86, 117–18,
    185, 207–8, 213
Lotman, J. M. 7–8
Lukacs, J.: *The Duel* 181
Lynch, D. 211, 221
Lyotard, J.-F. 184–7

MacCabe, C. 92–3, 100
Mailer, N. 179
Malory, T.: *La Morte d'Arthur* 74, 75
Marinetti, F. 162
*M\*A\*S\*H\** 195
*Matrix, The* 211
McLuhan, M. 189
**metafiction** 173–8, **235**
metaphor 14–15
metonymy 14
Milton, J.: *Paradise Lost* 122
**mimesis** 57, 61–6, 73, 81, 82, 83, 84,
    90–1, 92, 100, 144, 149, 156, 157,
    160, 167, 184–5, 211, 216, 220,
    221–2; defined 57–61, 104–7, **235**
**modernism** 3, 46, 90, 144, Ch. 6
    *passim;* 174, 183, 201, 208, 211, 217,
    **235–6**
**monstration** 156, **236**
montage 159–60
Murray, J. 202–6, 207–8
muthos see *plot*
myth 25, 32, 33–7, 38, 144; of Oedipus
    34–7, 164–5, 166

**narratee** 139–41, **236**
**narrative** and authority 7, 82, 86, 116,
    134, 135, 138, 174, 198–9, 206–9,
    216; defined 5–7, 9–10, **236–7**;
    'innateness' of 27–8; origins 23–8,
    Ch. 2 *passim;*
**narrative levels** *see* **implied author;**
    **implied reader; narratee; narrator;**
    **real author; real reader**
**narratology** 20–1, 217–18, 221–3, **237**
**narrator** 7, 43, 49–50, 66, 71–3, 82, 86,
    90–1, 92–4, 100–7, 108, 113, 134,
    138, 139–41, 147, 153–4, 155–69, 171,
    174, 177, 185, 199, **237; intrusive**
    **narrator** 108, 110, 116, 214, 217, **235;**
    **omniscient narration** 100–4, 107,
    108, 148, 149, 162, 199, 217, **238**
**naturalism** 108–111, **237**
Nebel, F. 112–13
news 29–30
Nicholls, P. 149–50
**non-fiction novel** 179–82, 198, **237**
Norris, F. 109–10
**novel** 3, 42, 47, 67, 73, 75–87, Ch. 4
    *passim,* Ch. 5 *passim,* 146–52, 157,
    163, 168–9, 171, 184, 206, 208–10,
    **238**

object *see* **sign**
Ogdon, B. 114–15
**omniscient narration** *see* **narrator**